D0310653

COUNTDOWN
TO LOCKDOWN

Also by Mick Foley:

The Hardcore Diaries
Scooter
Tales from Wrescal Lane
Foley Is Good
Tietam Brown
Mick Foley's Halloween Hijinx
Mick Foley's Christmas Chaos
Have a Nice Day!

COUNTDOWN TO LOCKDOWN

A HARDCORE JOURNAL

Mick Foley

Text © Mick Foley 2010
Photographs © Lee South

The right of Mick Foley to be identified as the author of this work has been
asserted in accordance with the Copyright, Designs and Patents Act 1988.

This edition first published in Great Britain in 2010
by Orion Books
an imprint of the Orion Publishing Group Ltd
Orion House, 5 Upper Saint Martin's Lane
London, WC2H 9EA
An Hachette Livre UK Company

1 3 5 7 9 10 8 6 4 2

A CIP catalogue record for this book
is available from the British Library.

ISBN (hardback): 978 1 409 11571 7
ISBN (trade paperback): 978 1 409 12389 7

Printed in Great Britain by CPI Mackays, Chatham ME5 8TD

The Orion Publishing Group's policy is to use papers that are natural,
renewable and recyclable and made from wood grown in sustainable forests.
The logging and manufacturing processes are expected to conform to the
environmental regulations of the country of origin.

www.orionbooks.co.uk

In memory of my father,
the original Cactus Jack

CONTENTS

INTRODUCTION

Yes, here it is — the book you've been kind of sort of waiting for. Okay, I know that four volumes of memoirs may seem like a lot for anyone (at this point, I think I have officially surpassed Churchill), but I prefer to think of this book as an action-adventure story. It's got all the elements: heroes, villains, romance, exciting combat sequences, clever dialogue, and a tense verbal showdown with former deputy secretary of defense Paul Wolfowitz. So maybe you could think of this book as less of a Churchillesque memoir and more of an Indiana Jones type of tale, kind of "Indiana Mick [I *am* a native Hoosier] and the Six Sides of Steel." As is the case in the latest Indy installment, the hero of this story (me) may have aged a bit since we last saw him, but he's still capable of telling a good story.

I've always considered the inside of the surreal world of professional wrestling to be *at least* as entertaining as what our fans see on their television screens. And I know that when I was a fan, I would have loved to have been given this access, to see what *really* goes on behind the scenes. Consider this book to be like a six-week backstage pass — the best possible place to view the cavalcade of curious characters who make up the world of professional wrestling.

Countdown to Lockdown is an in-depth look at the six-week period leading up to my biggest match in several years; a main event Six Sides of Steel (you know, a steel-cage match) showdown with one of my great all-time opponents — Sting. So, with this book as your admission ticket, I will take you on an all-access tour not only behind the scenes but inside my mind as well, as I try to find a way to regain the confidence, conditioning, and passion that will be so vital if I am going to be successful on this journey.

I was under a tremendous amount of pressure in the weeks leading up to this match — most of it put there by myself. Knowing that so much of the success of this *Lockdown* show depended on me, I was arguably the least confident I have been in my own abilities in more than a decade.

Many may think that this book is similar in feel to my last book, *The Hardcore Diaries*. It is . . . by design. Think of this as a companion piece to the *Diaries*, but I can assure you that the story is far different. It's my first book about my new company, and I will have plenty to say about both my arrival in TNA and my departure from WWE, as well as my thoughts on the wrestling world in general and many of the individuals who make up this world. I was told during the writing of my first book, the towering *New York Times* number one best seller *Have a Nice Day!*, that a memoir is not the right place to settle scores. So even though settling scores and slinging mud seems to be the easiest way to get attention, I've tried not to take the low road too often. As with *The Hardcore Diaries*, I've tried to make the entire book a PG-13 affair. Yes, there are a few stories that may be just slightly risqué, but I don't *think* I drop a single F-bomb in the entire book. I met a kid from Canada who was suspended from school for reading my last book. That act struck me as completely inexcusable, and I vowed to fight the school system on the kid's behalf . . . then I lost his phone number. But if you're thirteen or older and get suspended for reading this book, contact TNA via their website, or get hold of my publicist at Grand Central Publishing. I would love to intercede and do the right thing . . . and maybe even get a little free publicity while I'm at it.

Let me apologize in advance if I sound a little preachy every now and then. But in certain chapters, like "An Open Letter" and "A

Substance Problem," I found it very difficult to make valid points and passionate arguments without just a little bit of that preachy quality peeking through.

I don't feel like I'm doing my preaching to the choir, either. Occasionally, my opinions may strike some as controversial, or even flawed and wrong. Which is fine. I'm not attempting to be the sole voice of authority on any subject. But I do hope in a few cases that I will add a new voice to issues that need one.

As many readers of my other books may know, I have a variety of interests outside of wrestling, some of which I write about in this book. I think most people enjoy my observations on the outside world, and from a personal standpoint these chapters are fun and fulfilling to write, but I am aware that occasional fans will wish that I not veer so far off the wrestling course during certain chapters. I can certainly understand that, and thus I have come up with a handy **Wrestlemeter** to gauge the wrestling content of chapters that are not *Lockdown*-specific. For example, a chapter about the aforementioned tense verbal battle with Paul Wolfowitz has absolutely nothing to do with wrestling and would merit a zero on the **Wrestlemeter**, while a chapter about meeting singer Tori Amos actually has far more wrestling content than one might think and would therefore merit a surprising six. Many non-*Lockdown* chapters are very wrestling-specific (like the ones that detail my short-lived announcing career and subsequent decision to leave WWE) and would therefore rate a nine or ten on the meter. Armed with this valuable literary information, readers can now make up their own minds; read the chapters in the order they are presented (my personal favorite way), refer back to them at a later time, or skip them completely. Don't worry about hurting my feelings — I'll get over it...eventually. Occasionally, a reader (usually the mother of a wrestling fan) will pick up one of my books and find themselves completely engrossed by everything *but* the wrestling aspects. For these reasons, the **Wrestlemeter** is a valuable monitoring tool.

Before we get started, let me address this ugly rumor that has swirled about, hinting that I may have caved in to modern technology and written this book with the aid of a computer keyboard. I have several witnesses who will swear to seeing a large man with a marble composition tablet, scribbling frantically on coast-to-coast flights. So, I am proud to say that I wrote this book the old-fashioned way — the Foley way — with a trusty pen and several pads of paper. (Actually I did cave in to technology on my last two chapters — finally realizing just how slow and cumbersome that whole stupid handwriting thing is.)

So what are you waiting for? Start turning those pages, and we'll find out together if the Hardcore Legend has still got the fortitude required to tear the house down...or at least not embarrass himself too badly.

COUNTDOWN TO LOCKDOWN: 34 DAYS

March 16, 2009
Orlando, Florida

All right, all right, I'll admit it. I'm terrified of Kurt Angle. Not worried. Not concerned. Terrified. Absolutely terrified. Not like a "wow, Vince is really putting Koslov in a main event" type of terrified. I'm talking about an honest-to-goodness "Alastair Sim as Scrooge down on his knees begging the Ghost of Christmas Yet to Come for another chance at life" type of terrified. Yeah, I know I went with the same

Alastair Sim reference to describe my fear of my editor at Knopf, Victoria Wilson, who will no doubt love being mentioned in a second wrestling memoir, but I'm not sure that was real terror, more like intellectual insecurity. This, however — this thing I feel about Kurt Angle — is terror.

Don't get me wrong, I like Kurt. He's a caring, giving person and a genuine American hero; a guy who won a gold medal in the Olympics while competing with a broken neck. He is also one of the most talented performers in the history of our business, with a résumé of classic matches that rivals anyone's, of any era.

And later tonight, I'm going to be in the ring with him for the very first time. Okay, okay, all you nitpickers, I know I've actually "been in the ring" with him plenty of times — for interviews, angles, even an odd punch or really hard head butt or two. Granted, tonight is a tag team match, and really more of a door I must pass through to get me into the creative corridor leading to a different big match with a different big opponent.

But Kurt Angle really isn't interested in any talk about opening doors and creative corridors and big matches in the future. He's interested in tonight. And that same competitive fire that vaulted him to the top of the amateur wrestling world — possibly the most thankless and difficult world in sports — drives him to pull off the best match he is capable of, night in and night out, no matter how big the show, no matter how limited the opponent, no matter the physical or emotional toll to himself.

I respect that attitude. At one time I probably shared it. But I'm a different man now — older, weaker, slower — and a lot more realistic.

If anything, Kurt is more driven on this night than usual. Last night was *Destination X*, a TNA Pay-Per-View that held a world of promise. Following a February offering that looked flat on paper and, if anything, underperformed those limited expectations, TNA looked ready to regain its form with *Destination X*. Led by a complex, well-told, long-term story involving Kurt and his Main Event Mafia partner/ nemesis Sting, our *TNA Impact* show (Thursday at 9:00, Spike) was on a roll, recently eclipsing two million U.S. viewers for the first time. I liked the odds of Kurt and Sting pulling off a classic, and I was looking forward to my role as special guest enforcer at ringside, which more or less ensured me the best seat in the house (although technically I'd be standing).

But at *Destination X* on that particular night, expectation gave way to disappointment, reality couldn't compete with hope, and a good, hard-fought match simply wasn't enough for our fans...or for Sting or Kurt, especially Kurt. I was not without a disappointment of my own in the match, having shattered my own long-standing belief that I went up "light" for big moves — a necessity if one wants to avoid the worst of the injuries that the business can offer. Instead I went up like a 300-pound S.O.S. — figure out the acronym for yourself (I'm trying to stay PG-13 in this book) — for Kurt's Angle Slam, injuring my pride, and possibly Kurt's vertebrae, in the process.

Like I said, it was a good match, a point I kept reiterating in separate long conversations with both men after the show. I was trying to look at the glass as half full. But the glass-half-empty view was indeed troubling. Sting looked old. I looked like a 300-pound S.O.S. And Kurt Angle looked human. Apparently, a few voices on the Internet, I would guess a vocal minority, said that Kurt was washed up, his best days were behind him. I knew Kurt would be looking to prove himself. And guess who he'd want to do it with? Me. Great. Kind of reminds me of the night I wrestled Dr. Death, Steve Williams, in Saginaw, Michigan, in early 1990 — the same night Doc learned that WCW (World Championship Wrestling) intended to reduce his contractual guarantee. I remember how I felt that night. Pretty much the same way I feel tonight, over nineteen years later — terrified. Absolutely terrified.

How did this moment ever arise? I asked myself. Why hadn't I just stayed under the safety of the WWE umbrella? Sure, my situation with WWE hadn't been perfect, but it couldn't have been that bad, right? At least it was a certified Angle-Free Zone.

Well, to truly understand my story, I'm going to have to introduce you to an old friend of mine. Readers of my earlier memoirs will remember him well, if not fondly. Ladies and gentlemen, say hello to Al Snow.

Required reading.

REPACKAGING MICK

I think it might have been Al Snow's fault. For looking so darn good. No, that's not a misprint. At a certain point in time — 2000, 2001 — Al looked really good. No, not his ring work, which continued to be sloppy and juvenile. Not his facial features, either, which strike me as "Village People cop meets generations of inbreeding." But at a certain point, Al Snow's physique showed a marked improvement; leaner, meaner, more muscularly defined. Not that it affected his push in WWE, which continued to be almost unchartable, or his reaction from the crowd, which was nearly inaudible. But Al Snow, for a time, as a physical specimen, looked pretty darn good. The progress, according to Al, was a direct result of hundred-rep training.

Hundred-rep training seemed to fly in the face of all the conventional wisdom I'd picked up since my first gym visits in late 1979, when my dad used to drive my brother and me to the Gyrodyne Flowerfield, an isolated business development, where he'd park the car and catch up on his newspapers while his two children were tortured inside. Yes, after all these years, I can look back objectively and make a good case for the treatment we received constituting torture.

Neil's Gym was divided into two distinct areas. In one half was the free-weight section, where anyone in that part of Long Island who knew anything about weight training congregated, pressing barbells and dumbbells on equipment that would seem downright antiquated these days, but were cutting-edge by the standards of the day.

The other half, containing a full lineup of Arthur Jones's innovative Nautilus machines, was the only part of the gym my dad allowed my brother and me to venture into. Free weights were supposed to make people muscle-bound, which was an absolute no-no for anyone look-ing at athletic endeavors that didn't begin and end on the offensive or defensive line for the football team.

The notion seems downright primitive now, given the muscula-ture displayed by athletes ranging from LeBron James in basketball to Tiger Woods in golf. But the experts of the time more or less forbade experimentation with free weights. I have an old book, *Inside Basket-ball*, written by Dick Barnett, a member of the 1970 World Champion New York Knicks, that actually touted the idea of using kitchen coun-ter isometrics as its primary form of strength training.

These Nautilus machines, however, were supposed to be the athlete's answer to progressive strength training. Jones's machines fea-tured the philosophy of pre-exhaustion; each one was designed for an exercise isolating a specific muscle, followed by a second one that incorporated a larger group of muscles. For example, pectoral flies, which isolated the chest muscles, would be followed by an exercise simulating decline bench presses, which allowed the body to borrow strength from the triceps and deltoids to aid the pre-exhausted pecs. Isolated bicep curls would be followed by lat pull downs — both per-formed on the same apparatus, so there was absolutely no time for resting. Most daunting of all was the Nautilus leg station, where leg extensions were followed by seated leg presses. Adding to the agony were the trainers at the gym, who would move the athletes/guinea pigs of this physiological dark age through the circuit at warp speed, pausing only to incorporate little goodies like the sixty-second wall squat into the proceedings. The legs would start to throb at twenty seconds, shake at thirty to forty, and more or less cease to function just about the time the minute was up.

Indeed, if not for the encouragement/taunting/insults from the friendly staff at Neil's, I'm not sure I could have made it through a single workout. If memory serves me correctly, the instructors even had plastic buckets on hand, just in case an athlete/guinea pig couldn't quite make the bathroom in time to do what needed to be done.

Meanwhile, the guys on the other side of the gym — the free-weight guys — seemed to be the only ones making visible progress. And they seemed to be doing it at a much more leisurely pace; a set of six to ten reps of a single exercise followed by a few minutes of walking around, talking, and flexing in the mirror.

But all the walking around and talking added up, and by the time those free-weight workouts were over, it was not unusual for a couple hours to have passed — plenty of time to look down on the Nautilus guys crying and puking during their paltry twenty-minute workouts.

Thankfully, my dad caved in to my continual assault of free-weight requests, about the time a couple friends got their driver's licenses — sometime during my junior year of high school — and all those fears came to fruition; my body swelled almost instantly to Herculean proportions, eventually leading to my current status as muscle-bound stiff, my cartoonlike musculature proving useful only for impressing women and showing off on the beach.

Okay, so maybe even at my free-weight-pushing peak, my two-hours-a-day gym physique didn't show the slightest hint of training at all. But that didn't stop me from diving into the pool of bodybuilding literature that was getting deeper every day. I read everything I could find — *Muscle & Fitness, Muscular Development, Arnold: The Education of a Bodybuilder, Beef It!* — all in the quest to set free the ripped and ruthless body I knew I had locked away deep inside of me. Funny how none of those magazines or books seemed to make the slightest mention of things like genetic limitations — that some bodies just weren't meant to be buff, no matter how much protein was ingested, no matter how many hours were spent in the gym.

Over the years, I grudgingly learned to accept the weak hand that Mother Nature had dealt out to me. Sadly, I was never going to be Lou Ferrigno in the gym or Jimmy Snuka in the ring — a realization that no doubt played a role in developing my distinct pro-wrestling style. Somewhere along the way, I also took note of a direct correlation between how bad I looked and how much money I made: 220-pound Mick slept in his car. 235-pound Mick got a job in Memphis. 270-pound Mick became a player in Dallas and got a job in WCW. 300-pound Mick won a WWE title and wrote a towering *New York Times* best seller. 330-pound Mick pushed the theory a little too far, asking way too much of a lower back and knees that would have been far better off and lasted a few years longer at a far lesser weight.

Fast-forward to January 2007. I'm somewhere around 300 pounds, a weight I'd struggled to maintain for most of the previous five years, with the notable exception of a period in 2004 when I would get down to 272, my lowest weight since the late eighties, for a comeback that would yield the best match of my career — a brutal hardcore bout with a young Randy Orton.

A new book, *The Hardcore Diaries*, was due out in March, and it seemed to be practically begging to have its contents exploited for the good of a big match. Sure, the book detailed a frustrating six weeks in WWE in 2006 — a period of time that saw my high hopes for the second *One Night Stand* Pay-Per-View deflate, sputter, and fall to the ground like a childhood balloon released from thumb and forefinger. Even the accompanying farting sound of the sputtering balloon seemed appropriate.

Nonetheless, my name had surfaced as a possibility for a *Wrestle-Mania* main event, as Donald Trump's chosen "guy" in the highly publicized "Hair vs. Hair" match between Trump and Vince McMahon. Eventually, I was passed over in favor of Bobby Lashley, a world-class amateur wrestler and mixed martial arts practitioner with a massive chiseled physique and a world of potential — a guy who looked to be a huge part of the company's future…at least until he left WWE forever four months later.

Not to worry, I had a Plan B all lined up and approved by Mr. McMahon, and given the blessing of my publisher, Pocket Books. Plan B, I assured Pocket, was going to be a home run. While everyone else was vying for attention at *WrestleMania*, I would begin my big television push the day after the biggest show of the year, using the contents of the book to fuel a match with John Morrison, still known as Johnny Nitro at the time. I hoped that this match could do for John what my 2004 match had done for Randy Orton: move him up the ladder of success — give him an exciting Pay-Per-View opportunity with an opponent willing to help him make that big step.

We could even take advantage of the groundwork I'd laid down a year earlier, involving Morrison's real-life/on-screen girlfriend, Melina, who I still felt had untapped big-star potential.

But in order to have this big match with Morrison, I was going to need to be in top physical condition, or at least as close to it as I could realistically expect, given my knees and back…and neck…and pretty much everything else.

Enter Al Snow's hundred-rep training, specifically as it pertained to my legs. As I mentioned earlier, this method seemed to contradict everything I'd read about the subject over the last twenty-five years. Sure, specifics had changed, and I'd long since abandoned the training magazines and books that had once taken up so much of my time. But as far as I knew, the basics pertaining to repetitions remained the same — 1 to 2 for explosive power, 4 to 8 for size and strength, 8 to 15 for toning and endurance. I'd even heard or read that the legs were most responsive to reps in the 15-to-25 range. But a hundred reps?

According to resident expert Al Snow, the philosophy was actually quite simple. The weight should be light enough to limit strain on ligaments and tendons. But any weight starts becoming difficult at around the 25-rep stage. Somewhere around 50, my legs would start to burn. This was where testicular fortitude came in — and brother, if there is any one word that accurately described my testicles, it is *fortuitous*. At 75 reps, the exercise would seem almost unbearable. Only my legendary fortitude could see me through to 100, at which point I'd thank God for the forty-eight hours I'd have to rest before forcing myself to endure this kind of abuse again. Luckily, I had those experiences at Neil's Gym to fall back on — those extreme sessions of gratuitous suffering that even former V.P. Dick Cheney might have frowned on. "Dammit, man, get bin Laden off that Nautilus machine! Can't you see he's had enough?"

I didn't have a Nautilus machine handy for the task, even though my wife and I had donated a whole line of the classic Arthur Jones originals (which we'd bought used but in great condition) to a local church community center when we'd closed our gym in the Florida panhandle.

We'd opened the gym in late 1997 as a business to fall back on when my wrestling days were through. Fortunately, a couple of years later the wrestling business just exploded, and after the dust settled it became pretty obvious that unless we got completely stupid with our money (i.e., invested it in the stock market), we weren't going to need that gym as much as we thought.

Plus, I was a terrible businessman. In a business where a rule of thumb was to never under any circumstances offer a refund, my answer to every problem, big or small, was to offer people their money back. So when the State of Florida told us they needed our property to widen the highway, I did several Nadia Comaneci–like somersaults in my mind (despite outweighing the '76 Olympics sensation by some 240 pounds), followed by an incredible mental dismount. Of course, I didn't let the state representative witness my mental gymnastics. No, the state guy got a "but this was my dream, and now you want to take it away" story. All in all, we were paid almost enough to make up for three years of losses from running the gym, but perhaps more important, I understood that I should never ever think about running a business again.

We donated about half of the pieces we'd bought, sold some others at a steep discount, and had about ten Cybex machines moved up to New York and placed in the Foley garage, where they instantly set new standards in coat hanging, spiderweb clinging, and mouse feces collecting. Within about a year, I would donate half the pieces to the Homeless Veterans Residence Center in Queens, a place that wrestling legend Fred Blassie had visited regularly in the years before his death.

Among the pieces I hung on to, however, was a heavy-duty Cybex leg press machine — and brother, using Al Snow's hundred-rep routine as my guide, I began wearing that machine out, a hundred reps at a time every other day, in preparation for my big run the day after *WrestleMania*.

Heading into January, the world appeared to be my oyster. *The Hardcore Diaries* had received tremendous preorders, and Pocket Books was sure they had a hit on their hands. Sure, in some places the book was a little rough on WWE and on Vince McMahon in particular. But hey, Vince himself had given it his blessing, saying to his staff "Well, if that's the way he feels, just print it" after concerns were raised about its not completely pro WWE content.

We'd taped some cool commercials for the book, centered around an unsubstantiated rumor that I was something of a name-dropper — a charge I'm pretty sure *CBS Evening News* anchor Katie Couric, who has interviewed me twice, would refute.

And thanks to Al Snow's hundred-rep training, I was starting to get in serious shape. Every day I was feeling stronger, leaner, more determined, more punctual, sexier, more empathetic, and far humbler. I was about to have another best seller on my hands — and a return to WWE television that would go down in history as one of the most *recent* returns to WWE in history. What could possibly go wrong?

Umm, how about everything?

I was somewhere around my sixtieth rep when I felt a sharp pain in my lower back. A sharp, burning pain. But "Hell's Bells" was on the boom box — the same boom box that had been given to me in 1999 (when the boom box people were our sponsor) for being featured in the "boom of the week" just about every week — and Angus Young, the armadillo hiding in Brian Johnson's trousers (read *Hardcore Diaries* for more info on the armadillo), and the rest of the gang in AC/DC still had a couple of minutes of uplifting Christian folk rock to deliver.

Plus, like I'd mentioned, Al's hundred-rep training was so foolproof that one could just gut their way through the pain — even if that pain happened to be a rupturing of the L4/L5 disc in the lower back. So, instead of getting off the Cybex leg machine — as common sense would have dictated — I gutted my way through those last forty horrible reps using the image of some incredible moment of upcoming Pay-Per-View glory to see me through.

As usual, I climbed out of this modern-day torture apparatus, holding on to some other piece of former "Foley's gym" equipment to keep from falling over due to dizziness and complete exhaustion of the thighs. I walked the little hill from my detached garage, savoring the light-headedness and total muscle expenditure, but a little concerned about that burning pain in my back. *You know,* I thought as I opened the door to my house, *I think I may have hurt myself.*

A week later, I was looking for some major relief. I'd tried ice, rest, heat, hot tubs, stretching. Thankfully, I'd fought off the quick-fix pain-pill urge. Pain medication has always been a last resort for me — an admission of failure in the battle against pain. And I wasn't ready to raise the white flag of surrender just yet. I realized that all of my measures in this battle had been defensive. Ice, rest, heat, hot tubs, stretching? All weak counterpunches. I needed to go on the offensive, to go deep into the tissue, the spasms of the muscle, to confront the source of pain head-on. I needed a surge of sorts. A deep tissue massage. A massurge.

But who to go to? Where to turn? I knew from the summer of 1993, when I had suffered a bruised shoulder after being thrown down a flight of stairs by Randy Orton, that I couldn't go to a spa. Much too nice in there, much too gentle. Kind of like a UN peacekeeper with those intimidating sky blue helmets; it might keep the issue from getting worse, but it really wasn't going to solve anything.

So I ruled out the spa possibility, opting for Healing Hands Physical Therapy. I told them I'd just about reached the end of my rope, that I'd be willing to do just about anything to feel better…except, you know, let a guy touch me. Because it feels weird. And there's always the remote possibility of having to deal with the psychological aftermath of "it" moving during the male therapist encounter. Just ask George Costanza.

So I had no idea who would be working on me when I got to Healing Hands, and I didn't really care, just as long as the person doing the work didn't have a penis. I scanned the room wondering who my new ally in this battle against back pain might be. The attractive blond by the desk? That would be cool. Or the brunette with the well-defined biceps? Yeah, I bet she could really dig in deep.

Then I heard a high-pitched little voice: "Hello, Mickey." I turned to see a tiny Asian woman with dark glasses, maybe five feet tall, maybe a hundred pounds — not likely to be much of an ally in the battle against pain.

"Hi, I'm Jessie," she said. She led me down a hallway, to what I was sure would be the least helpful massage of my life, not to mention my most wasteful expenditure of money since picking up that *Best of the Curry Man* DVD. As I watched the tiny lady in front of me, I could tell she was having trouble navigating the hallway, seemingly unable to see where she was going, using her hands to touch walls and furniture as she went. Suddenly it made sense. The dark glasses, the difficult walk down the hall. Oh, great, not only was my therapist tiny, she was blind, too.

But the moment the little lady put her hands on me, it was like, *bam,* Mr. Miyagi, the wizened martial arts expert/spiritual mentor/ apartment complex custodian from the original *Karate Kid* movie, who was able to heal Daniel-san from the injuries he suffered at the hands of Sensei Martin Kove's Cobra Kai bullies.

As I lay on the table, appreciating Jessie's deep-tissue-probing hands and elbows, realizing this woman might just be my greatest weapon in the war against pain — I had a separate, borderline-indecent thought.

A massage recipient is almost always given the option to wear or not to wear underwear during the massage. No undies offers the benefit of allowing the gluteus maximus (buttocks) to be worked on — a valuable and large muscle group for a therapist to have access to for the most effective massage possible. The commando downside? Being completely naked, which I'm not totally comfortable being in front of anyone, including my wife. Even while covered by a towel, there's too much that can go wrong — camera phones, secret video, the human gag reflex. So, glutes or no glutes, I'd always exercised my right to keep my undies on.

I say the recipient is "almost always" given the option, because in September 1994, while suffering from some pretty acute sciatic pain while on a tour of Austria, I was told in no uncertain terms that I absolutely, positively had to remove my undies, sparking the following dynamic Deutsche dialogue between the future Hardcore Legend and a male Austrian therapist with particularly bad teeth. You need only know that *Unterhosen = underpants.*

MICK: *Ich möchte auf meinen Unterhosen halten.*
BAD TEETH: *Nein, sie können seine Unterhosen nicht tragen.*
MICK: *Ja, Ich möchte auf meinen Unterhosen halten.*
BAD TEETH: *Nein, sie können seine Unterhosen nicht tragen.*

Oh, don't worry, *Ich hatte mein Unterhosen getragen.*
Good thing I had those *Unterhosen* on, too. Because "it" moved

during the course of my time with that bad-toothed therapist. Oh, yes, it moved!

It would take several months of semiregular massages with Jessie before I would become confident enough to discard my *Unterhosen*, providing unrestricted access to my long-suffering gluteals. And with that historic discard of the *Unterhosen*, Jessica at Healing Hands became the first woman — in my limited history of being naked around women — that I felt comfortable being naked around.

And if "it" happens to move once in a while? No big deal — I mean, how's she going to know?

I would come to see Jessica as not only an incredible massage therapist but as something of a modern-day superhero. Life cannot have been easy for a blind orphan from Vietnam, especially when her husband took off on her — returning for good to his native Mexico, leaving her to raise their three small children by herself.

Despite those troubles, she refused to stay down, putting herself through massage school, riding trains, taking buses, doing whatever it took to make her own living. And now...she gets to put her hands on the naked Hardcore Legend. What an inspirational story!

After a few massages from Super Jessie, I was feeling good enough to start anew, even seeking the services of a personal trainer for the first time. I kept hearing about the advantages of training the core, those muscle groups surrounding and including the abdominals and lower back. No doubt about it, I was going to be in really good shape for this big return.

I would actually be making a couple of WWE appearances before my *big* return a day after *WrestleMania* — just enough to fan the flames that were starting to surround the release of the *Diaries*. Pocket Books continued to be pumped about the release.

Speaking of pumped, my first personal training session went well. Sure, that exercise ball stuff seems a little, you know, wimpy at first, but when done correctly, that stuff will wear a guy out, especially when it's hitting muscles I didn't even know existed. I still had a small amount of back pain to contend with, but keeping in mind for a moment that I'm the guy who single-handedly dealt the mighty Cell (as in Hell in a Cell) a major ass kicking, I really didn't think that a small amount of pain was worth worrying about.

It was March 2, 2007, when lower-back-disc disaster struck — just three days before my official return to *Raw*, my first WWE appearance since I was "fired" by Vince McMahon and WWE Diva Melina over six months earlier. What a great day for WWE fans. They were going to eat up this return. Please stow those previous two lines away with "Wait until Otis sees us! He *loves* us!" from the 1978 classic *Animal House* under the heading "Returns that didn't quite live up to the returnee's expectations."

I had one more personal training session to complete before heading out to Phoenix. In the backseat of my car, I had a box of books, each of them addressed and signed to people I had written of in *The Hardcore Diaries* — people like Dee Snider, the legendary Twisted Sister singer; John Irving, America's greatest novelist; Victoria Wilson, editor of my novels at Knopf; and Christy Canyon, iconic eighties adult film star (with a brief mid-nineties comeback).

I had some reservations about including John Irving and Victoria Wilson in my book. What if they didn't want to be in a wrestling book? As it turned out, my concerns were unwarranted; both Mr. Irving and Ms. Wilson kind of enjoyed it. A little later in the book, I will include a story about meeting one of my favorite performers, and my similar concern that this performer might not care to be included in a Mick Foley memoir. Who was it? How did it work out? Well, you'll just have to keep reading, won't you?

So, I drove out to the training studio, did an hour's worth of elastic bands and rubber balls — challenging stuff, sure, but nothing compared to the agony I'd endured at the old gym as a teenager or on the trusty Cybex following Al Snow's leadership.

Somewhere during the course of that hour, however, I felt a distinct burn in my lower back. Just a little one, like, let me see — like if someone had some kind of access, via teapot spout maybe, to the inside of my body and poured just like a thimbleful of hot water into my spine. Just a thimbleful. No big deal. Besides, I thought I knew just what that slight burning was; the final small burst of pain needed to complete the healing process. I mean, what else could it possibly be?

I headed to the post office to send out those books, relieved that the healing was finally complete. But as I stood in line at the post office — a fairly long line — I got the distinct feeling that the little thimbleful of hot water seemed to be growing in volume, as if that little teapot had been upended and completely poured out. I felt a steady stream of pain cascading down my leg…and I didn't like it. I looked at my books, no longer caring much about what John Irving or Victoria Wilson might think about me. Following that happy post office visit, I still had to pick little Hughie up at preschool. Even with my most precious cargo in the backseat, I began to seriously weigh the merits of running red lights on the way home, in order to get there that much quicker.

Let me see, risking my life and the life of my child versus getting home five minutes quicker? I'll take that risk! No, I guess I'd better not. But I swear, it was a tough decision.

I stumbled into the house and headed right for my minor stash of hard liquor — a half-pint bottle of 100 proof Rumple Minze that will usually last me a good six months, given the infrequency of my imbibing and an almost childlike inability to down more than two shots without getting overly sentimental. I retreated to the relative comfort of the Tempur-Pedic bed, where, curled up in the fetal position, I let out the type of low moaning sounds usually reserved for particularly difficult childbirths.

You know who I felt sorry for? Me? Yes, that's a given. But mostly I felt bad for my daughter, who had previously seen her dad as some type of tough guy. Boy, that image disappeared in a hurry, kind of like that budget surplus we had for all of about ten seconds back in 2001.

Finally, after hours of unrelenting agony, I lay down in the back of my beat-up Chevy Venture and let my wife take me to the emergency room.

"Tell me how much it hurts on a scale of one to ten," I was told.

"Ten."

"No, on a scale of one to ten."

"Ten."

"Ten?" A question; a little skepticism.

"Yes. Ten. Ten, as in the worst pain I've ever felt in my life."

"Really?" Look, I knew what they were getting at, and I'm sure the ER gets their fair share of pain med junkies faking injuries for the sake of prescriptions. And I realize I have long hair, I'm missing my front teeth, and I don't dress well. But doesn't a guy deserve the benefit of the doubt?

"Look," I said, pulling up my hair on my right side, showing them a stump where once upon a time an ear had been. "In 1994, my ear was ripped off my head. When I was asked at the hospital how bad the pain was, I said four. That was a four, this is a ten!" Technically, I said *vier* in that hospital, because it was in Germany, but I think you get the drift.

I was sent home a little while later, diagnosed with a "muscle strain," given a prescription for the weaker-level — 500 mg, not 750 — painkiller, by a doctor who just wasn't interested in hearing about my history of disc herniations.

(A week later, an MRI would show four disc herniations and two bulging discs — a hollow victory of sorts, especially given that my fight to avoid payment for the incorrect diagnosis was unsuccessful.)

I was about three hours into the five-hour flight from New York to Phoenix when my double dose of pain medication wore off. I had weighed the pros and cons of taking the flight at all, and in truth, had it not been for my monumentally important return to *Raw* to promote my latest literary effort, I might have opted to stay home.

Two more seemingly interminable hours in the air, followed by an agonizing taxi ride to the arena, followed by a couple of the most painful conversations of my life. Painful, as in I was in so much pain during the course of them, though the content may have been quite painful as well.

Then a visit to the doctor, who suggested inserting a needle about a foot long into my spine. The shot, he told me, had about a 50 percent chance of working. Fifty percent? No thanks. Not a real big fan of any needles, let alone really big ones. Don't like pricks of any size entering me, let alone twelve-inch ones. Wait! I probably could have put that a little better.

I was back at the doctor's in ten minutes, no longer quite so picky about things like foot-long spinal injections or 50 percent odds. You know, I never did ask what that other 50 percent might entail. Paralysis? Death? A lifetime of impotence? I didn't really care. I wanted the shot.

A considerable part of my left leg went numb to the touch and stayed that way for a while — like for about a year. And I didn't care. The pain went away, with the aid of another double dose of pain medication.

The doctor told me the pain might come back in ninety days, or it might not come back at all. I'm not afraid to admit that I lived in fear of that most unwanted return for weeks, months, even years. To this day, I don't want to do anything that might hasten its return. Like work out too hard. Or train my core . . . at all. Seriously. I know how to interpret a sign from God when I get one. And God does not want me to work out too hard, not even for a Kurt Angle match.

I made a decision back in 1988, before heading out to Tennessee for my first full-time wrestling job, that I wouldn't mess with pain medicine unless I was really, really in a lot of pain. Even as a young guy in the business, I'd heard way too many tales of wrestlers falling prey to the allure of pain medicine. So over the years, I would see guys take more shots than Kobe on a hot streak, and would see pills popped like cherry Pez — all the while extending my definition of what "really really in a lot of pain" meant. For those of you keeping score at home, here are the only three occasions that merited the taking of more than one pain pill in a single day:

1. Bruised shoulder — Cactus Jack and Maxx Payne versus the Nasty Boys, May 1994
2. Veritable laundry list of injuries — Mankind versus Undertaker, June 1998
3. Multiple disc herniations — taking bad advice from Al Snow, March 2007

Following my visit with the doctor and the needle, I had a deep talk with Joey Mercury (now wrestling as Joey Matthews), who was coming back to WWE after a difficult drug rehabilitation. Joey thanked me for a couple of letters I had sent him during his rehab, citing them as a great help during a very tough time. I nodded numbly, recognizing the irony of accepting heartfelt thanks for helping with a dependency problem while being more or less stoned myself.

But hey, at least I had my big return to look forward to. That returning-star pop that would do wonders for both my ego and my book sales. Right?

Let's revisit Otis of "Wait until Otis sees us" fame. Remember the gang in *Animal House* who showed up at an all-black club and were under the mistaken impression that Otis Day was going to love them just because he'd played at their frat party? Well that was my big return in Phoenix, possibly the lukest of all the lukewarm responses I'd received in my career.

It was odd being out there, almost like being in a parallel universe. I'd already done a couple book signings for *The Hardcore Diaries*, and they'd been big — my biggest since 2001. Recognition in public was right up there at near 2001 levels, too. Maybe not quite up there with my real glory days, but bigger than 2003–2005, for no easily digestible explanation. Yet, in my big return, the most recent of all big wrestling returns, I'd received a smaller reaction than the basketball team's mascot — the Phoenix Gorilla. Imagine that, the Hardcore Legend playing second banana to a gorilla. Yes, at least I've still got my best-selling author's gift for wordplay! Banana — gorilla? Good stuff, right?

A couple of days later, I received a consolation of sorts — *The Hardcore Diaries* entered the *New York Times* Best-Seller List at number seven. It would peak a week later at number six. Sure it wasn't number one, like the other two had been, but the playing field had shifted since 2001. A large number of wrestling books were being released every year, making it highly unlikely that any one of them would ever see number one again. Still, I was happy and relieved to be on the list at all. Besides, this book had a long-term marketing plan — it was going to be on that list for a long time to come.

A conversation a week later with the Texas Rattlesnake, "Stone Cold" Steve Austin, would prove to be prophetic. I just realized that Austin had more than one nickname, kind of like the old days on *Monday Night Football*, when Howard Cosell would refer to "Dandy" Don Meredith as "Danderoo," apparently not realizing that "Dandy" was quite possibly enough nickname to go around.

Anyway it was Washington, D.C., and Stone Cold/Texas Rattlesnake/Austin 3:16/World's Toughest SOB/Stunning Steve/Hollywood Blond/Steve Austin came over to me, brandishing a big grin, like he had a story he'd been wanting to share, and the HCL (Hardcore Legend) was the only guy suitable for the task at hand.

Warning: It's tough to find a balance between keeping a book PG-13 and staying true to the authenticity of Stone Cold's dialogue. You know what, I'll go PG-13 here, but I will affix a little asterisk to the words I've altered, allowing you, the reader, to use your knowledge of Steve Austin and your imagination to authenticate it yourself.

Here we go:

"Hey kid, did you see that promo I did on ECW last week?"

Indeed I had, and told him so.

"Gosh darn*, wasn't that the drizzling poops*?"

"It wasn't that bad."

"Not that bad? Shoot*, it was the freaking* poops*. Now listen, kid, I'm not trying to put myself over, but last week on *Raw*, gosh darn*, I went out there and got a heckuva* reaction. Then the next night on ECW? Shoot*, freaking* nothing."

I laughed and told Steve that it probably had more to do with the crowd being drained by the time ECW went on the air live at 10:00 p.m. Eastern. *SmackDown*, clearly the A show, was taped first, and would end whenever it happened to end, sometimes as early as 9:00 p.m., leaving an often tired crowd to wait up to an hour for the B show to begin. Kind of like watching the Yankees play a game at Yankee Stadium and then being asked to wait around an hour for the Scranton/Wilkes-Barre Triple-A farm affiliate to take the field.

I had a great time for most of that night, reconnecting with some old friends — Scott Armstrong, Kane, and too many others to list — as well as making some new ones, like Shelly Martinez, who had heard, quite accurately, that I had found her vampire character Ariel to be quite entertaining.

I was always grateful for the tremendous respect I received from the younger wrestlers, whether they'd met me or not. It's a special thrill for me to talk to guys like Ray Gordy and Harry Smith, whose dads I had worked with before their untimely deaths. I feel a special bond with those guys sharing stories about their dads they may never have had occasion to hear or, in some cases, just liked hearing again.

Yes, it was a good night, until I went out there for the ECW show, just about an hour after the A show closed up shop. I was looking for a way to explain the treacherous actions I had taken almost a year earlier on ECW stalwart Tommy Dreamer. I wanted to portray my actions as doing Tommy a favor, giving him a gift of a barbed-wire bat shot to the back as a way to focus public attention on him.

ECW writer Dave Lagana asked me if I had some ideas for my upcoming promo.

"How about some honesty?" I said.

"What did you have in mind?"

"Well, what if I just go out there and say, 'Look, I could have made a fortune if I'd hit Batista in the back. I hit you instead!'"

Lagana nearly choked. Too much honesty, apparently. I told him I'd work on something.

Shoot*, I could have used a little of that freaking* honesty out there. The reaction was even luker than that lukest of lukewarm reactions I'd received a week earlier. Gosh darn*, it was, like, really freaking* luke. Had it not been for a cricket I heard faintly chirping at the three-minute mark, or a pin dropping in the upper balcony a couple minutes later, I'm not sure my appearance would have been accompanied by any sound at all.

At one point in the promo, I pointed to Sabu, a true ring warrior if ever there was one, and told him he'd never gotten his full due; that he should have been one of the biggest stars in the business.

Later on backstage, he hugged me and thanked me, and I noticed he was doing his best to fight back tears, and failing. Finally, a tear fell down his battered, scarred face.

"Sorry," he said, wiping the tear away quickly. "I had to do my best not to break down out there in front of the fans."

Wow, tense moment, begging for some levity from the Hardcore Legend. "I wish you would have, brother," I said, slapping Sabu playfully on the collection of keloids that is his deltoid. "It would have proved that someone was listening to my promo."

I didn't take the failure too personally, even laughing to myself at Steve Cold's earlier words. I had given the wrong promo in the wrong place, at the wrong time. Hey, poop* happens, right?

Besides, I'd get 'em next time, right? Well, not exactly. By my count, this would be the second-to-last, honest-to-goodness, microphone-in-hand, making-a-real-point promo I would give as a member of WWE. Not until sixteen months later, in my last appearance for the company, would Vince McMahon allow me any real promo time.

Looking back on it, I'm pretty sure my D.C. promo was the final nail in my WWE main event coffin. Not sure that metaphor even works. Let me see: I'm lying in a coffin, trying to get out in order to do a main event, but nails keep being pounded into the coffin, making it harder to get out to do a main event, then *bam*, there's one more nail, making sure I never get out again. Okay. It works well enough, even if I did get to do one more main event only three months later, but I never really did get that microphone back until that final day.

But I do believe it's safe to say that the powers that be behind the scenes who were not big fans of mine finally won out that night over the powers that be who still felt I had something major to offer.

I had read off and on for months that I had heat with people behind the scenes, and that my depictions of the WWE creative process hadn't won me any new friends within the company. The *Wrestling Observer* hinted that Triple H was not among my biggest fans, which struck many as odd since I'd been fairly influential in his career in 2000, when he was making the transition from popular performer to legitimate main-event bad guy.

To which I say to Triple H . . . brother, . . . that's okay. Honestly. First of all, I was paid for those matches with Triple H. Paid really well, too. It wasn't like I helped him move into a new apartment, or lent him money when he was down.

Second, whether I was helpful to his career or not, Triple H is a part of the McMahon family — he owes it to Vince and Linda, and Shane and Stephanie as well as the shareholders and fans to offer his best opinion, based on what's best for the company, not based on who may have been beneficial to his career.

So let's forget about the idea of anyone owing me anything. If, however, someone wants to start a discussion about how wrong WWE's judgment was, or how they chose to ignore all the big reactions I received in favor of a couple of those cricket chirpers . . . well, I'm willing to listen.

A day after *WrestleMania*, Vince pulled me aside. He had two issues to discuss. One, I was no longer exempt from the WWE dress

code. After years of coming and going pretty much as I pleased —
flannels, sweats, sneakers — I would be expected to wear a sports coat,
slacks, and shoes. I heard the part about the sports coat, but not really
the words *slacks* and *shoes*, choosing to pretend they'd never left his
mouth at all.

Two, I needed to be "repackaged." Fans "no longer connected with
me." There would be no angle, no match with Morrison, no follow-up
on the book. I did a pretaped promo for the Make-A-Wish Foundation
that took me nearly twenty takes — probably because my confidence
was shot — then drove to the airport and caught a flight home, leaving
behind a long legacy of making a difference with the company.

I received a phone call from my editor at Pocket Books a couple
days later. What happened to my big push on TV? she asked. Where
was the big angle?

I told her I'd been sent home for repackaging and recited Vince's
line about not connecting with the fans anymore.

"What?" my editor yelled in disbelief. "You don't connect with the
fans? You're number six on the *New York Times* list!"

COUNTDOWN TO LOCKDOWN: 33 DAYS

March 17, 2009
Orlando, Florida
8:55 a.m.

I've got a bowling ball in my stomach, I've got a desert in my mouth. Figures that my courage would choose to sell out now. That's what's going through my head as I make my way down to ringside for the match I need to do that will get me where I want to go — Philadelphia, Pennsylvania, for my April 19 *Lockdown* match against Sting. Those words are from "Crucify," a song by Tori Amos, who is now making her third appearance in a Mick Foley memoir. Why? Because almost literally, I feel like I have a desert in my mouth. Like an entire desert. Sure, my courage feels like it's been selling out every time I've stepped through the curtain for a big match over the last nine years. My legs always feel like Jell-O; quivering, soft, no real strength upon which to move with the slightest authority. Just walking upright feels like quite an accomplishment come match time. I'm always worried about my wind, too, figuring I haven't done the proper cardio for matches of any magnitude. Usually I'm right, too. My wind goes, and my legs go, and I'm left to rely on a few big moves, a little creative forethought, and a little compassion and understanding on the part of my opponent to carry me through. It worked like a charm at *WrestleMania 2006* with Edge. It worked pretty well at *One Night Stand* in June of '06, too. But that was before that "desert in my mouth" problem started acting up.

*Look, before we move forward, there is something you need to know about my writing style. When I write about wrestling matches that have occurred in the past I nonetheless often refer to them in the present tense, as if they are taking place in my mind. Which, come to think of it, they usually are. Other times I will shift back into a past tense, sometimes without warning. I will leave it up to you as the reader to navigate this particular nuance.

The match is just minutes old, four or five, when Kurt picks me up for an Angle Slam on the concrete. I can almost hear you guys saying, *On the concrete, Mick? Are you crazy?* No, I'm not crazy, but Kurt needs a big move, something drastic and obviously painful to dramatically turn the tide, put me in a world of hurt, and create immediate sympathy. I'm simply not in good enough shape to fight out from underneath, stage comebacks, and hit any kind of impressive offensive moves. I need something quick, efficient, and convincing. Angle Slam on the concrete.

I'm only halfway up and I already feel redeemed. What a difference twenty-four hours can make. Hello, old "light" Mick. So long, you

S.O.S. My back lands with a sickening thud on the concrete — the cold, hard concrete, if you want me to go into details about it. Growing up a wrestling fan, I know concrete just wouldn't be concrete without the adjectives *cold* and *hard* in front of it. I hear the collective groan of the crowd in the Impact Zone, and I know I've got a chance to tell this story. If only I could swallow.

What is it about this pace that makes it such a task? It can't just be nerves. Often, since joining TNA back in September, I've needed only to cut a promo in the ring — and I've found myself barely able to talk. At our live *Impact from Las Vegas*, I was almost in a state of panic, looking at our smoking-hot floor director, Stevie (who is a woman, by the way, a woman "with flaming locks of auburn hair, with ivory skin and eyes of emerald green" — a little Dolly Parton "Jolene" lyric for you), to give me the five-minute cue, and feeling, absolutely feeling, that I had less than a minute of moisture in my body before my mouth just sealed shut, like the slamming of some forbidden tomb.

At least then I was just talking. Now I have to face the prospect of being beaten up by the world's most intense, driven athlete while worrying about my legs, my wind, and my damn saliva. I have a vivid thought, a question that I ask myself as Kurt rolls me into the ring. *If I had a choice between a million dollars and a bottle of water, what would I choose?* It's a million-dollar question, literally. Kurt is putting the boots to me for several seconds when I answer my own question. *I would take the million.* But I had to think about it. Really, really think about it.

There's only one way to make this work. I need to look as helpless as possible — defenseless, incapable of any hope of offense. But I can't just lie there. I've got to be animated in my helplessness. Show my despair to the camera, let the fans in the building and at home feel my pain. Kurt just needs to stay aggressive, ruthless. Not really a problem for Kurt.

I look over at Sting, Kurt's partner for the match. "That's enough, Kurt," he says. "He's had enough." Bingo. There it is. My incentive. My rationale for whatever action I might take. It all goes back to what "Freebird" Michael Hayes told me so long ago: "A heel has to believe he's right." Not that I think my potential actions will turn me heel. I don't really want to be a bad guy. I just want to paint my character with a few shades of gray. For I think it's within these shades of gray that the battle for TV ratings and Pay-Per-View buys will be fought, hopefully won. The ratings have been up for TNA. But these ratings have not been translating to Pay-Per-View buys. I don't know if a match with Sting can be part of the solution. But I think it can. Maybe I'm naïve or slightly delusional. I think there's always been a fine line between self-confidence and self-delusion in our business. Any guy bold enough to think he can make a difference is probably just barely on the right side of that formula. I've seen top guys toward the end of their run fall on the wrong side of that line, and it's not pretty.

I may have little to no confidence in my in-ring abilities, but when it comes to getting people involved in my matches, getting caught up in my stories, I'm like the Little Engine Who Could. I think I can, I think I can. So, if I can just make it to *Lockdown* to face down Sting in about a month, I can hope for those few big moves, that creative forethought, and that understanding and compassion from my opponent to at least give me a chance to pull off some kind of April surprise.

Besides, I have a little over a month to improve my situation. Increase my wind, strengthen my legs, find a solution for that desert in my mouth. Maybe it's a medical condition. Dry mouth. Or, as I've long suspected, it may be the special-effects fog — the smoke that accompanies our entrances — that causes the problem.

I've been searching for answers on the Internet, looking up "dry mouth" and "leg fatigue," as if some magic formula exists for all these things that ail me. I know my name and *Internet* usually go together like Al Snow and *Hall of Famer*, but I'll try anything at this point.

Just about a minute left. Another merciless minute at the hands of Kurt Angle before I can finally harvest the fruits of my labors. Kurt goes for a pinfall but pulls me up at the count of two. How heartless, how diabolical. Sting once again pleads for clemency, but Kurt's compassion well has been dry for quite a while. I know I'm kind of mixing in facts and stories, characters and human beings here, but that's indicative of my mind-set. It certainly feels real to me.

Jeff Jarrett has seen enough. Like a real-life Popeye, the TNA founder has stands all he can stands, and he can't stands no more. (I wonder how many children over the decades have flunked an English test or two due to the influence of the grammatically incorrect sailor?) Jeff fires up his own comeback while I lay prone in the ring. "Bam, bam, bam," or "ga-bing, ga-bing, ga-bing" — depending on which wrestler's vernacular you go with. Down goes the ref. It's an overused but valuable cliché, and it gives Kurt a chance to scamper out to ringside for a metal folding chair. Something else happens, but I'd be lying if I said I had a clue what it is. I'm too tired to really follow everything. My head is starting to clear, enough to realize that a million dollars could be an awful lot to pay for a bottle of water. Still, I'd probably give Stevie about a thousand dollars for just a swig — that would be a pretty good deal.

Jeff has his guitar in hand, but Sting grabs it from him in midswing. I can now concentrate on the action. Sting has the guitar. Jeff may be the founder, and he is a tried-and-true good guy in TNA, but he is not above backpedaling with his hand extended in the face of danger. That "wait a minute, let's talk about this" gesture that must be second nature to a guy like Jeff, who grew up with the business in his blood, a second-generation wrestler who's seen the sneakiest heels in the business do the Memphis backpedal. No one did more backpedaling than a classic Memphis heel — Eddie Gilbert, Jerry Lawler, Robert Fuller — not counting that horrible moonwalk Michael Hayes used to do during all his matches. I never could tell whether Hayes really thought his moonwalk was good or whether he did it just to get heat. But I guess the same could be said for his singing.

I pick up the chair, seemingly looking for vengeance on Angle, the man who bounced my head off the concrete. I make a move toward

Kurt, but he bails from the ring — a noticeable disappointment for all the fans in the Impact Zone. Jeff has stopped backpedaling, Sting has lowered his guard, the situation has seemingly settled. Not so fast. Moving in a little semicircle, maybe a six-foot arc, I wheel my body around, facing an unguarded Sting, and bring the metal chair down over the Icon's head. It's a good shot — maybe not my best, but I think it's good enough. It was probably more of a lunge than a wide-open, have-no-mercy blast, the kind of blast I've given and received (usually received) many times over the course of my career. But he's Sting, he's a legend, he's got a family. Those weren't conscious thoughts in my head, but I wouldn't doubt they were clanking around my subconscious when it came time to pull the trigger.

Maybe I'll feel differently when I have a chance to watch the video, but for now I feel like the contact made is solid enough. If the crowd reaction is any indication, it certainly was. Besides, it's the surprise and outrage that I'm looking for, that "shock and awe," as the previous administration might have said. Hey, say what you will about George W. Bush, but I honestly believe that of all our ex-presidents, he is the most recent. I cover the body of the fallen Stinger, just as our referee conveniently arises from his temporary slumber. One...two...three. I have a lot of explaining to do. I can't wait to start.

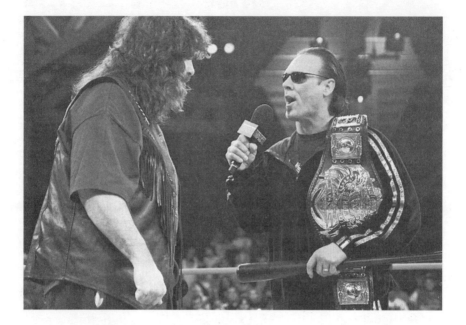

COUNTDOWN TO LOCKDOWN: 32 DAYS

March 18, 2009
Orlando, Florida
12:15 a.m.

I had really wanted to wait a week to make any type of comment regarding the chair shot heard round the world. More accurately, I guess, I had wanted our fans to wait a week to hear my explanation. Maybe the treacherous act could even attain a certain status almost impossible for pro wrestling in 2009 — perhaps it could become "watercooler" cool, the subject of conversation at workplace watercoolers.

"Hey Jim, why ya think Mick Foley hit Sting last night?"

"I dunno. Maybe he's just plain crazy, but come on, we gotta get this tranny fixed before we balance and rotate the tires."

"Jim, why don't ya balance and rotate this...whoa!"

or

"Dr. Stevens, are you bothered at all by Mick Foley's actions on last week's *Impact*?"

"Troubled, deeply troubled, Nurse, but we can talk about that later. That can wait — this heart transplant can't."

or

"Cut, cut. You seemed preoccupied out there, like your mind wasn't on your scene."

"I'm sorry. I guess I was thinking about Mick Foley, wondering what his motivation for attacking Sting could have been."

"Listen, Trina, maybe you could just text him or e-mail him, find out for yourself. Right now I need you concentrating on business. These group scenes aren't cheap, you know."

Still, I understood TNA's concern. They needed to make this match public as soon as possible, to give them an extra week to advertise and promote it. Which meant I needed to come up with a reason in a hurry. A reason I could grab hold of, make people believe in. More important, it had to be a reason I could believe in myself.

Sometimes, out of necessity — dollars and cents, or time — interviews are pretaped and inserted where needed in our two-hour show. One of my tendencies is to lose sight of the context the interview will be placed in and use too much humor, because it feels good at the time. It's a tendency I have to continually be mindful of — which can be difficult when looking at Jeremy Borash holding the microphone with those bulging Ralph Furley eyes. Sometimes I wonder whether Don Knotts had some kind of dalliance with a Borash ancestor during a break on *The Andy Griffith Show* set, or possibly during the filming of *The Ghost and Mr. Chicken*, the critically acclaimed smash film Knotts bailed out on Mayberry for.

Fortunately, on this particular occasion, we're doing this shot more or less live. Less live than if it was being aired live — more live than if it was pretaped earlier in the day. The promo is shot in real time, and I'll be responding to Sting's postmatch challenge to face me for the TNA World Heavyweight Championship at *Lockdown*.

So what's my motivation? It's got to be plausible and I've got to believe.

Ever since hearing of this possible matchup with the Stinger at *Lockdown*, I'd been trying to think of the go-home promo — that last interview people would see before making that choice. To buy or not to buy, that is the question. Honestly, it's a question that way too many of our viewers answer the wrong way — they go with choice B, the "not to buy" option. Don't get me wrong; we're thankful for their viewing support, but the percentage of viewers who go with choice A is too small for our liking. We've got to get that percentage up and it hasn't been easy.

Up until I actually sat in Jeff Jarrett's chair — a symbolic act if ever there was one, a little subtle foreshadowing of things yet to come — I wasn't sure where I might go with my explanation. I just knew my previous idea for a go-home promo, an "I respect you, Sting, but you have to understand, when I get inside that cage I only know one way to wrestle, brother!" type of deal, complete with handshake, was a recipe for a mighty bland entrée. I needed a different recipe — one with a little more spice.

"Okay, I've got it," I told our producer, Vince Russo. "Let's just roll and see how this thing goes."

They began shooting.

J.B. is holding the mike, his eyes not Furleyesque but always on the verge of being so. He's trying to get answers from Jeff Jarrett, who is pacing, irate, confused. Sting had been this close (sorry you can't see it, but I'm holding my thumb and forefinger about half an inch apart, which is pretty close indeed) to leaving Kurt's Main Event Mafia, and now I'd ruined, or at least greatly jeopardized, that possibility.

"Hell, J.B.," Jarrett says, "for the last time, don't ask me, I don't know what the hell is going through his brain."

"I'm here with Jeff Jarrett," J.B. says. "I'm here with Mick Foley, and Mick, you heard the challenge from Sting, you versus Sting, Six Sides of Steel at *Lockdown*, in Philadelphia — and Mick, what happened to you out there?"

Okay, here it is, my big explanation. Ready…and go.

"Do those eyes, J.B., do those eyes for me, J.B." I'm holding my head, I've got an ice pack on my neck, and I'm calm and joking, asking J.B. to show off those Furleys for me.

I'd asked him to show me those eyes earlier in the show, but the mood was lighter then. I'd told Jeff I needed just one match to satisfy my wrestling craving, comparing an occasional match to a slice of pumpkin pie or a sporadic ride on the Incredible Hulk Coaster at Islands of Adventure, the Universal theme park about fifty yards from our studio. The pumpkin pie and coaster were things I could never completely do without but could manage in moderation. But now, this one slice of pie, this one loop-the-loop had turned into something far from moderation.

"The eyes?" J.B. and J.J. (Jeff Jarrett) say in simultaneous disbelief. I mean, how could I take this turn of events so casually?

"Hell, I don't know what happened out there," I say, kind of chuckling to myself. "It was a gut decision. If I had to do it over again, would I? I don't know. But I'll tell you what — I'm proud of my actions. I guess you could chalk it up to inspiration. Sting went out there and he said, 'What inspired you, Mick?' and I think if I had to use one word to explain what inspired me it would be…Sting. Sting inspired me."

Time to get serious now, time to make my point. I take my hand off my head and get a little more animated.

"Make no mistake about it, J.B., Kurt Angle beat the crap out of me — it was on *Impact*, it was live [not technically true, but cut me a little slack]. Worse than I'd been beaten in a long time — and that's fine! That's how the game is played. You know what's not fine, J.B.? Out of the corner of my bad ear [usually it's eyes, not ears, that are associated with corners, but continue that slack cutting, please] I hear Sting say the words, 'That's enough, Kurt, he's had enough, just pin him, Kurt, just pin him.'"

Here it comes. If it was an adult film, they'd call it the money shot. If it was any other business in the world, they wouldn't.

"'Just pin him'?" I repeat incredulously, this time in a yell, and throw my ice pack at the wall. "Just pin him? You condescending little son of a bitch, Sting! Who the hell do you think you are? Who the hell are you to tell me when I've had enough? Are you making all the decisions now? Are you the decider? I'll tell *you* when I've had enough! And it's not yet! You want to issue a challenge like a big man? You want to go back to school? Old school? You want to lock me up inside a steel cage? Are you sure that's a good idea? Because what you call hell — I call home. I was looking for happiness, J.B., and by God, I found it! Stinger, you and I at *Lockdown* ... and I will tear you apart!"

There it is. My reason. A reason I can believe in. Aside from the Colonel Trautman "what you choose to call hell, he calls home" reference from the 1985 movie *Rambo: First Blood Part II*, I really liked it.

First Blood, by the way, was the movie I went to on my very first date — a true romantic gesture. Come to think of it, my last date, too, with that particular young lady, except for the Superdance debacle about a week later, which I fictionalized, but only slightly so, for my first novel, *Tietam Brown*.

I wouldn't have another date for almost three years — my first real girlfriend, my college sweetheart. It only lasted a couple of months, until she graduated from college, but, man, that was a good time in my life. I hadn't really thought about that college love in a while — until right now, that is. So, instead of thinking about my return to Promoland, I'm thinking about my first love, wondering what she's doing, where she might be, if she remembers those memorable seconds (almost thirty, I believe) of passion we shared.

Thank goodness for wrestling — it cushioned the heartbreak, gave me something to love that occasionally loved me back in those next couple of years between dates. Yes, that's right, a couple of years, until a charming coed stepped into my life and closed out the last two weeks of college life in memorable fashion. Really, really memorable fashion. Memorable as in I remember every second — and this time there were almost sixty of them! Yes!

In the interest of full disclosure, there was the motel manager who seduced me in Pittsburgh (really knew her stuff) and the hitchhiker who massaged more than my ego while her boyfriend slept in the back-seat of my Ford Fairmont. But that was it. You know, I don't believe this thought has crossed my mind in twenty-three years, but I believe that motel manager would have been up for seducing me a second time if I'd only made a phone call. My loss — she really, really knew her stuff.

So, I lacked a little in female companionship. A lot of people did. And they dealt with it in different ways. Some retreated into little fan-tasy worlds, be it *Dungeons and Dragons*, a fifty-seventh viewing of *Star Wars*, or the precursors of Internet porn — videotape rentals. Back then, it wasn't so easy to be a pervert. You had to actually enter a store, make your way into that forbidden back room — eighteen and older, please, we do check ID — and make a person-to-person videotape rental transac-tion. There might even be eye contact, provided you could take your eyes away from your shoes for just a fleeting moment before heading out that door, hoping you hadn't been spotted by a former teacher, the parent of a friend, or any living soul, before making it to that trusty VCR and see-ing what Kay Parker had to offer before Mom and Dad got back home.

But, I had another world to retreat to. A place I still visit from time to time. A place reserved for big guys in tights who pretend to fight. A place where one guy in tights can think of ways to tell that other guy in tights what's going to transpire when they finally meet up... and pretend to fight. I know the place well. Some of you might have enjoyed the trip you took there with me in *The Hardcore Diaries*. And after a three-year hiatus, I'm going back. Back to Promoland!

COUNTDOWN TO *LOCKDOWN*: 27 DAYS

March 23, 2009
Washington, D.C.
2:40 a.m.

I'll admit it. I was a little nervous about seeing Linda McMahon. I've been a USO volunteer since November 2003, when I made my first trip to the Walter Reed Army Medical Center to visit American troops wounded in the conflicts in Iraq and Afghanistan. I really thought my first visit would be my last, but I felt inspired by that first visit, feeling as so many do who visit with our injured troops — that I'd gotten so much more out of my visit than I'd actually given. And so I continued going — every month for a couple of years, every few months in the years that followed.

I was never completely sold on the logic behind going to war in Iraq, but nonetheless, I had the deepest admiration for the men and women who willingly put themselves in harm's way, doing what our country asked of them. Probably because I wanted to be a soldier or marine for the longest time, wearing my hair in a crew cut back in the late seventies and early eighties, when literally no one else in school did, visiting military recruiters every year from age seventeen to twenty, even holding out a distant dream of being an officer and a gentleman, just like Richard Gere. I guess you could say that I turned out to be neither. So, while I never did serve my country in uniform, I did get my applications to West Point and Annapolis rejected.

It really wasn't until I was a sophomore in college that I gave up the dream, realizing that the military look just wasn't going to work with the new look I was working on. You know, the look I have now. The same look I've had since late 1985, with the exception of a mid-2000 buzz cut, when I thought I would never, and I mean *never*, be in the public eye again. I think I cut it again sometime in 2002, but those haircuts were just two bumps in an otherwise smooth twenty-four-year road of unkempt, unchanging, completely unflattering long hairstyles.

Despite this lack of military style, I have been thoroughly embraced by the USO and in the process have met luminaries and dignitaries, four-star generals and secretaries of defense, senators and congressmen, celebrities and journalists. And, of course, I've met so many fine young men and women, people I've talked with and laughed with, held hands with and prayed with, all the while learning lessons about perseverance and bravery, honor and dignity, and a loyalty to country that someone like me, who's never served, will never be able to completely comprehend.

I have been a part of the annual USO gala every year, save one, since my first in 2004. So, I've been to five of the past six, breaking out the tux every year, except for the one year when I just simply forgot it was black tie and never did grasp how underdressed I was until photographic evidence showed what appeared to be a large man in an ill-fitting sports coat, sporting the always-winning combo of sweatpants and work boots.

WWE has been a part of the gala for the past several years. In 2004, they were awarded the first Legacy of Hope Award (named in honor of the legendary comedian Bob Hope), in recognition of all the time and effort WWE had put in on behalf of the troops. On that night five years ago, I gave the acceptance speech, quite an honor given that Triple H, Batista, and Linda McMahon were there with me on the stage accepting the award on behalf of the company.

Even during the years before I "officially" rejoined WWE in 2006, I was always kind of with them when it came to these types of things. This would be the first year that I would clearly be not "kind of" with them. In fact, I wouldn't be with them at all. Which presented a potentially awkward scene — WWE would be presenting the Legacy of Hope Award to the NFL Alumni Association while I would sit there and watch as WWE history was conveniently reinvented.

So, like I said, there was the potential for a little awkwardness. A few weeks ago, I had asked the USO who would be there from WWE.

Gary Davis, they said. That was cool; I'd known and worked with Gary for years — had even gone to China with him a couple years ago. Ken Anderson would be there, too. Hey, I like Ken, and I've always hit it off with him. Much to my daughter Noelle's embarrassment, Ken had reminded Noelle that her favorite word during the filming of *Beyond the Mat*, when she was three and four years old, had indeed been *nipples*.

A couple of years ago, Ken and I had the opportunity to tour Walter Reed with then Miss America Jennifer Berry. Jennifer was real cool, couldn't have been nicer, and even let me hold her crown while on the bus ride over to the hospital.

The Polaroid camera is a ubiquitous (there's a good SAT word) presence on these hospital visits; a photo is taken in every room visited. One time, I arrived for my visit just a day after Al Snow had toured the hospital and spotted many a prestigious Al Snow Polaroid gracing the bottoms of garbage cans throughout the premises. I know Polaroid went bankrupt a few years ago, but the USO must have stockpiles of film somewhere, as the photos are always around.

On this day, however, our USO guide was briefly delayed, as Ken, Jennifer, and I found ourselves in the room of a wounded soldier, the Polaroid camera in Jennifer's possession. I *think* I know what she *meant* to say. Something like "Mick, why don't you take a photo of me with this soldier, and then I will take a photo of this soldier with the two of you?"

Once again, that's what I *think* she *meant* to say. What Miss America actually said was this: "Mick, why don't you do me first, and then I'll do both of you at the same time?" Ken, the soldier, and I just looked at each other, startled, not knowing exactly what to say. This was, after all, a suggestion from Miss America. Fortunately, we opted not to say anything, not even a sophomoric *whoa ho ho* or a Hank Kingsley–like *Hey now!*, opting instead to let Miss America grasp the weight of her own words.

"You know," Jennifer finally said. "I'm not sure that came out the way I wanted it to."

Then we chimed in with all that sophomoric stuff: "Whoa ho ho, hey now," etc.

So, yeah, despite the fact that we worked for different companies, Ken and I, having shared a male bonding moment like no other, were going to be cool.*

Anyone else? I asked the USO.

Linda McMahon, they said.

Ouch, that one could sting a little. I'd always had the deepest respect for Linda, as a businesswoman, as a mother, as a person. Darn it, she'd been in my corner at *WrestleMania 2000*, my retirement

---

*Of course Ken is now a major star with TNA.

match after my other retirement match, before I un-retired four years later. But I really didn't know what I'd say to her. I knew she'd be at the cocktail reception for some of the special guests a little later in the evening…and I had no idea what I would say.

It was in the back of my mind all day, from my flight into Baltimore, to my ride into D.C., to my attempting to play wheelchair basketball with some of the outpatients, who knew their way around the court a whole lot better than I did.

I arrived fashionably late for the reception, wondering what I might say, dreading the thought of trying to piece together a conversation with someone who had been such a big part of my past. Okay, maybe that sounds a little dramatic, because I didn't know Linda all that well, despite the fact that she'd been in my corner at 'Mania, but nonetheless, she is a major part of WWE, which had been a major part of my life — ergo, Linda was a big part of my life!

I walked into the room. Thankfully, no Linda. Over in the corner was my security blanket, the guy I would cling to emotionally to get through this trying time. Rick Yarosh, as fine a man as you're likely to meet anywhere. I met Rick a year ago, when he and *The Daily Show*'s Jon Stewart laid a wreath at the Tomb of the Unknown Soldier.*

Rick had suffered incredible burns following an explosion in Iraq in September 2006. His nose and both ears were gone, several fingers had been incinerated, and even after dozens of major operations, his face was still a mask of scars, a document to suffering I can't even begin to gauge.

But within a few minutes of meeting him last year, he put us all at ease. We no longer saw him for his scars, but rather for his laugh, his easygoing manner, his infectious optimism, and his love for life. I'll never forget that day with Rick and Jon: touring Arlington National Cemetery, getting a behind-the-scenes tour of the Tomb, making

---

*Solely because of this experience, I was later chosen to be *The Daily Show*'s Senior Ass Kicker.

a vow to myself that I would never again complain about the little things in life. A vow I kept for almost a day.

So there I was, the Hardcore Legend, clinging to Rick and his mom and dad, hoping they'd protect me from that big bad Linda.

I started to relax. I talked with Al Franken (now Senator Al Franken) and his wife, Franni, for several minutes. Senator Kay Hagan from North Carolina stopped by for a few minutes as well. I even shared a story with actress Renée Zellweger. (Man, is this good name-dropping stuff, or what?) I mistook actress Leeann Tweeden for the current Miss America, an error she gently corrected me on after about the seventh time I made it.

"You know, I don't think I am who you think I am," she said.

"You're not?"

"No, I'm not Miss America."

"Wow, that's kind of embarrassing."

"Don't worry about it," she said, a big smile on her beautiful Danish/Filipino (what a great combination) features. "As far as mistakes go, that's a pretty flattering one."

By the end of the night, Leeann and I would be pretty good buddies.

Uh-oh, there she is. Coming toward me. Linda. What will I say?

"Hi, Linda." Good one, Mick.

"Hello, Mick," she says.

And we share a little hug. All in all, the meeting with Linda went pretty well, and all that trepidation seemed unwarranted. Keep that word *trepidation* in mind — I'll get back to it.

I told Linda about a nice surprise I'd received a few days earlier. Where a fan had asked me to sign a big coffee-table book, a *WWE Encyclopedia*, which had a two-page spread of me in it. I looked through the book. Not too many guys getting the two-page spread. Only the really big shots: Steve Austin, the Rock, Hulk Hogan, Undertaker, Triple H, Shawn Michaels, a few more, but not too many. I looked at the front of the book, inside page three, looking for a publication date, figuring 2006, 2007. I was momentarily stunned to see

the number 2009, meaning that the book had been published several months after I'd left. Certainly, if he'd wanted to, Vince could
have personally pulled (or reduced) my spread, kind of like he'd done
with the *SmackDown vs. Raw* and *Legends of WrestleMania* video
games. To be honest, given the choice, I would have preferred to
have been shut out of the book and kept in the games, as those video
game royalties can be significant. Still, I had to admit that being
given such a spread in the *WWE Encyclopedia* was a very pleasant
surprise.

"To be honest, Linda, I thought I'd get a postage-stamp-type layout."

Linda smiled, knowing, I think, that I was sincere. You don't get as
far as Linda McMahon has in the wrestling business, or in life, without being able to spot insincerity a mile away.

"Mick, you were a very big part of our company," she said. "You
deserve to be recognized in that book."

Bam. Just like that, all the tension disappeared. I hung out. I enjoyed
the night. So what if I was introduced to the gala audience immediately after Rick's incredible list of heroics had been rattled off? From a
standing O to a polite smattering of applause in a matter of moments.

Even watching Ken and Linda present the award I'd once accepted
didn't feel all that awkward. Besides, I later learned that Elaine Rog-
ers, the president of USO Metro Washington, had asked WWE if
they were cool with me being there. I don't know if WWE would
have the power to bump me from the event, but they sure could have
made things a lot more difficult. But Elaine assured me it was never a
problem, that WWE knew how big a deal volunteering for the USO
was to me.

Al Franken gave a nice speech, vowing that if his Senate confirmation process ever did come to completion (which it has since this writing) he would "fight to make sure the troops get whatever they need,"
both during and after the fighting.

And Renée Zellweger gave a beautiful speech, noting how "trepidatious" (see, there's that word, or at least the root word with a different

suffix) she'd been while waiting outside the door of the first injured service member she was scheduled to encounter.

Later, I congratulated her on a wonderful speech.

"Thank you," she said, her Texas accent soft and sugary, like honey.

"You had me at *trepidatious*."

Not much you can do after a line like that except go upstairs and write about it.

Young and innocent days.

A SURPRISE FOR DIANE B.

Somehow the talk in the dressing room turned to tattoos. These days, a guy in wrestling is considered something of an oddity if he isn't inked, but back when I was in high school, even college, a guy was really making a statement if he had the slightest little mark on his body. *An Officer and a Gentleman* even had Richard Gere's on-screen dad, Robert Loggia, pleading, "Zack, come back...officers don't have tattoos," when given the news that Gere's Zack Mayo character is off to OCS — Officer Candidate School — seemingly unimpressed with his dad's graduation present of two willing women, still dozing peacefully in bed after an implied father-son tag team contest.

I once used a line from that scene with Al Snow in Las Vegas — consoling the Prince of Hardcore after a long line of embarrassing losses. "Kind of like that night we banged those two stewardesses in Manila," I said to Al, as we rode the Big Shot roller coaster atop the Stratosphere Casino, one thousand feet in the air. Later, after giving the "Manila" line a little thought, I asked the WWE producer to put the kibosh on that particular piece of footage, just in case any members of our viewing audience (my wife, Al's wife) weren't completely up to speed on Loggia and Gere's unique brand of father-son bonding.

Years later that scene still resonated with me. Even after becoming an unlikely orange juice pitchman, all I could picture when I saw Loggia were those two stewardesses in Manila. I guess an actor could be remembered for worse...just ask poor Ned Beatty.

Anyway, Zack headed off to OCS with a big bandage on his arm, where his secret is discovered by Lou Gossett Jr., as Drill Sergeant Foley (no relation), who immediately recognizes the work as being from Subic Bay, in the Philippines.

Suffice it to say, the tattoo, circa 1982, my junior year in high school, was solely the domain of the bad boy, the badder girl, the drunken sailor, or the prison inmate. Of which, Diane Bentley was none.

Sting was the guy who asked me. "Mick, you don't have one, do you?"

"As a matter of fact, I do," I said. "I have a black panther on my hip."

A bunch of heads turned. This was a surprise to some of the biggest names in the business, including Kevin Nash, who I thought would have known, given his propensity for surreptitiously staring at me while I showered over about a two-year period — from early '92 through the end of '93, when he left WCW to become "Diesel" in WWE.

"Yes, it's true," I said, pulling my sweats down just a wee bit to show off a faded Huey Newton portrait on my left hip.

Okay, maybe it wasn't *that* kind of black panther...and I'm pretty sure Nash never surreptitiously scoped me out.

How long had I had the tattoo? Oh, I guess, about twenty-seven years. Why had I gotten it? To impress Diane Bentley — what other reason could there possibly be?

To this day, I don't think it was a romantic gesture. I'm not claiming I hadn't at one point had a little crush on her, but I'm pretty sure it was over by the time the tattoo tale transpired. Diane was like my super-cool friend. Not supercool as in cheerleader-type popular. I mean cool as in doing my math homework for me without even being asked, giving me free Carvel scoops, and absolutely loving Springsteen. In return, I would write humorous songs and poems about her ("Bentley and the Jets" being one of my best), and even did a few essays for her in Mr. Biggers's poetry class, which received considerably better grades than the assignments I turned in under my own name. I saw Biggers last year at a local college basketball game and called him out on it, finally asserting my long-held feeling that he'd been judging a book (me) by its cover (my appearance). I even told him that the limerick he'd liked so much years earlier had not rolled off the pen of Jim Arceri at all, but off the pen of the Hardcore Legend.

In a little side note to that little side note (to go off on a tangent from the tangent I'd gone off on), Biggers's wife, Miss Stefanic, had been my third-grade teacher in 1973, when I'd had my mouth badly busted in a friendly game of Kill the Guy with the Ball and realized I didn't completely dislike the sensation of turning my white Chicago Bears sweatshirt an instant shade of red — a story I told during a famous 1997 *Raw* interview with Jim Ross.

So, anyway, Diane Bentley paused from whatever pressing poetry need was at hand to tell me her intention of getting a tattoo. Like I said, back in '82 only real bad girls got tattoos — and Diane, while being supercool, didn't strike me as the type. Although, come to think of it, she wasn't all that squeaky clean — smoked a little, gave out free scoops, and in the long run probably hurt me more than helped me by doing all my math homework.

I looked up at Diane and calmly informed her that I already did have a tattoo, which was absolutely not true. As a matter of fact, I'd never even thought about it. Not a single thought, ever. But that didn't stop me from venturing out that very day, to a seedy part of Long Island, to one of only a few places in my county that dared to do such dubious work.

And I never even mentioned it to Diane. Certainly I didn't mention how I whimpered in pain at the first hint of needle poking flesh. I didn't even know how tattooing was done. I guess I thought it was like a painless superpermanent marker — just something that was drawn on.

A good two weeks passed, maybe even more. I didn't say a word about tattoos and neither did Diane. Maybe the trip to Medford had been a total waste of time — the most foolish needle-related experience since Leo DiCaprio hit the hard stuff in *The Basketball Diaries*. It wasn't as if I thought Diane Bentley was going to swoon and slowly melt like a scoop of Carvel in the sun. I just thought she'd have a supercool reaction. Even when I was in high school, I needed that reaction, that positive feedback, that pop from the crowd. Sure, running out to get a tattoo for the sake of a single girl's reaction might seem a little extreme, but was it really any worse than taking back body drops on gymnasium floors in front of only slightly larger crowds?

Mr. Biggers pulled a no-show. Absent for the day. Half the class decided not to show up, too, and the sub for the day just let the remaining students read, study, or even talk quietly among themselves.

"So, Mick?" Diane Bentley said, a mischievous little smile on her face.

"Yeah."

"How's that tattoo?" Yes, there it was — the question I'd been hoping for.

"Oh, the tattoo?" I said. "It's good."

"Oh yeah?" Obviously cynical.

Diane went back to writing, possibly cranking out my next geometry assignment.

"You know, Diane," I finally said, "I don't think you believe me."

In an odd way, looking at it now, her reaction reminded me of Victoria Wilson, my editor at Knopf, telling me in a fairly declarative tone that the rewrites I'd turned in couldn't possibly be any good.

"Why not?" I'd asked Ms. Wilson.

"Because you cannot rewrite a book in one day."

That's the same tone Diane Bentley took with me: "Mickey...I know you don't have a tattoo." Calm, but fairly declarative.

"Mickey, I know you don't have a tattoo," she repeated.

This was going to be fun.

"Well, I do have one," I said, turning in my seat to face the front of the class, hoping she'd continue with this line of questioning.

"Okay, Mickey, let me see it."

"What?" I said, pretending not to hear.

"I said okay, Mickey, let me see it."

Diane Bentley had a huge smile on her face, toying with her good friend, calling his bluff.

That smile disappeared the moment I took my trousers down — a theme that would remain constant with women throughout my life. The moment she saw that first black panther paw peeking out of my undies her entire demeanor changed. The smile disappeared, replaced by that look of wonderment and disbelief a kid gets looking at the magician at a birthday party: wondering how it was done, but not quite accepting it as true magic.

But what could she do? As the unveiling proceeded, Diane had to accept that her shy friend Mickey — the kid with the out-of-style crew cut, the limited wardrobe, the never-kissed lips — was a bad boy in disguise.

"Mickey...I...am...freaking out!" There it was, the reaction I'd been hoping to get — not necessarily the freaking-out part, but the surprise, the excitement.

"So what do you think?" I said.

"I'll tell you what I think, Mickey...I think I...am...freaking out!" she practically yelled.

I called Diane Bentley a few days ago, just to see if she had any qualms about being in my book. It had been a few years since I'd seen or talked to her, since I'd heard her distinctive voice yelling out "Hey Mickey" at an appearance at an upstate New York minor-league baseball game. She had just come to the game as a spectator with her family, having no idea that the Hardcore Legend would also be among the attendees.

"I'll be honest, Mickey," she said during the phone call. "I never thought people would stand in line to meet you."

"Hey Diane, do you remember that tattoo I showed you in high school?"

"Yeah."

"Did you know the only reason I got it was to impress you?"

She asked me if I ever regretted it, much in the same way I'd asked wrestler Stevie Richards if he regretted the weak, homemade-looking Mötley Crüe tattoo on his shoulder. "Every single day," Richards had told me. "Every single day."

"You know, Diane, there are probably months at a time that go by when I don't even think about that tattoo. But I've never regretted it once, not a single day. Your reaction in Biggers's poetry class made it all worth it."

A reaction, any reaction, I learned — be it laughter, disgust, dismay, or the look of shock from Diane Bentley in Mr. Biggers's poetry class — could be a very powerful...and addictive...thing.

COUNTDOWN TO LOCKDOWN: 24 DAYS

March 26, 2009
Long Island, New York
11:01 p.m.

"Stinger, I don't blame you for being angry with me," I said. "You asked for an explanation and doggone it, I'm going to give you one and I think in a few minutes we're going to be laughing about this because it's really quite simple. It was a big misunderstanding. Now, I've put together a tape, I had Keith Mitchell in the back put together a little video to straighten things up, but before we see this video, I want to make it clear that I had taken a heck of a beating at the hands of Kurt Angle. Stinger, I'd been Angle Slammed, right out there, by the announcer's desk, my head literally bouncing off the concrete floor. I'd been battered from pillar to post, so I may have been in a slightly altered state when I saw the following scene take place. Let's take a look."

I was thinking of going with an exaggerated "Ralphie" from A *Christmas Story* — trying to whip up some fake tears, but instead, I opted for a little simple overacting, making sure everyone knew just how disingenuous I was being. I smile while I play and replay the scene in my Christmas room. *Impact* has just ended and I think the show went well.

"There is Jeff Jarrett — he is going for the guitar. Remember, I don't know this, I am out, I see nothing, Jarrett wielding the guitar and there's Sting — here is where things take a turn for the worse. Because you, Sting, you grab the guitar, now watch, when I come around, when I finally come to, it appears to me as if you are threatening the life of the founder, Jeff Jarrett. I believe you are going to wind up, I believe you are about to take his life, so in an act of desperation, oh, I save the life of the founder, lashing out to protect the man who founded TNA."

There are some faint boos, and some looks of bemusement in the crowd. Not too many people are going to buy me as an honest-to-goodness bad guy, but I think they enjoy seeing this other side of me. Clearly, I'm energized and enjoying this new tweak in my character.

Sting doesn't look like he's enjoying this ludicrous explanation — at least not on camera. "You think this is funny, Mick?" the Stinger asks. "You think it's some kind of a joke? It wasn't funny last week when you hit me with that chair. I wasn't laughing then and I'm not laughing now, Mick. Don't you get it, Mick, last week, I was trying to protect you, Mick. That's all I was trying to do. Mick, let's face it, I understand the physical pain that you are in. Mick, I've seen what it's like, the pain on your face just trying to get up and out of a chair. Mick, your body is ravaged. You left a piece of yourself right here in the middle of the ring, all over the world, Mick, and you did it for these wrestling fans right here. Mick, you didn't just do it for the fans, but you did it for all the boys, all the wrestlers in the back, Mick. You even did it for me. And last week when I tried to protect you, I did it because I respected you, but I'm starting to get a little bit pissed off now. And I'm starting to lose the respect right now."

Sting has used my first name ten times in a one-minute time frame. You know who would be happy? Vince McMahon — he hates pronouns. Really.

"Well, aren't you the humanitarian, Stinger," I say sarcastically. "Make no mistake about it, times are tough out there. A lot of people are down. The stock market is spiraling out of control. Foreclosures are forcing people out of their homes. The job market has never been worse. A lot of people out there could use your help, Stinger, but I'm not one of them. Who the hell are you to pity me?

"Now, maybe a couple of weeks ago I could have used that pity. Let's face it, Stinger, it was a sad sight, me sitting there in a director's chair reliving my glory days, talking about Hardcore History 101, whoopee!"

For several weeks, I had been doing a segment on *Impact* called "Hardcore History 101," telling stories about my glory days. This was a Vince Russo idea, and a good one, laying down a solid foundation for my return to the ring. The segments may not have been popular with some fans (who thought I spoke too much about current WWE star Randy Orton or revealed too much about the inner workings of the wrestling business), but as a long-term character builder I thought they were effective; illustrating an inner fictitious desire to once again step back inside that ring.

"But since last week's *Impact*, Stinger, things have changed, because from the moment that steel chair made impact with your skull, the tables of time have turned. You can feel it in the air.

"No one is talking about that other wrestling show in April anymore, Stinger. They are talking about *Lockdown*."

I regretted saying this the moment it came out of my mouth, knowing it was not only factually incorrect but might be perceived as a slap in the face to anyone at WWE who works so hard to make *Wrestle-Mania* such a great event. It's the type of comment I would have hated and found disrespectful when I was a WWE guy. But that's one of the drawbacks of visiting Promoland — you don't know every word that might come out. You've got a feeling, you've got a general idea, but it's not rehearsed and not predigested. Therefore, it's sometimes not as smooth as it might be — a little lump in the creative pudding. Which is probably why politicians so rarely veer off script these days. With cameras following those poor guys 24-7, no one wants to get caught in one of these gotcha moments. This line was especially lumpy, but nonetheless probably better than "The statistical percentage of people talking about *Lockdown* as compared to the other show has changed to a slight extent." Okay, enough of the explanations; let's get back to the promo.

"They are talking about you versus me, Icon versus Legend, which is exactly the way it should be. But make no mistake about it, when that cage door slams shut and you and I are locked inside the Six Sides of Steel, it won't be some pathetic loser crying about the old days like some drunk in a corner bar, talking about the night he copped a feel at the homecoming dance. No, Stinger, you and I, we're not going to be *reliving* history. We will be *making* history. Oh yeah, as far as those big dives off the cage, Stinger, as far as those big dives, I've still got a couple left. Bang bang, bang bang...." (This line would later come back to haunt me.)

Yes, I did it! A few visits to Promoland, and *bam*, I'm at the top of my game. I have no doubt, absolutely no doubt in my mind, that if *Lockdown* merely required me to come out and tell people how good I was going to be at *Lockdown*, that I would tear the roof off the place.

Unfortunately, it's not that simple. *Lockdown* is actually going to require some physicality — a one-on-one matchup that will be among the biggest challenges of my career.

My legs have no strength. My cardiovascular conditioning has been weak to nonexistent. I've got that "desert in my mouth" thing happening. And Promoland can only get me through TV tapings — it can get me *to* but not *through Lockdown*. For that, I'm going to need some inspiration. This looks like a job for Tori Amos.

*There's more wrestling in this — my favorite chapter —
than you might think.*

MEETING TORI AMOS

(Really Deep Thoughts from an Unlikely Fan)

I almost passed on the chance to meet Tori Amos. I'd been thinking a lot about this opportunity for two days, since learning of her
two-hour promotional appearance at the San Diego Comic-Con. I'd
made appearances at this convention in two previous years — in 1999
to promote Chaos! Comics' new *Mankind* comic book, and in 2006
to create an initial buzz for my third memoir, *The Hardcore Diaries*.
The convention had been big back in 1999, and it provided me with
my first real look at the bizarre subculture of the comic-book fan:
people who traveled hundreds, sometimes thousands, of miles to buy
and sell comics, talk shop, attend seminars, and walk around for hours
dressed as their favorite sci-fi characters or superheroes — kind of like
a slightly nerdier version of my own fan base. By 2006, though, it had
just exploded and had transcended the boundaries of mere comic-
book convention to become a legitimate pop-culture phenomenon.
Indeed, the Con, as it had come to be known, had become a place
to make deals, where A-list stars and directors premiered trailers for
new films, where advance buzz, or the lack thereof, could either make

or break a project. Nonetheless, the Con struck me as an odd place to find Tori Amos, singer of beautiful songs and the most unlikely inspiration in my professional wrestling career.

I'd been nervous about this Con, anyway, even before beginning my great two-day internal Tori Amos debate. Those two previous appearances had been a piece of cake — two hours in 1999, one hour in 2006 — both heavily promoted by WWE and the Con. No real chance of seeming like anything but a big star. No chance of looking like Mickey Rourke in *The Wrestler*, sitting at his table in near solitude, at a legends convention the whole world forgot to attend. This Con would be different for me — three days of signings, four hours a day. No project to promote, no financial guarantee — you sign what you sign, you get what you get, you hope for the best.

Three days, as it turned out, was one day too many. Or maybe, more accurately, four hours on that third day was about two hours too many. Pretty much anyone with any desire to meet me had already done so, leaving plenty of time for doubts, nerves, and Tori-fueled trepidation to get a good grip on me. Simply put, I was afraid to meet Tori Amos. On the surface, this fear might seem foolish. After all, I'm six four, weighing in around 300. Tori, five four, maybe 110, 120 tops. Besides, I'd met big stars, lots of them. Sports Hall of Famers, Academy Award–winning actors, eighties adult film icon Christy Canyon. I've even got photographic evidence that some of these meetings took place — those "look at the camera, smile, act like you've known each other more than five seconds" types of photos. Look, there I am with Secretary of Defense Robert Gates; with baseball's all-time hit leader, Pete Rose; with lovable, foulmouthed rapper Snoop Dogg.

Some of these meetings are memorable or even touching. Katie Couric closed out a *Today* episode on Halloween 2001 by holding my then one-year-old little Mickey, who was dressed as a pumpkin — a moment I once referred to as the best of my career. I actually feel fortunate and blessed to have met so many talented and famous people, some of whom I'd admired for years. But I wasn't actually afraid to meet any of them. This was different. For of all the artists, athletes, and other dignitaries whose work has in some way touched my life, none has done so on a more personal, emotional level than the music of Tori Amos.

I can still remember the first time I heard that voice. Sitting in the back of Maxx Payne's (the wrestler, not the video game, comic, or Mark Wahlberg movie character) colossal '79 Lincoln two-door Coupe Mark V, embarking on some otherwise forgettable road trip in the Deep South — Alabama, Mississippi, Louisiana, it doesn't really matter — in the fall of 1993. In another lifetime, Maxx had been Darryl Peterson, an All-American heavyweight wrestler at Iowa State. That was 1985. By 1993, Darryl was Maxx, six foot six, nearly 400 pounds, a mountain of a man with waist-length, jet-black hair, a booming, gravelly, baritone voice, and one of the nicest dispositions of anyone in the wrestling business, or probably any business for that matter. And in 1993, Maxx was all about the music. Along with Brian Armstrong (WWE's "Road Dogg," TNA's "B. G. James"), referee Nick Patrick (our copilot for this particular road trip), and 350-pound, Mohawk-wearing bass player Dr. Squash, Maxx had put together a first-rate rock-and-roll band — part heavy metal, part grunge, part insightful social/wrestling commentary — and spent most of his nonwrestling time holed up with the band in a sound studio, working on an album that never did quite materialize, although legendary rocker Steve Miller (*The Joker, Fly Like an Eagle*) gave the demo a listen and once referred to it as "the album Pink Floyd should have put out, but never did."

Some of the guys called Maxx "Maxxguiver" — a nod to the TV show whose hero seemed to escape death on a weekly basis with the aid of a paper clip — for his propensity for collecting random gadgets that seemed to serve no useful purpose. But when it came to his Lincoln, that passion for gadgetry seemed to find its useful purpose. Equipped with every technological innovation known to man, and possessing the type of wattage normally reserved for the sleep deprivation of captured South American drug lords, Maxx's gas-guzzler, affectionately named Miss Christine, was like a rusting two-ton boom box on wheels, as we barreled down some unknown Southern highway, heading for a tour I can't recall and a show I have no memory of.

But I remember that music, that all-out audio assault that Maxx and Nick Patrick subjected me to for so many hours on that night so long ago. Megadeth was there — and I must admit that singer Dave Mustaine had a way with a phrase, although those phrases were delivered at a volume just a little too loud for my liking. Then there was some Rage Against the Machine, where Maxx and Nick knew the words to every angry, socially conscientious song — every song. I'm not sure Zack de la Rocha knew the words to *every* song . . . and he was the band's lead singer! Then, something called GWAR, and a few other offerings so raucous and raw they made the guys in GWAR seem like sensitive song stylists by comparison.

Finally, I tapped out, picking a spot in between menacing musical offerings to meekly request something a little less combative. As a veteran of the wrestling business — eight years as of that moment back in 1993 — I fully understood that the selection of the tunes was almost always the sole dominion of the automobile's driver and his chosen copilot. Over the years, a few backseat passengers have voiced disapproval at my choice of Christmas tunes in July — and ended up getting an extra dose of Nat King Cole for their trouble. But by this point, I was willing to usurp wrestling protocol; I was almost begging for some aural relief.

Maxx briefly turned off the system as he considered my request. "You know, Jack," he said, baritone booming (remember, I was Cactus Jack back then), "I have something you might like."

Those words turned out to be something of an understatement.

I always thought I had an appreciation for diverse musical styles. As a halfway-decent college DJ from 1984 to 1987 I had been exposed to some great progressive stuff, and I always took a certain amount of pride in unearthing and exposing unheralded musical gems or dusting off some forgotten classics.

But, up until that night with "Miss Christine," Tori Amos had eluded me. I was vaguely aware of the name but most definitely not the voice, which instantly struck me as an instrument of unique and incredibly emotive beauty. By turns haunting, tender, defiant, angry, vulnerable — sometimes within the same lyric, the first four songs of that Maxx Payne selection *Little Earthquakes* were altogether unlike anything I'd ever heard.

And then there was "Winter." Is there such a thing as falling musically in love — love at first listen? If so, I fell helplessly, hopelessly, in love with that song from that very first time:

Snow can wait, I forgot my mittens
Wipe my nose, get my new boots on...

The sound system that had earlier seemed so invasive, seemed suddenly transportive, as if the Lincoln's backseat was my own intimate concert hall, as if Tori Amos were sitting next to me on that cracked leather interior, singing her heart out for an audience of one.

When you gonna make up your mind? she asks me, accompanied by the gentlest, tenderest of notes from the Bösendorfer piano she has somehow managed to sneak into the backseat of Maxx's car. *When you gonna love you as much as I do?*

Maxx and Nick had seen her play the song on Leno or Letterman, and were attempting to interrupt my private concert by describing her unusual piano-playing style. Apparently the late-night appearance had created quite a visual memory for them.

I didn't even know what she looked like.

But I thought it was the most beautiful thing I had ever heard.

I think it would be safe to say that I became a passionate fan of her music. But it wasn't unusual to find passionate Tori Amos fans. Her music — too personal and thought provoking for true mass

consumption — imbued a fierce loyalty in her fans. But the vast majority of the passionate were female and were unlikely to do what I did
for a living.

I saw placards and posters for her tour in several German cities I
traveled to with WCW on our March 1994 tour of Germany. I thought
about snagging a poster or two from a wall but opted not to, thinking
it wrong to in any way jeopardize her potential audience for the sake
of my own personal gain. I could almost hear a promoter say, *Sorry,
Ms. Amos, the show would have done better, but apparently some wrestler was going around town, taking down all your posters.*

I regretted that decision on March 17, 1994, when a wrestling ring
mishap resulted in the infamous loss of my right ear, leaving me with
nothing to listen to, read, or look at for two interminably long days in
a Munich hospital. One of those Tori Amos posters on my hospital
room wall would have made the experience a little less tenuous.

Two weeks later, April 1, 1994, with my head still swathed with
enough gauze to pass for Boris Karloff in *The Mummy,* I took in my
first Tori Amos show from the third row of the Center Stage Theater
in Atlanta, using my WCW connections (we held our Saturday night
television tapings at the venue) to gain a great perspective on what
really did strike me as an unusual piano-playing style.

But it was not until leaving WCW, while on a tour of Japan in
January 1995, that Tori and her music, particularly "Winter," started
playing a unique role in my wrestling career.

Willingly leaving WCW had been a bold move, one that had not
been particularly popular with my wife. We'd just had our second
child, and the thought of leaving a job with a guaranteed six-figure
income (low six, but still six) for the uncertainty of the independent
circuit didn't seem like the greatest example of responsible parent-
hood. Especially during my first tour for IWA Japan, a small promotion with a heavy emphasis on wild matches — barbed wire, fire,
thumbtacks, and blood — lots of blood.

I've got my own little theory on Japan, with its samurai traditions

and warrior ethos — and how the WWII defeat and subsequent dis-
mantling of its military caused that warrior ethos to reemerge in other
areas of its culture, like IWA Japan wrestling.

While some of the tools of this unique trade were new ones to me,
the idea and practice of putting on wild, physical matches was not,
and my baptism into this strange world of Japanese extreme wrestling was seamless and successful. Still, despite that initial success,
the thought of the tour's final night, a no-rope barbed-wire match with
Terry Funk, was an ominous mental presence. Despite being twenty
years my senior, Funk, a mentor and something of a father figure to
me, was a veritable wild man in the ring. He was a genuine hero to
Japanese wrestling fans who had come of age when Funk was a top
foreign star for All-Japan Wrestling, at a time when that promotion did
monster ratings in prime time.

Only 180 fans braved the cold to attend that last show in the small
city of Honjo, in the prefecture (similar to a state) of Saitama. But
the national wrestling media were there, and Funk and I both felt
that an exciting match, captured in full color and seen within a few
days by up to half a million fans (Japanese wrestling magazines were
incredibly popular at the time), could serve as a foundation on which
to build this small promotion. I understood that an exciting match
would almost certainly lead to a regular role with the promotion — a
valuable incentive for a father of two small children with a mortgage
to pay. I also understood how dangerous these types of matches could
be. The Japanese fans were sticklers for detail and authenticity, so the
barbed wire would be the real stuff, sharp and uncaring, capable of
catching and tearing flesh in a hurry. There was the distinct possibility
of returning from this match in far worse shape than I'd entered it.

The conditions were near freezing in the dressing room (and not
much warmer inside the gym). All the *gaijins*, sans Funk, huddled
around a small kerosene heater just to get warm. Terry was on the
other side of the building, leaving me no opportunity to speak with
him, to talk over possible ideas for the match. I guess the reasonable

goal, looking back on the match all these years later, should have been just to get through it. Be safe and return home in approximately the same condition I'd left in. Unfortunately, my goals tended not to be all that reasonable back then. I wasn't willing to settle for just getting through it. My goal that night was simple and nonnegotiable — to have the best no-rope barbed-wire match ever.

There was only one basic problem. I was terrified — a normal human response to the very abnormal prospect of being dropped headfirst, neck first, and yes, even balls first on hungry strands of jagged metal barbs. How exactly does a basically gentle, caring man (me) transform himself into a willing balls-first participant in a match of this barbaric nature? Inspiration — lots of inspiration.

I looked out the dressing room door and saw the Japanese preliminary wrestlers (from this point on respectfully referred to as "the young boys") taking down the ropes, beginning the process of barbed-wiring the ring. I knew I had about thirty minutes before the wiring process was completed — thirty minutes to undergo some type of drastic mental transformation.

I took out my battered Sony Walkman, and after great deliberation selected a cassette, bypassing more obvious hard-rock selections in favor of something a little less conventional. I moved away from the warmth of the crowded heater, finding comfort in the solitude of a far corner of the backstage area, seeing a cloud of my own breath as I pressed the Play button.

Snow can wait, I forgot my mittens. Wipe my nose, get my new boots on. Like I said, far from conventional, but there was just something about that song, that voice, that touched me in a way no other song ever did...or likely ever will.

When you gonna make up your mind? Tori Amos asks me inside that frigid dressing room in the tiny city of Honjo. *When you gonna love you as much as I do?*

And then I realize I'm going to be all right. Headfirst, neck first, balls first — it really doesn't matter, because by the fourth listen, I know I'm going to tear that place apart.

Tracy Smothers, a veteran wrestler I'd known for years, had witnessed my prematch disposition — rocking, shaking, fighting back tears — and correctly surmised that I might have something special on tap for the audience in Honjo. "Cactus, promise me you won't do anything crazy out there," he said.

At the time it struck me as the most absurd request ever made.

"You know I can't do that," I said as I stepped out into the gymnasium, fully intent on making hardcore history.

Looking back, after all these years, it is probably the match I'm proudest of. Funk once told Barry Blaustein, the director of the acclaimed wrestling documentary *Beyond the Mat*, that it was possibly his favorite match, quite an accolade given the Funker's storied, legendary four decades in the business.

Sure it was bloody — but that's kind of a given. Every barbed-wire match is. But aside from the almost obligatory forehead laceration, there was so much innovative if ridiculously dangerous stuff, not done simply for the sake of being dangerous or ridiculous but with the sincere belief that a classic match could put our small promotion on the map. Make no mistake about it, some of this stuff (fire chair, flaming branding iron, that balls-first barb-drop I made mention of) was ridiculously dangerous.

Perhaps most ridiculously of all, I fully intended to hang myself in the barbed wire that night in Honjo. Well, maybe not literally hang myself, but close enough: propelling my body over the top strand of the wire, while catching my head between the second and third strands — creating a very realistic illusion of hanging. Unfortunately, this *illusion* of hanging requires...um, you know...the actual act of hanging — and the ramifications of such a move were bound to be severe. After all, it was this same move, sans barbed wire, that had been responsible for the loss of my right ear. The same move done in barbed wire? Probably not the best idea I'd ever had, even if I did have the foresight to concoct what seemed like a foolproof exit strategy.

In addition to the buckets of water and wet towels to be used in case of any type of fire mishap, each of the young boys had their own personal wire clipper, and were under direct orders to start clipping in earnest the moment I got hung up in the wire.

But, those poor young boys never got the chance. I nailed the move, but never foresaw the possibility that the wire wouldn't hold. Instead of holding me, supporting me, hanging me, the wire sagged and tore under the stress of my weight and momentum, sending me down to the gym floor in a precarious seated position, my arms extended, stubborn barbs still lodged inside both pinky fingers.

A quick tug was all it took to break free of my predicament but not without serious consequences. Angry chunks of flesh peeked up at me from both my pinkies. After the match, Tracy Smothers, he of the absurd request, would help me drip stinging antiseptic into the holes and pack the chunks of flesh back into the fingers with the benefit of white athletic tape.

Back at the Con, I take a close look at both my pinkies. Gone are those angry chunks of flesh, transformed over the years into something oddly beautiful: distinct souvenirs commemorating a night where Terry Funk and I overcame the small crowd, the frigid conditions, and the foreboding specter of near-certain injury to lay down the foundation on which our little promotion was built. They're my little "Winter" jewels and I wouldn't trade them or take them back (especially the left one), even if I could.

It's not like I'm proud of every scar, either. Some of them do serve as evidence of sacrifices worth making while others are minor sources of shame, reminders of a time when I thought more was always better instead of usually just being…more. Those scars are like gaudy tributes to excess — the keloidal equivalent to the gold rope chain you can't just remove, the bell-bottoms you can't just take off, or the embarrassing mullet you can't just clip or hide the photos of.

Not that I have a lot of room to talk about fashion faux pas. Especially on this day at the Con, where the attire I've selected for the day — cutoff red flannel, light blue Grumpy (of Seven Dwarfs fame) T-shirt, and tie-dyed sweats that my wife snagged on eBay — strikes me as a particularly weak ensemble, even by my relaxed standards.

A security guard approaches my table. "You can go up there anytime you like," he tells me. "Okay, thanks," I say. "I'll be over in a few minutes."

Despite my trepidation and limited sense of style, I'd made a couple of moves in preparation for this possible opportunity. About a half hour before the Tori signing began, with a large line of her fans already beginning to form, I'd introduced myself to the guards in charge of her queue. Thankfully, they knew who I was.

"I've written about Tori Amos in a couple of my books," I said. "Do you think I'd be able to come over and say hello?"

I'd also given fifty dollars to a particularly avid wrestling fan, asking if he could go purchase a copy of *Comic Book Tattoo*, the massive coffee-table collection of stories inspired by Tori's songs that was her reason for visiting the Con. Sadly, the fan came back empty-handed — *Comic Book Tattoo* was all sold out. Yes, he did give me the fifty dollars back.

Maybe a swarm of rabid Mick Foley fans would descend upon my table, eager to purchase each slight variation of an eight-by-ten photo depicting me with my thumb in the air, the classic pose I stole from the Fonz... or Siskel... or Ebert. It would take the decision out of my hands. I simply would be unable to go. That swarm never materialized. I push back from the table, take a deep breath, then begin the long journey, a pilgrimage of sorts, to Tori's side of the massive convention hall.

What exactly was her reaction supposed to be? As far as I could guess, there wasn't any really good choice. It was either:

A. She'd never heard any tale of a wrestler preparing for matches by listening to her music. "Hi, I'm Mick and I'm a wrestler, and I used to listen to 'Winter' before some of my matches." I'd get a polite but wary "Hello," maybe even a mildly amused "Thanks," and I'd be on my way.

B. She'd heard about the wrestler and didn't really care much one way or the other. A polite but wary "Hello," a mildly amused "Thanks," and I'd be on my way.

C. She'd heard about it, and didn't appreciate the odd paradoxical beauty of the situation. In that case, I might be the recipient of a mild Tori Amos reprimand, maybe even a stern finger wag.

If I was a betting man, I'd have gone with A, although all of them seemed like distinct possibilities — each of them sending me back to my table in worse condition than I'd left it.

I'd been a big Jethro Tull fan for many years before meeting Ian Anderson backstage at the Westbury Music Fair in Long Island. Ian seemed slightly underwhelmed by my presence, polite but apparently not impressed by my legendary status. Which was fine, because I can still enjoy "Locomotive Breath" without any palpable reduction in listening pleasure. But "Locomotive Breath" wasn't "Winter." And Ian wasn't Tori.

Bruce Springsteen once said "Trust the art, not the artist" in response to fans who seemed to expect too much from Bruce, the person, when he was selling out football stadiums in two hours, on the heels of "Born in the U.S.A.," back in the mideighties. I wondered perhaps if I should have heeded Bruce's advice as Tori Amos came into my view. There she was — bright orange hair, high distinct cheekbones of a Cherokee ancestry, and a warm smile for each fan who posed by her side. Maybe I, too, could get one of those smiles even though I had no book to sign, and I'd be cutting in front of her line, several hundred fans strong.

"Okay, your turn," I'm told, and suddenly I think of Burgess

Meredith in the first *Rocky* barking out "Time," indicating that it's uh, you know, time for Rocky Balboa to hit the ring for the inevitable beating at the hands of Apollo Creed. I also think back to 1976, the championship game of the Northern Brookhaven Little League. Not quite eleven, I was scheduled to bat in the final inning, our team down by two, the bases full, two men out. Man, that was one long lonely walk from our bench to home plate. I swung and missed badly on the first two pitches. Then choked up on the bat, like our coach Will Grey had taught us to do, and with a short, compact swing, doubled in two runs to tie up the game. Over the past thirty-two years, I've thought of that game a bunch of times, pausing to wonder how life would have worked out if I'd missed that third pitch. Life is like that, I think — made up of moments that interconnect, a fast-moving spiral that somehow helps shape the people we become. I don't mean to suggest that I would have become a predestined loser if I'd gone down on strikes, but I do think there are special moments in life that, for better or worse, go on to define the people we are.

I'm about ten feet from Tori, when she looks over at me...and gets up from her chair...and extends both her arms. I have to admit, I never saw this one coming — never considered the chance that there might be a choice D, the possibility of Tori hugging Mick. It seems so far-fetched, even a mere second before contact, that my official first words in the presence of Tori Amos are in the form of a question.

"I can hug you?" I ask, in almost total disbelief (*not* "Can I hug you?" which would have been a request), and then Tori puts her arms around me, and though I tower over her and probably outweigh her by close to 200 pounds, I feel very much like an innocent child in the arms of an angel. Hey, I'm not making this up. This is how I remember it. I was a child and she was an angel.

"You know who I am?" I say, unable to grasp that this beautiful woman, this sensitive soul, whose music has meant so much to me over the years, not only knows who I am but apparently finds me worthy of hugging.

And then Tori Amos looks straight at me and, moving her hands in small, majestic opposite arcs (think Mr. Miyagi teaching Daniel-san to wax on/wax off, but with far more pageantry and beauty), says six simple words: "I know exactly who you are."

Tori, it turns out, has a nephew who is a big wrestling fan, and he apparently had clued Aunt Tori in about the wrestling guy who used to get motivated for big matches while listening to her music. I'm not trying to claim that she was a fan. In fact, I just can't seem to get a clear mental image of her on a couch watching *Impact* or *Raw* with a beer in one hand, a remote in the other, and a bowl of chips in her lap. But she definitely knew, and she seemed kind of flattered.

I return to my table, almost impossibly happy, maybe even giddy, thinking about that hug and those words. I think of the old Jim Croce song "Time in a Bottle" and can't stop wishing that such a thing could exist. And no, I'm not talking about taking those lyrics too literally — no saving "every day till eternity passes away just to spend them with you." I just want to have a way to keep that special moment, to think back to it, to remember how it made me feel. I also think about writing a little note. A simple one. I thought I had some appropriate words:

"If I live to be a hundred, I will never forget how special you made me feel."

Pretty nice, right? Except I never wrote it.

I returned home from the Con, still high on my meeting, a feeling I'd keep with me, at least in small part, for months afterward. I even treated myself to a little Tori-themed expenditure party. I bought a couple CDs, a DVD, and her book, an autobiography so honest I felt fully secure trusting the artist as well as the art. I even promised myself I'd donate the money I made on the day I'd met her to RAINN (Rape, Abuse and Incest National Network), the foundation she'd helped found in 1994, to offer invaluable aid to victims of sexual abuse.

Wouldn't it be cool, I thought, *if Tori looked at my books?* I didn't expect her to run out and purchase one, or to pick up a T-shirt, or start watching our show. But maybe, I thought, the impression I made was just good enough to merit a brief bookstore visit or a quick Google search.

I flipped through the pages of *Have a Nice Day!* There we go, page 306. Oh no! Look at the words: "As the beautiful images in her song peaked, so did my ability to see brutal images in my mind."

"Brutal images"? I sound like a psycho! How about *Foley Is Good?* Try as I might, I couldn't find her in that one. But I knew she was in *Hardcore Diaries*, near the end, where I wrote about psyching myself up for my big match with Edge. Yes, there it is, page 341. Come on, Mick, let it be nice. Oh, no, please, don't tell me! This one is even worse: "I had found a private corner of the building and rocked back and forth for minutes, listening to 'Winter' by Tori Amos, a beautiful, haunting song that for some reason continues to give rise to goose bumps and thoughts of hardcore destruction, thirteen years after first being touched by it in Maxx [Payne]'s car on a long-forgotten WCW road trip."

"Hardcore destruction"? Good grief!

Remember that high that I wrote of? The one that lasted for months? Well, that may be true, but from the moment I read my own words, that high I felt had emotional company. Guilt. In my first book, I'd borrowed a line directly from Tori's song "Crucify": "Got enough guilt to start my own religion." Which is basically true. If somebody, some-where, is suffering somehow...I'm pretty sure I'm at least partially responsible. Homelessness on Long Island? Should have sent some more money. Fifth grader bullied in Bellport? Should have talked at more schools. That second Bush term? Should have knocked on more doors.

I didn't want to go down in musical history as the guy who ruined "Winter." What if Tori herself stopped liking the song strictly because of the words I had written? What if she got only as far as "Snow can wait" and broke down onstage, thinking about that guy at the Con with the flannel and tie-dye? Hey, it could happen.

Look what happened to "I Love," the Tom T. Hall song about "little baby ducks, old pickup trucks, slow-moving trains, and rain" (my wedding song, no less). It's now the basis for a beer commercial, a seeming endorsement for not only getting hammered at a football game but also harboring a thinly veiled fantasy of a possible tryst with identical twins.

And then there's Mick Foley, who took the most beautiful song ever written and turned it into his own twisted ode to suffering and woe. Okay, maybe that's overdoing it a little, but I did feel kind of bad, did worry about what Tori might think, and did spend many hours wondering why such beautiful words could serve as such an odd motivation.

What was it about that song? The question gnawed at me for days, then weeks, then months. It never consumed me; I was never clinically obsessed with this quest. Instead, it would pop into my mind at various times — while reading, while driving, while watching TV. Sometimes the thought was just fleeting, other times it hung around for an hour or more. Always leaving me wondering, *What is it about that song?* So while it didn't consume me, it continued to take tiny bites from my conscience for a very long time. Like I said, it gnawed at me.

I thought for a while I could boil it all down to simple emotion. That if I put all the factors into a metaphorical pot, those factors, or ingredients, would all boil down to a simple emotional connection. Indeed, when listening to "Winter," at least a few hundred times over the last sixteen years, I have never failed to receive that tingling in the scalp, that sense of electrification, that magnificent rush. There have been times on long road trips when I've put the disc in the dash, that I've been slightly nervous, figuring this might just be the time when the magic runs out. But somehow, every time the rush is still there, the tingling remains, the magic lives on. Yes, it must be emotion.

But wait, other things in life make me feel that same way. Like that scene in *Rocky* when Adrian closes her eyes after watching her man hit the deck in that big fourteenth round. Or when John Coffey brings Del's mouse back to life in *The Green Mile*. Or once every year, for as long as I can remember, when that train with square wheels, the ostrich-riding cowboy, that annoying clown Charlie-in-the-box, and the rest of the gang on the Island of Misfit Toys hear that first jingle of bells in the distance and realize heroes do exist, that Rudolph has kept his word and that Santa has not forgotten them. Come on, admit it, that scene gets to you, too.

But I've never watched *Rudolph the Red-Nosed Reindeer* and thought about barbed-wire barbarity. *Rocky* used to make me do weird things like go jogging at midnight, but it never inspired a single wild match.

Lots of music moved me; there have been hundreds of non-"Winter" musically inspired magnificent rushes while I logged so many miles in my car — over a million, by my own estimation. I'd listened to some of those tunes before matches, even before big Pay-Per-Views. I was never a guy who needed music night in and night out to get myself pumped. Still, I know there were songs other than "Winter" that I used for big matches — songs that gave me an emotional rush. "Copperhead Road" by Steve Earle, "Diary of a Workingman" by Blackfoot, "Danger Zone" by Kenny Loggins — all right, I'm kidding about that last one. But I specifically remember Nils Lofgren's guitar solo on the live version of Springsteen's "Youngstown," and how after listening to it I felt like I could take on the world.

But, for the life of me, I can't specifically remember the name of the city, or the guy that I wrestled, or the name of the show that I used "Youngstown" for. Same with "Copperhead Road" and "Diary of a Workingman." I don't have a clue. I'm sure if I puzzled and puzzled till my puzzler was sore, I might think of a few song titles — I might even eventually connect one of them to a specific time, place, or match.

"Winter" is different. I remember the times. I remember the places. I remember the shows. Every single move that took place. January 8,

1995, the no-rope barbed-wire match with Funk in Honjo, Japan. August 23, 1995, the infamous King of the Deathmatch tournament at Kawasaki Stadium in Yokohama, Japan — a day that left me with forty-two stitches (distributed over six separate body parts), second-degree burns, and hundreds of tack holes. April 26, 2004, my first singles match in four years, the best match of my life, Edmonton, Alberta, Canada. And April 1, 2006, with Edge in Chicago — my favorite *WrestleMania* memory, the match that was voted by WWE fans as the best of the year.

That was it — only four matches. Yeah, I know, you might think given all of the time (about twenty-two hours so far on this chapter, on the first draft alone) that I've given this story, that I'd cranked up the Tori before every big show. And it would be easy to lie — how would anyone know? — and pick out some more crazy matches to add to my list. Just toss in Hell in a Cell for history's sake.

But I think, and I believe and I honestly feel, that it's the song's rarity on my life's list of matches that makes it so special. Four matches out of approximately two thousand. But the song has become such an indelible part of my memories of those four that in my mind, at least, I can't separate the matches from the song.

Again, though, why that song? And why the near nine-year absence from the prematch headphones? It wasn't as if "Winter" had been banished from rotation in my cavalcade of crummy cars. I still listened to Tori, still listened to "Winter," just not before matches.

I think it comes down to confidence. For most of my full-time years in WWE (1996–2000), I remained fairly sure that I was pretty good at my job. I still needed music to help me think while I drove, and once in a while I listened to something somewhere before I wrestled someone in some kind of match. Music that helped me get over the hump.

But "Winter" did more — it battled my fears and helped me believe in myself during times when the need for believing was at its most vital.

In all four of those matches, my anxiety was sky-high, my confidence low. All four matches offered not only the possibility but the near certainty of injury. And in all four of those cases, I sat down by myself, rocking back and forth slowly, letting that voice, so haunting and pure, take me far away from that place where my doubts and insecurities lie.

When you gonna make up your mind, when you gonna love you as much as I do?

Most listeners would interpret "Winter" as a song about a father's love for a child. But I think for me, those words, that question it asked, always appealed to that insecure inner child, the scared part of me, the part that believed I wasn't strong enough, or big enough, or good enough. It never *made* me think of "brutal images" or "hardcore destruction" — it helped me *believe* that I was strong enough to realize those images, to do the things I already knew needed to be done. I didn't visualize new ideas while I listened; ideas I'd already formed that seemed destined for doom came dancing back to life.

I wish that I'd used different words in my books. Some might look at those matches and think they were indeed brutal and violent. But my intentions were never bad, or brutal, or violent. I just wanted to leave my best artistic impression on the abstract canvas that pro wrestling can be.

Besides, I don't think about matches anymore when I listen to "Winter." I think about the world and what I can do to save it. Honestly. And every year on July 22, for as long as I am blessed to make a decent living, I will send a check to RAINN for that same amount of money. We need people in our lives who make us want to be better people. Even if they're only in our lives briefly.

It's been a few days since I started this chapter, though I'm still seated at the same hotel desk in Dublin. Earlier tonight at the TNA show, I was talking to a couple of guys about their "me" walls — those tributes to oneself that every wrestler has. Kurt Angle couldn't even guess, but estimated that he has forty grand tied up in framing costs alone. Brother Devon guessed he had about a hundred photos on his "me" wall.

Sometime in early fall 2008, I received a package in the mail. A package from Steve Woolf, the guy who'd booked me for the Con. I knew just what the package was, and dug in with great anticipation. Yes, there I was with Tori Amos, a couple different eight-by-tens, really sharp photos. We're looking at the camera, in both of them she's smiling — these are a full grade above the average photo op. I'm so glad that Woolf was there to offer up visual evidence that this meeting really did take place.

But wait, there's one more photo. You can't even see my face, just my head and shoulders, and that cutoff ragged flannel. But I can clearly make out Tori. Her eyes are like merry little magical half moons, and her mouth is parted slightly, as if she had been speaking when the photograph was taken. And her hands are in the air, seemingly suspended in midmovement. Immediately it dawned on me — this was my special moment. Tori had been speaking and I knew just what she'd said: "I know exactly who you are."

My wife, Colette, thought it was a great photo, too; she said it had great energy. She later said it was the very moment that Tori Amos had cast some type of spell over her husband. I cut the photo down to five-by-seven size, put it in a wooden frame, and placed it on a bookshelf inside the Foley Christmas room, where it instantly became the only "me" photo in my house. Okay, that's not quite true — there's an old magazine cover of me dressed as Santa Claus; the title reads "St. Mick." But I swear, I'll take it down if it makes my story more legit.

Every time I look at it, my day gets just a little brighter. Sometimes I walk over to the photo, and it literally makes me smile, helping me relive one of my life's favorite memories — my little moment of "Time in a Bottle."

COUNTDOWN TO LOCKDOWN: 22 DAYS

March 28, 2009
On board Continental Flight 1033, New York to Houston
10:50 a.m.

"Seems like a big mistake." I texted those words to Vince Russo, TNA's head writer, just minutes ago, before buckling up for the three-hour forty-minute flight to Houston, where I will do an appearance for Booker T's Pro Wrestling Alliance organization. I've known Booker for fifteen years, and several months ago promised I'd do a show for him gratis in appreciation of his friendship. It sure sounded good when I said it, almost magnanimous, if I do say so myself, although saying it and doing it are obviously two very different things.

Wow, that's a long way to go for free, I kept thinking. Not to mention a long time to ride in coach, probably somewhere around seat 26C, more likely than not a mere row or two away from the crapper. I had e-mailed Sharmell, Booker's wife, asking for the possibility of an aisle seat, maybe even an exit row. She e-mailed me back, "Mick, we love you and we're flying you first class."

Well, that little e-mail changed everything. Suddenly a long, depressing voyage, sure to be unpleasant for both my aching joints and my nasal passages, seemed like a place to sit back and relax, do some serious *Lockdown* thinking, and spend some quality time putting pen to paper; my little private office at twenty thousand feet. Plus, I'll be able to sleep in, fly out at a reasonable hour, and get more quality pen time in during my day off in Orlando, before our pivotal pre-PPV tapings on Monday and Tuesday. Three weeks of taping in two days at Universal. Two days that will either make or break the buy rate for *Lockdown.* And, deep in my gut, I can't help think that one of Russo's ideas seems like a big mistake.

I already feel like last night's TV show was a little bump in the road — like that recap video that just didn't happen was a lost opportunity. Sure, I was happy with the in-ring promo, but Russo's intention of mixing in another story line — Abyss versus Matt Morgan, one that's been running awhile and thus far hasn't caught fire — seems like a really good way to water down the product we're trying to sell. Like the TNA consumer will be asked to scarf down two bland entrées instead of savoring one really good one, and passing on the other. To paraphrase the old Michael Hayes adage about the steakhouse, we've got to remember why our TNA diners are coming to the *Lockdown* Café. Sure they love the baked potato, but that's not why they put down their hard-earned Pay-Per-View dollars. They want that steak. And I'm really concerned that instead of getting one really good-looking steak and a delicious potato, we'll be serving up two heaping helpings of a Who-hash. Look, I'm a big fan of Abyss and appreciate the sacrifices he has made to create compelling matches, and I think Matt Morgan has a world of potential. But their story line is just not clicking and I don't want it to make hash out of mine. Now whether or not that steak really tastes good is the big question Sting and I will have to answer on April 19. I sincerely hope it's delicious, and I'm looking to find ways to ensure that it is. I'll be looking for a little seasoning, maybe a barbed-wire bat or a chair to spice up that steak. Yeah, I'll try my best, but the truth is, if that steak is indeed going to be bland, I'd feel a lot better knowing that a lot of people ordered it. That's right, if I'm going to stink up the arena as well as the airwaves, I don't want that stinking to be a well-kept secret.

I've always been a fan of Vince Russo's ideas, and I give him major credit for pioneering the action-adventure television format that helped launch WWE into the ratings stratosphere in the late nineties. Sure, I once wrote that he needed somebody to reign in some of those ideas, and I think even Russo knows deep down that his WCW World Title run may not have been a high point for the business. But I've always respected his ability to create ideas and book compelling television shows. And I do think that adding a struggling story line into my very personal issue with Sting and expecting a heaping double helping of overdone hash to attract diners to the *Lockdown* Café is a little too ambitious.

My son Dewey, who believe it or not is seventeen now, went with an amusement park analogy. Longtime readers of my multitude of memoirs might remember seven-year-old Dewey as the little guy with the pro-wrestling fixation, the avalanche of action figures, the voluminous collection of videos, and the plethora of Dad posters. Or they might remember the ten-year-old Dewey as the guy who took down those Dad posters and replaced them with new heroes — Sammy Sosa, Shaq, Olympic bobsledder Mike Wasco. But over the last couple of years, Dewey has gotten back into wrestling. He watches WWE but prefers TNA, and he seems to have a good head for details, like what works and what doesn't, who deserves a little more attention, who deserves a little less. A few months ago, my wife and I went to one of Dewey's basketball games, looking on with great parental pride as our son rode the bench for the duration of the contest. Over the course of the season, I learned to show up only if his team was playing a really bad school or a really good one — to view a little Foley mop-up time in a lopsided win or loss. But on this occasion, before I'd learned to properly weigh playing-time potentials, I made an astute observation during the course of a close game and decided to share it with my wife.

"Dewey's haircut looks kind of ridiculous."

"Stop it, Mick," Colette said. "He's just trying to have his own style. We don't say anything about your hair."

"But he looks like a jerk, the way it's combed up and gelled in the middle."

About a month ago my youngest son, six-year-old Hughie, went to the barber and traded in his shoulder-length blond hair for a similar stylistic debacle. Sure, I'd felt bad for the little guy and had even become a vocal proponent for change after hearing a couple hundred too many *dear, honey, sweetheart,* and *princess* references from well-meaning but gender-confused onlookers. I heard the poor little guy say "I'm not a girl" so often that it kind of became his nickname. So I'd been in favor of just about anything, from a bowl cut, to a buzz cut, to a 1950s astronaut cut similar to the one WWE Hall of Famer Jerry Brisco sports. But this gelled thing, this faux hawk, was a little much, even if it did solve all these gender-confusion issues. I mean, what exactly were my kids thinking? A few words from Hughie cleared up the whole thing.

"Look, Dewey, now we both look like Alex Shelley."

Alex Shelley? Alex Shelley? My children wanted to look like Alex Shelley? Don't get me wrong — Shelley is a great wrestler. Along with his partner, Chris Sabin, they are the Motor City Machine Guns, probably the most exciting team in the business. They can wrestle any style — Japanese, Mexican, European, submission. And I'm a big fan of Shelley's quirky facial expressions and subtle sense of humor. I just never saw him as a setter of fashion trends or as a guy that kids would want to emulate. But at least for my family, Alex Shelley has become both. Probably because my son Dewey has a good eye for talent and is just slightly ahead of the public opinion curve.

Like most dads, I've had my ups and downs when it comes to relating to my teenage kids. Well, not really Noelle, who's like a straight-A angel, one of the least problematic kids around. See, witnessing those eleven unprotected chair shots from the Rock back in 1999 wasn't so traumatic after all. But this teenage boy parenting thing has not been without its struggles. Recently, however, a new gift from the programming gods has descended. The gift of Kenny Powers (of HBO's *Eastbound & Down*), possibly the most lovable, foulmouthed, insensitive, egotistical loser to ever bathe us in the brilliant blue glow of HDTV. Yes, Kenny has been good to us, opening up the lines of father-son communication that had once seemed closed for good.

So it was with that Powers-imbued confidence that I spelled out Russo's scenario to my oldest son, after picking him up at 12:30 a.m. — his latest night out ever — following his junior prom.

"Dad, that's all wrong," he said. "That story line is kind of like a carousel at an amusement park; people might enjoy it, but that's not why they buy the ticket. They want to ride the roller coaster."

I looked over at my son, who was wearing an all-white suit, a hot pink tie, and his Alex Shelley haircut. He looked completely ridiculous. But he was right. Now how do I explain all this to Russo?

COUNTDOWN TO LOCKDOWN: 21 DAYS

March 29, 2009
On board Continental Flight 786, en route from Houston to Orlando
10:50 a.m.

"It's the haircut, stupid. The haircut is the answer — the answer is the haircut."

I spent most of my Houston hotel downtime desperately trying to get ahold of Russo. A couple of detailed voice messages — a soliloquy about not mixing in the casts of *Platoon* and *Tropic Thunder* because two good movies about Vietnam would turn into one lousy one. Even a mention of Mike Brady's (Robert Reed) rules of comedy; it's okay to have a soldier with a brain injury who *thinks* he's a superhero on the old seventies classic *M*A*S*H*, but the moment a real superhero shows up on the battlefield, all credibility goes sailing down the pipes. I threw in a little *Happy Days* as well — how the show was never quite the same for me after the bucolic Wisconsin town from the fifties received a visit from a real alien from the planet Ork. I know the Fonz has received a ton of heat over the years for that unique moment in time when he jumped the shark — yes, literally jumped a shark — while waterskiing in his traditional aquatic attire of leather jacket and white T-shirt. Although, if I really think about it, the show's true shark-jumping moment for this particular *Happy Days* enthusiast involved a weight-training session in which the Fonz, arguably the toughest fictional guy on the planet, was seen bench-pressing somewhere in the neighborhood of 70 to 75 pounds of those cheap, plastic, sand-filled weights, sporting a set of pipe-cleaner biceps and what appeared to be the slightest hint of man boobs beneath the iconic plain white T-shirt. Heyyy!

Okay, where the hell was I? Oh, yeah, haircuts and phone messages. Well, I finally got a call from Vince, just as I was heading out to Booker's show. I thought about talking over the whole thing in the car until I verified that the guy driving me was a huge wrestling fan who probably shouldn't hear such extensive information about upcoming *Impact* episodes. So I said I'd call him from Booker's show, hung up, and did my best to shrug off the emotional blow of seeing a Whataburger on the highway, only minutes after settling for Taco Cabana. Man, I love Whataburger; the mere sight of that majestic W reaching up into the Texas sky is enough to make my mouth water. It might just be my favorite thing about Texas — excluding, of course, my memories of a buxom thirty-nine-year-old Australian woman who worked the front desk at a little motel in Fort Worth, back in the winter of 1988. She'd be sixty now. Cool.

I did get through to Russo, and we had a solid talk. I think the memories of my last big creative battles — the ones detailed in *The Hardcore Diaries* — left such a negative impression on me that I forgot how the give-and-take with the writers and other powers that be can actually be fun, and beneficial, and invigorating.

I offered up my idea in detail. I knew from past experience that Russo dreaded — and rightfully so — the wrestlers who demand changes an hour or so before cameras roll. Back in the late nineties, when Russo helped pioneer (hey, I'm not kissing his butt; this is historical fact here) the action-adventure format for WWE, those two-hour melodramas that got people talking and eyeballs viewing, some of the biggest stars in the business would question Russo's creativity, even his integrity — thinking in some cases that a segment or two not to their liking was some grand conspiracy to make them look bad. I remember seeing Russo despondent at the *WrestleMania XIV* after-party, usually an event of great celebration, due to an intense tongue-lashing he'd received from Shawn Michaels (remember, this was back in the "bad Shawn" days) in regard to a match on the show (which happened to be mine) that he felt made DX look weak. One night later, on a live *Raw* where Terry Funk and I were left battered and beaten, DX was stronger than ever. I don't really know if any post-*Raw* apologies came Russo's way, but if so, I doubt the apologies arrived with comparable vociferousness.

Russo liked my idea but wondered which opponent could take the place of Matt Morgan, who he had originally suggested.

"I don't think it really matters," I said. "Just as long as it's a guy who's been here since the beginning — a guy who wouldn't like me trying to usurp Jeff [Jarrett]'s authority." Yes, I really do use words like *usurp* occasionally.

Russo thought about it momentarily. "You know who'd be perfect, Mick?" he said.

"Who, Vince?"

"You really want to know?"

"Yeah."

"You wanna know?"

"Yeah, I wanna know!" I yelled.

"Okay, I'm gonna let you know," Russo hissed. "Because you had the talent to be a good fighter. But instead of that, you became a tomato; a leg breaker for some cheap, second-rate loan shark."

"It's a living," I said weakly, unconvincingly.

Russo paused, dropping a verbal hammer: "It's a waste of life."

Okay, I went off on a wild *Rocky* tangent, refiguring dialogue that Burgess Meredith and Sylvester Stallone had shared in 1976. Actually Russo just wanted to suggest Alex Shelley as my opponent on *Impact*.

The idea clicked right away. Shelley and I had a little history on the show, a little generational misunderstanding where I didn't think he was showing proper respect to the Hardcore Legend. That little issue hadn't gone anywhere, which was fine, because in my mind not every hint has to merit a full answer, just like every flirtatious line or gesture from an older Australian woman doesn't have to end in unrivaled physical pleasure — even if in my case, it certainly did twenty-one years ago. Yes!

But was my limited history with Shelley enough of a reason for fans to tune in to our main event? Was it going to be a big enough issue for kids like my own, all around the country (no, I don't mean that I have kids all around the country), to ask for just a little more *Impact* before they go to bed?

For some reason, I don't think children's bedtimes are factored in when discussing and analyzing ratings trends in wrestling. As I write this, we're on something of a ratings roll in TNA — hitting 2 million U.S. fans a week for a few weeks running. Sure, it's a way off from the heyday of the Monday Night Wars, where WWE and WCW were regularly pulling in a combined 10 million fans on Monday nights. Then again, back then, YouTube, the Internet, and digital video recorders weren't such staples of the viewing diet. These days, it's so easy to punch in a few letters on a keyboard and see the highs and/or lows of a two-hour show in a matter of several minutes. So, I understand that it's a continual weekly challenge to engage our fans with the proper mix of action/drama/comedy.

Ideally, a two-hour show will peak in the last ten minutes so that the maximum number of possible eyeballs are tuned in at the most vital time — the big win or loss, the surprise, the swerve, the turn, the cliff-hanger.

I think, in truth, most wrestling shows build an audience as they progress. Let's face it, by now fans know the deal about those final few minutes. But these shows undoubtedly lose an audience, too — kids like my older ones, who have to get up at 6:15 in the morning, who would love to see what happens but simply can't or shouldn't be allowed to. Wrestling shows aren't like *CSI* or *Law & Order*; they can be enjoyed on their own merits for ten minutes, fifteen, an hour, without seeming like a waste of time should the conclusion not be seen. The secret, then, is to gain more viewers than you lose throughout the course of those two hours.

Sometimes I think too much emphasis is placed on the ratings at the expense of wrestlers who might have a valuable niche audience, like Shelley or Sabin, or Jay Lethal or the Curry Man. Okay, not him. I remember a time several years ago when Jeff and Matt Hardy were almost thought to be ratings poison, especially when featured in television main events. Yet in a live setting, fans went absolutely crazy for them. Maybe they weren't connecting with every demographic, but certain slices of our audience loved them. My former publicist at HarperCollins, Jennifer Robinson, told me that their book signings felt like Beatles concerts, yet the powers that be always seemed hesitant to really get behind them. I don't want to sound mean here, but maybe they should have figured out that many of the Hardys' die-hard fans were in bed way before the show ended.

I see the Machine Guns and guys like them as a new wave of Hardys, guys who may not appeal to every demographic but certainly should be given a shot at climbing that ladder of success. I'm hoping that this match on *Impact* will be one step up that ladder for them, even if the real goal of the match is to get me one step closer to Sting at *Lockdown*. So here's the challenge — how do we keep the ratings rolling with Sabin and Shelley in the main event when much of their fan base is tucked up in their bedrooms fast asleep?

It's the haircut, stupid. I need to convince our fans that those faux Machine Gun Foley haircuts make this situation very personal — like it's a parenting failure on my part. Like the Motor City Machine Guns have invaded my house and I don't like it. I'm thinking of throwing in the line, "Even Ted Nugent wouldn't want *those* guns in his house" — my attempt to reach out and hook those Second Amendment enthusiasts who stopped watching *Raw* when Stone Cold retired.

Here's my big tagline. Ready? "When I'm done tonight, no child will want to look like Alex Shelley again." Hopefully that line, delivered at 10:00 Eastern, will be enough for the Guns' base to beg for another hour of TV time. If not, maybe it will entice those kids to willfully disobey their parents.

Hey, do you mind if I pat myself on the back a little here? Back in 1998, when I had the chance to do *The Three Faces of Foley*, my first video with WWE, I asked the director, Steve Cooney, if I might get a couple of the wrestlers to sit around in the seats at Nassau Coliseum, listening to my exaggerated stories of personal glory, instead of just talking to the camera. Cooney liked the idea. "Sure, who were you thinking of?" he said. I told him I was thinking of Matt and Jeff Hardy. "That's funny," Cooney deadpanned. "Really, who were you thinking of?" I told him I was serious; I wanted the Hardys in the video. "Okay, why?" Cooney asked, his face a mask of dread, as if these two kids were going to single-handedly ruin the shot simply by being in it. Keep in mind that in 1998, the Hardys were talented but underutilized extras, guys who did a great job making other guys look good. I looked at Cooney and said, "You know, Steve, I think one day these kids are going to be really big stars."

Sure, I might have had doubts when I heard that Jeff missed a show because his pet raccoon had gotten out of the house, climbed up a tree, and refused to come down, but overall I think time has proven me to be correctomundo — a little Fonzieism for you. Now about that time when I thought that Dwayne Johnson kid just wasn't going to cut it? Well, I might have been wrong about that.

Try it. You'll like it.

REALITY STAR

They never even knocked. Hughie and Mickey just burst through the door, catching their mom and dad at a most inopportune time, seeing their father in a way they had never imagined him. Yes, my children walked in on me and my wife while we were right in the middle of... watching the original *Rocky*, and saw their father... sniveling, choked up, fighting back tears.

It might have been understandable if they'd caught me in the middle of the fight scene; as I've already mentioned, that moment where Adrian closes her eyes in the big fourteenth round always gets to me. Even though it hadn't actually gotten to me in about ten years. Yes, for all my talking about *Rocky* as my all-time favorite movie, I hadn't actually seen it in ages. But Colette and I resolved to watch *Rocky* in its entirety before setting out to see *Rocky Balboa* in the theaters. The film had been getting incredible buzz, and we wanted to be filled with the Rocky spirit before heading out to the cinema.

I guess I wasn't prepared for my little trip down memory lane; scenes that previously hadn't affected me at all now tugged at my heartstrings. Like the scene my kids walked in on. The one where Mickey (the curmudgeonly manager, not my son) pays the Rock a visit. When I was eleven, or twenty-one, or even thirty-one, it seemed like the visit was merely a vehicle for Stallone to yell "What about my prime, Mick? At least you had a prime!" Suddenly, in my forties, the scene seemed like an incredible metaphor for vulnerability, acceptance, and forgiveness, practically an allegory for potential world peace.

My little guys wanted in. Wanted a piece of the Rock, so to speak. At first I resisted, thinking they would only laugh at my fragile emotional state or lose interest after a few minutes. With my luck, Mickey would be farting "Take Me Out to the Ball Game" under his armpit just as Stallone started his "I can't do it, I can't beat Apollo" soliloquy. Yes, my son really can fart "Take Me Out to the Ball Game" under his arm.

But the little guys surprised me. Their interest never waned. And they were cheering on our hero as he struggled valiantly to beat the count in the big fourteenth round, thankfully so caught up in the action that they missed out on the spectacle of their hardcore dad very nearly losing his battle with tears the moment Adrian closed her eyes.

They were so caught up in the excitement that they thought Rocky actually won the big fight. It wasn't until several days later, while watching *Rocky II* on DVD, that they learned the sad truth — creating the perfect parental opening for a discussion on moral victories and the importance of trying one's best. Fortunately, my kids have a dad with one of the worst win percentages in the history of modern sports entertainment — the living embodiment of that old adage "It doesn't matter if you win or lose, it's how you play the game."

"Movie night," a weekly staple of the Foley family viewing diet, became "Rocky night" and then "Rocky every other night," before briefly morphing into "Rocky twice a day, every day" as the little guys and I (my older kids have never seen a single *Rocky* movie) breezed through Stallone's Balboa oeuvre in less than a week. Colette bailed on me after *Rocky III*, perhaps finding the homoeroticism of Rocky's half shirt and the uncomfortably long hug shared by Stallone and Carl Weathers in the California surf to be a little much to take. Funny how the first two movies seem so timeless, yet *III* and *IV* didn't fare quite so well over the long haul.

It was during this full-blown Rocky renaissance that our home was invaded by swarming reality-show production teams, each working eight-hour shifts, meaning the cameras were fixed on me and the family from the moment I woke to the time the final light went out and every "Good night, Mary Ellen; good night, John-Boy" (1970s *Waltons* reference) had been said.

I know I said in my last book that participating in reality shows was not for us — and I meant it. Just as I mean it now when I say reality shows are not for us. But man, that's a tough path not to cross, given all the potential benefits waiting on the other side. At the time, Hulk Hogan's laundry hadn't gotten quite so dirty and certainly hadn't been aired quite so publicly. Though I don't know Hogan well, I did tell him I was sorry for all the trouble he was going through. The two crews from A&E were part of our lives sixteen hours a day, for eight long, exhausting, but exciting days. It was a great experience, paid fairly well, and most important, spared me the nagging what-ifs: What if we'd tried it? What if it had been a hit?

We tried it, we liked it, and everyone involved seemed to like it, too. Marcus Fox had directed *The Osbournes*, *The Newlyweds*, and other successful entities in the reality world and therefore knew a hit when he saw one. He thought he had one with us, his *Wrestling My Family* cast, thinking he had the modern-day Huxtable family on his hands, a functional but slightly quirky cast of characters.

There was Dewey, the oldest child, an underachiever in school, who honestly felt that owning twenty-three pro-style major-league baseball hats was about seven too few and was determined to become the first pitcher to star in the majors without throwing a single fastball. Nothing but junk for the Dewster.

Noelle, the little girl who cried in *Beyond the Mat*, was nearly grown up — a young woman looking for more freedom than her mom was willing to give her. Her on-camera look of surprise, disgust, and humiliation when Dad handed her a twenty to go clothes shopping was a thing of beauty.

Colette, the mother and loving wife, whose decision to have two children in her forties occasionally comes back to haunt her. She loves those children dearly, but oh, what she wouldn't give for a little break from the hectic pace she's set. And then there are the two little guys.

By now, I guess it's common knowledge that A&E didn't pick up the show. Yes, the network that green-lit *Billy the Exterminator* passed on *Wrestling My Family*. Ouch.

I just wish it could have aired once — just the pilot. If only for the Rocky scenes. If only to see the phone calls from "Rocky." First, let me explain that in the world of my little guys, *blood* is not a noun. It's an action verb. The definition, more or less: "to cause bleeding." As in Rocky Balboa leaving a message informing two small children that he was going to be stopping by "to blood you a little bit."

I'd really just meant it as a joke — a way for my kids to say, "Come on, Dad, we know that was you." Except they didn't know it was me. I may only do three good imitations, but Rocky is one of them. The other two? Terry Funk and Vince McMahon. The Vince imitation is really good.

The unintended consequence of my little message is that my children were terrified. "Rocky's coming over," Hughie said. "And he's going to blood us!"

My wife pulled me aside. "Great work, Mick. Your children now think Rocky Balboa is coming over to beat the crap out of them."

"Well, what do you think I should do?" I asked.

"Have Rocky leave another message, telling them he's only kidding."

I walked out the front door and placed the call.

"Hi, you've reached the Foleys," the machine said. "Please leave your name, number, and a short message, and we'll get back to you as soon as we can."

"Hello, Hughie, Mickey, this is your good friend Rocky Balboa. And I just want you to know that I would never ever blood you guys."

"Hello, Rocky?"

It was Hughie, thinking he was in fact talking to the real Rocky Balboa. "Are you going to blood us?" he asked.

"Of course not, little buddy. You know why? Because Rocky Balboa is a friend of yours."

"When are you coming over?"

Think up a lie, Mick, think it up quick. Think of the Grinch and Cindy Lou Who. "You know, Hughie, the Rock is in training right now, so he's kind of busy."

"What time will you be here?"

"Um, well, your friend Rocky is going to be training for quite a long time, like two or three months."

But the questions kept coming. I was running out of things to say. So I just started quoting random lines from the first movie.

"It's a cold night out here, you know?" Even though it was about seventy-five degrees. "Good night for a basketball game."

WWE had called me during our first day of filming, offering me a main event match at *Vengeance*, about five weeks away. A five-way match for the WWE title, each entrant being a current or former world champion. A five-way? I thought I could handle that. Plenty of opportunities to take creative restaroonies. Plus, through the magic of WWE repackaging, I was now ready for a Pay-Per-View main event. The repackaging had apparently been so magical that I didn't even realize it had taken place.

A nice little reality-show story line had just fallen into our laps. I would do a little training at my old buddy Mikey Whipwreck's gym. Perhaps a Rockyesque training sequence, provided I didn't have to run, climb steps, do one-armed push-ups, or hug a muscular black man in the pounding California surf for an extended period of time. As part of the show, I visited my orthopedic guy, Dr. Segreto, for a full range of X-rays. I probably could have used an MRI or two as well, but I'm guessing those might have run afoul of the A&E budget.

I actually have a couple orthopedic guys, Segreto and Dr. Legouri, who I first saw when I was twelve, his first patient of the day on the very first day of his practice. His first patient ever! He put me in a cast up to my elbow for a broken thumb I'd suffered two weeks earlier, the victim of a Little League injury behind home plate, back when my knees were still capable of lowering my body into a crouch. Actually I think I could still get into the crouch. Getting out would be the tricky part.

Segreto was concerned about the buildup of arthritis around my knees, the same way Legouri had been years earlier, when he'd called his staff over to marvel at the thirty-four-year-old guy with the eighty-year-old knees. As it turned out, not wearing knee pads for the last three years of my full-time career wasn't the best move I could have made.

But he reserved his greatest concern for the state of my pubis and ischia bones in the pubic symphysis area — or lower pelvis, for those of you who feel uncomfortable with that particular phraseology. I had often wondered about the long-term consequences of dropping elbows off of ring aprons onto concrete floors. Ironically, when I used the move almost weekly at the Sportatorium in Dallas (which actually had a wooden floor, not concrete) in late 1988 and most of 1989, "the consequences" had been the name of that move. Not that the name ever really caught on. Usually it was just called a flying elbow on the concrete, back in my near Bob Beamon–like days when I could put my opponent upward of fifteen feet from the ring apron and still make some kind of contact. Maybe it was a forearm or palm of the hand, but at least I was traveling some distance on the move.

By the time I left full-time wrestling, the move was almost a vertical one; just a 300-pound frame dropping straight down, accompanied by the thud of ass covered in sweatpants, hitting the concrete.

Most reasonable onlookers predicted a hip replacement in my future. Sure, my hips hurt, but not as bad as my neck or back, and

certainly not as bad as my knees. To tell you the truth, I thought
destiny was going to look the other way when it came to hundreds of
high-impact elbow drops. Yes, I thought Mother Nature was going
to give me a pass. And while it's true that I do vividly recall specific
momentous elbow drops that resulted in temporary numbness in the
area of my weenie, until I saw those X-rays it had never really dawned
on me that the consequences of that particular move would be con-
centrated in the *inner* and not the *outer* part of the hips.

Dr. Segreto had never seen anything like it. The repetitive trauma
had apparently caused multiple small fractures with resultant additional bone growth in the area. According to him, *no one* had seen
anything like it, making me something of a one-man control group
for studies on the long-term effects of launching one's body onto concrete. By the time I got to WWE, in 1996, the elbow was for TV and
Pay-Per-View purposes only, but by that time most of the damage had
already been done. The bone, through constant impact, had been
chipped away at — the fragments floating freely in my system like the
meteoric waste of some great interplanetary explosion... a condition
Segreto warned could eventually lead to paralysis.

Luckily, over time, these types of injuries heal themselves, revers-
ing the aging process, leaving little sign that... wait, what's that you
say? Time doesn't heal these particular skeletal wounds? They're only
going to get worse? Oh great. I can't wait.

Wrestling My Family seemingly had everything going for it. Humor.
Warmth. A wrestling comeback match. That threat of paralysis. Everything you could ever want. Everything, that is, but conflict.

I'd had a few concerns when A&E first expressed interest in the
show. "I don't know," I'd told Marcus Fox, our director, during
our initial phone conversation. "I don't really yell the way most of
those reality guys do. Our family doesn't really get in big fights or
anything."

"Don't worry about it," Marcus said. "That type of thing is passé. A&E is looking for a new type of family."

At the time they probably were. But in the end, I think they (the network execs, not Marcus) opted for more of the same. I may be giving American viewers too much credit here, but I think people are a little more capable of detecting subtleties than reality television producers give them credit for. Conflict comes in many forms; it doesn't need to be embodied by outbursts, drug habits, teenage pregnancy, or nude modeling. Our home is actually filled with conflict. Most homes are. It's there if you look — you just have to look a little harder. American viewers can accept those types of subtleties. It's time that reality television stopped dumbing down life for them.

Wait, what's that you say? *Rock of Love* is a huge hit? So is *Flavor of Love*? Scott Baio's show was renewed? In that case, I take back what I said about American viewers. Dumb it down, brother, dumb it down. The dumber the better.

You know, I think we had the answer to our conflict problem right in front of us. Shelly Martinez (ECW's "Ariel" and TNA's "Salinas") called me a few days into shooting, saying she'd been released from WWE because the creative team was out of ideas for her. That was something of a surprise for me, especially because I thought her character was a high point of the ECW television program. Certainly I watched her unique entrance with great interest, thinking that maybe, just maybe, this woman really was a vampire. Either that, or she *thought* she was a real vampire, which was just as impressive.

A few weeks earlier, I'd interviewed her on Dee Snider's *Fangoria* satellite radio show, and she'd been great. Rumor had it that she'd actually been let go following a rather spirited verbal exchange with a top WWE star. Which is a shame, but perhaps, I thought, WWE's loss could be A&E's gain.

I offered my idea up to Marcus, who loved it but had reservations about whether my wife would share our enthusiasm. I gave it a try.

"Colette, you know I'm friends with a lot of the WWE Divas, right?"

"Yes, Mick," she said, rolling her eyes, sensing something really stupid was about to come out of her husband's mouth.

"Well, one of them is a vampire." Yes, there it was, that something stupid.

"No, Mick, don't even think about it."

"Just listen. She was just released by WWE."

"No, Mick."

"What if she slept over? When you wake up, you come downstairs, and Mickey and Hughie are eating breakfast with a vampire!"

My wife just wouldn't listen to reason. But if Billy the Exterminator has breakfast with a vampire, you'll know where A&E got the idea.

A few weeks later, my wife paid fifteen hundred dollars for a feces-eating dog. Too bad Marcus and his team had already left. For there was plenty of conflict in the Foley house during Pom Pom's short tenure.

I don't think I'm a hater. But man, did I hate that dog — a tiny little Pomeranian that scarfed down pieces of poop as if she were a canine Takeru Kobayashi at the Nathan's Hot Dog Eating Invitational. At one point I saw her looking like Groucho Marx working on a giant stogie. Except Groucho didn't eat his cigars.

My older children, who had previously never heard their dad drop a single F-bomb, heard the dropping of several during Pom Pom's stay. It was the "shock and awe" campaign of paternal profanity, prompted not only by the sight of feces going down the gullet, but by the feel of bare feet settling into the warm ooze of fresh dog poop that Pom Pom left around the house.

Fortunately, I had an out. At a certain point, my wife agreed that the Pom Pom experiment had been a failure. Maybe, she thought, I could sell her to a previously interested buyer, a woman who thought that the spirit of her recently deceased Pomeranian lived on in Pom Pom. I called the number on a letter she had written — the one containing the theory on Pom Pom's spirit.

But the owner didn't outwardly express an urge to give me fifteen hundred dollars for my feces-eating dog. Instead, she gave me the name of a medication to apply to Pom Pom's food, which would cause the feces to taste foul. Of course, how could I have been so dumb? It was in fact the same medication my parents had placed on my food, when in my early teens I began to mistake my own feces for warm apple pie à la mode — just like Grandma used to make. Mmm, delicious.

We tried the medicine. It failed, apparently unable to fully mask the down-home goodness of fresh-baked turds, right from Pom Pom's oven.

I called that same number a few weeks later. I begged the woman to take Pom Pom. I made no mention of money. Mickey went into his room and had a good little cry, before coming with me to the safe house. He held little Pom Pom in his lap, petting her, telling her he'd always love her.

Pom Pom's new owner had about five other dogs in the house. On the wall in the kitchen was a large framed photo of all the dogs sitting in chairs, celebrating a birthday. They had party hats on.

"You know, Mickey, I think Pom Pom's going to be okay," I said as I headed for the door, pretty sure I could go another fifteen, sixteen years without dropping an F-bomb in front of my kids.

Hughie didn't take the departure well, claiming that he'd loved the dog and didn't want to talk to me ever again.

"What if I buy you a toy?" I said.

"Okay." Sadness and anger, you see, are no match for a new Rey Mysterio figure.

Sometimes — not often, but sometimes — I think of Pom Pom. I think of the look on her little face after polishing off that last savory morsel. It almost looked like Pom Pom was smiling. A big, ol'-fashioned shit-eating grin.

COUNTDOWN TO LOCKDOWN: 20 DAYS

March 30, 2009
Orlando, Florida
9:30 p.m.

Sometimes I envy the Machine Guns. Not just because my kids like them more than they do me. But also because they court the nerd contingent, the way I used to in my late-nineties Mankind days. But the Guns are more aggressive in their courting — they're more active, more inclusive. I was like a nerd in hardcore clothing, trying to lead by example. Sabin and Shelley, by nature of their promos, are almost running for nerd presidents. "Hi, we're Chris Sabin and Alex Shelley, and we want your vote."

Sting was inside the ring as *Impact* began, voicing a reasonable grievance about me; that I had forced him to wrestle Samoa Joe a week earlier, as a tune-up to *Lockdown*, while I, the other participant in the big Philadelphia main event, sat on my sizable butt. Which technically wasn't true, as I'd actually been quite impressive in a decisive victory over a cardboard cutout of Rocky Balboa. By the way, the Don West call of the Foley/Balboa showdown was a thing of broadcasting beauty.

The Guns came out, accompanied by what may be TNA's worst entrance tune (sorry, Dale; sorry, Serge) to rectify the situation.

"Chris and I were in the back playing *Resident Evil 5* and *Street Fighter IV*, and we couldn't help but hear what you were saying, Sting," said Alex. "Quite honestly, our hearts go out to you. We completely agree with you, it is not fair that you had to wrestle Samoa Joe last week and Mick Foley had the night off, but I guess that's what happens when Mick Foley's the boss around here. However, if you wanted to make things right, Jeff, the Motor City Machine Guns aren't just the most attractive tag team in TNA, we are a tag team for hire tonight."

Resident Evil 5? Street Fighter IV? I've never even heard of these games. Shelley then reached back to a long-forgotten angle — the one that almost got the Guns fired — to tie the frayed threads of logic together.

"Thanksgiving Eve 2008 was one of the worst days of my life," Shelley explained. "And do you know why? Because I was humiliated, okay. I had to put on a turkey suit that was extremely itchy. It smelled like burnt hair, I don't know why, and on top of that I get sucker-punched and double-arm-DDTed by Mick Foley. And not one day has gone by that I haven't thought about that. I've been waiting a long time for a night with Mick. You weren't doing anything and the Motor

City Machine Guns weren't doing anything, and you want to give Mick Foley a tune-up match for *Lockdown*, well, how about the Motor City Machine Guns versus Mick Foley in a handicap match? What do you say to that, boss? I mean, you are still the boss around here, you are the one with all the stroke? Get it?" This was a slick reference to the name of Jarrett's finishing move. "Do I have to talk to you, do I have to go talk to somebody else, do I have to text them, e-mail them, smoke signal, you tell me, huh, what do you say, Jeff?"

It was ironic in a way that Shelley was talking to Jeff about that particular instance — the Thanksgiving turkey suit extravaganza. Because Jeff hated it, absolutely hated it! More specifically, he hated the way Shelley sold his feathery fate.

Jeff had literally grown up in the business, and knew, just knew, that the best way, the only way, to project fear and unhappiness was to really *project* fear and unhappiness. Project from the front row to the nosebleeds (even if technically there are no nosebleeds at the Impact Zone). Shake your head vehemently. Put out those hands in protest. Whoa! Whoa! Hold on a minute. I am not putting on that turkey suit!

Instead, Shelley made little birdlike faces, and said something about his MySpace page — how donning the suit might jeopardize his status on the social networking website.

I later learned that the MySpace comment was the final straw on the camel's back — that Sabin and Shelley, who'd had heat with the office over a misunderstanding from over a year earlier, were facing possible termination by TNA.

Meanwhile, not being privy to any of this, I had been singing the Guns' praises, talking to Russo about big plans I had for these guys, how much potential I saw in them. But that night, after the turkey suit incident, I got word of the imminent firing. The Hardcore Legend leapt into action...you know, figuratively speaking. Because it's been awhile since I leapt anywhere.

I talked to Jeff about the guys and how things had changed since the days of the territories, the days of having to project to every soul in the audience, like the ring was our little theater in the round — or hexagon, in TNA's case.

"You know, Jeff, his reaction caught me by surprise, too," I said. "But remember, people are sitting home watching this show on big screens, in hi-def. Those little expressions work. Those guys are funny — their humor is just a little more subtle than what we grew up on."

The next day, I sat down with both Guns and asked for the whole story behind the big misunderstanding from a year earlier. I know readers will want to know the story behind the misunderstanding, but after giving the subject much thought, I decided that the details are for them to tell, not me. Their rationale was pretty intricate but completely understandable, and I asked them if they'd ever explained their side of the story to Jeff. They had not.

"Then you need to go right now and tell Jeff exactly what you told me. Now off with you, you little muskrats." Okay, I didn't call them muskrats.

The talk must have gone okay, because four months later they're all in the same ring, making nice.

"Oh, you got the right guy, Alex," Jeff said. "You got the right guy. You hear that, Sting? He's got the right guy. You and Sabin and Foley in a handicap match tonight. You want him, you got him."

A few minutes later, announcer Jeremy Borash (J.B. from now on, unless I refer to him as "Jeremy," "Borash," or "Jeremy Borash" again) is looking for my reaction in his own inimitable style that makes Gene Okerlund look subtle by comparison.

"Mick, I gotta be honest, I did not see this coming," J.B. said. "You, tonight, in a handicap match against the Motor City Machine Guns. Looks like Jeff Jarrett tried to one-up you there, huh?"

"I don't know what to say, J.B., I'm at a loss for words, so I think it's best if I borrow the words that K.C. and the Sunshine Band gave us so many years ago. Because that's the way, uh-huh, uh-huh, I like it." (Yes, K.C. makes an appearance in another Foley book — the third,

I think [tying him with Tori Amos, though K.C. is unlikely to get his own chapter], including a novel.) "Did you see Jeffrey out there, taking command, just like I knew he could? He is back in the game, J.B."

"I'm a little confused," J.B. said. "He just booked you in an unscheduled handicap match tonight — you and the Motor City Machine Guns."

"I know that, and I'm looking forward to it. Have you seen the Guns lately? Fire, J.B.! Pizzazz! [This is a little tribute to an ECW promo I cut in early 1996.] These guys are great white meat babyfaces. Boy, have I got my work cut out for me. But if you don't mind, I need some time. I'm going to tweak that match a little bit, I'm going to tweak it."

"What do you mean? You're going to *tweak* what?"

"Tweak it," I reiterated.

There it is, the birth of a catchphrase, or at least a catchword. The word had actually been Russo's idea, his ball, more or less, that he handed to me. But I pumped that ball up, shined it, nurtured it, and ran with it.

A few minutes later, Jeff entered his office, the one I'd kind of requisitioned from him. I was trying to be the cuckoo bird of TNA — the guy who moves into a nest another bird has built and kicks the original nest builder out.

Common sense would state that a regular guy would be upset at the prospect of wrestling a two-on-one match against two nerds hell-bent on vengeance. I intended to prove to the world that this version of the TNA shareholder was no regular guy.

"Yes, that's what I'm talking about," I say to Jeff, guitar in hand, seemingly unfazed by the big match he'd booked. "Two weeks ago I told you to turn that frown upside down, and that's just what you did. You found your smile tonight, brother, you booked yourself one heck of a main event, and if you don't mind, I'd like to add a little sizzle to that steak by...tweaking that match a little bit."

"*Tweak?*" Jeff says, savoring the sheer ridiculousness of the word. "Mick, whatever you want, but...*tweak?*"

Here it is, one of my great career moments, modifying the Michael Jackson/Eddie Van Halen hit "Beat It" to meet my own needs. Sing along if you want. "Tweak it, yeah, tweak it. Just tweak it... Just tweak it."

Meanwhile, Sting was doing a great job of showing the wrestling world another side of Mick Foley — the side that needs to be taken seriously at *Lockdown*. In a pretaped sit-down interview with announcer Mike Tenay, Sting shed some valuable light on our past — long past and recent past — and possible future. I thought it was very effective.

Announcer Mike Tenay said, "Sting, I think it's pretty obvious that when it comes to Mick Foley's recent actions, you have probably been as surprised as the rest of us. I have to admit I never saw that chair shot coming, and judging by your reactions I don't think you did, either."

"I was surprised the first time he hit me with the chair," Sting replied. "Only because there is a twenty-year friendship, a twenty-year history there, between Mick Foley and myself, matches against him from all over the world and here in the United States. So I was surprised about it, but if you had to try to put logic to something that Mick Foley was doing, from one old salty veteran to another, I know that he is smart enough to start at the very top, he's going to start with the World Champion. That is why the chair to the back of Sting's head, because right now, I happen to be the World Champion."

"I'm going to have you play psychologist if I can," Mike said. "What do you think is going through the mind of Mick Foley?"

Sting replied, "To be a psychologist and try to get into his mind, I think that is impossible. I would have to be a schizophrenic, I think, to be able to get into the mind of Mick Foley. I know better what Kurt Angle is going to do from one moment to the next, but Mick Foley, no idea what he is going to do next."

"On several occasions in the past you and I have talked about your potential retirement," Mike said. "When it comes to *Lockdown,* is this a case where it's more about your well-being than it is about wins or losses and how concerned are you?"

Sting said, "That's a good question. You know, I'm no spring chicken, that's no secret. In 1990 my left knee was reconstructed and I came back five months later. That same kind of injury happens to me now, there is no comeback. It doesn't matter how good the doctor is, there is no comeback, and going into this match, I'm reminded of 1994. In 1994, in Germany I saw Cactus Jack [my ring name for the first eleven years of my career] wrestle a match against Vader. I was one of those guys at the back, peeking through the curtain to see what was going to happen in this match with Cactus Jack and Vader and the next thing I know, Cactus was tangled up in the ropes. There was blood. I saw blood on his head, but didn't think much of it because it's like an every-night thing, you see blood it seems like. Gary Cappetta, who was the ring announcer that night in Germany, he came into the locker room with a human ear in his hand. He came up to me and said, 'Sting, I think I have Cactus Jack's ear,' and Cactus came into the locker room a few minutes later, blood all over the side of his head, pulled back his hair, no ear. I said, 'Cactus, are you all right?' This is exactly what he said. He said, 'I think I lost my frickin' ear — bang bang,' with the big smile, the missing teeth, the whole picture. That pretty much sums up who my opponent is at *Lockdown*. He's out of his mind. He's going to be in his element, steel cage, the right crowd, so when I say that when I go into *Lockdown* against Mick Foley, it very well could be my last match, I know that."

We're at the midway point of the two-hour show. Time for a little promo — the one I hope will give Guns fans reason to plead with moms and dads across the land for just one more hour before going to bed. I need to make fans understand why this match matters. And to do that I'll need my six-year-old son.

Here it is, the hard-earned fruit of my negotiating labor. All those hours in Houston — e-mails, texts, and phone calls — coming to fruition in my big in-ring promo.

"To tweak or not to tweak? That is the question," I begin. Yes! You can never go wrong when paraphrasing/bastardizing Shakespeare in wrestling! "Now some might say, Mick, why feel the need to tweak a great main event like you in a handicap match against both Motor City Machine Guns? After all, both Shelley and Sabin are tremendous wrestlers." Always build up your opponents. If you lose, you've lost to *someone*. If you win, you've actually beaten *someone*. "It's a match that would push me to my absolute limits, but I have, after all, decided to tweak because of what is right here in this notebook, containing the beginnings of my next book." A cheap plug for this book? Absolutely. "That's not why I'm out here." No, of course not.

"A couple of months ago I was at my son's basketball game. He's seventeen years old. Some of you might remember Dewey." An idiot in the crowd yells out "Cane Dewey" in reference to one of the most intense promos of my career, circa 1995, in response to a fan whose sign had read "Cane Dewey." One of the few drawbacks of the Impact Zone is the tendency for jaded fans to try to get themselves over at the show's expense. "I've been writing about him and talking about him since he was just an infant. I looked over to my wife and I whispered in her ear, and I said, 'Jeez, Colette, Dewey looks kind of ridiculous out there with that haircut.' She said, 'Mick, why don't you let him have his own style, leave him alone, after all, we don't bother you about your hairstyle.' I said, 'Point well taken,' but then I saw this little thing on my refrigerator. It was a birthday card, legit, this was on my refrigerator. When I opened it up, there was this picture right here and it said, 'To Dewey, have a great birthday, P.S. MMG 24-7, 365.' When I came home, I asked my son what the deal was, and he said, 'Yeah, that's why I wear my hair like that, I want to look like Alex Shelley.'

"If I may, let me call for a photo. You guys don't know my six-year-old son, Hughie. Let's have a photo of little Hughie up there on the screen." The little guy's face pops up on the screen and he is absolutely adorable; shy little smile, shoulder-length blond hair. "Look at that face, oh, give me a collective ohhhh." The crowd actively *oohs*. "I went away on the road for a few days, I came back and found my six-year-old son Hughie looking like that" — a photo of the faux-hawked

Hughie — "and he said, 'Dad, now I look like Alex Shelley, too.' Well, is that a fact, kids?"

I start showing a little anger here, about to apply Freud's principle of transference — switching the heat from my children to Alex. "See, this is where the tweaking process comes in. Sure, we could have a great main event on our hands with a normal match, but I've decided to *tweak* it a little bit so tonight's main event is a first blood match." A big *oohh* from the crowd, excited at the prospect of this First Blood match, in which the first person to bleed loses. "And to make sure there is no interference and to make sure that the Stinger has a great view of what's on tap for him at *Lockdown*, I want Sting to be down here as a special guest enforcer. And you know what, as long as I'm at it, I'd like Jeff Jarrett to be down here to do whatever the hell it is that founders do at ringside. Jeff Jarrett, come on down." Even though, as it turned out, Jarrett never did come down. "And here's my promise to all of you — now I've tried hard to make my home a Machine Gun–free environment. I doubt even Ted Nugent would want *those* particular guns in his home."

Yes! There it was, the Nugent line! So what if it elicited only a couple muffled chuckles. It was my line and I got it in! Mission accomplished, or so I tell myself. I've got about forty minutes before my match. Forty minutes to figure out a way to at least be presentable against one of the best tag teams in the business. "So by the time I'm done tonight," I conclude, "no child will ever want to look like Alex Shelley again, because I will carve that kid up like a Thanksgiving turkey." A subtle tie-in to Alex Shelley's Thanksgiving nightmare — the one that smelled like burned hair.

Bell time, and my goal has never been clearer — just get through it. Actually, I've had a separate goal throughout the course of this march to *Lockdown*. I am aware of the distinct possibility that I will look like a tired old man inside that cage at *Lockdown*. But if that tired old man shows up in Philadelphia inside that cage, I want *Lockdown* to be his debut. No one's going to pay to see a tired old man (Ron Jeremy and

Ozzy Osbourne exempted), so I will do whatever it takes to keep him in hiding until *Lockdown*.

The best way, I figure, is to let the Guns do their cool stuff, be their punching bag, let them fly around me, like jet fighters taking down a bruised and battered King Kong. So it's the Gun show out there — double kicks, double tope, double Ds, Doublemint gum.

Amid the general fun, there's a moment that I will watch back several times on DVR. A moment that gives me cause for great concern. It starts out innocently enough: by capping off a simple sequence of moves from the Dynamic Kid/Tiger Mask series of matches from Japan from the early eighties — one of the greatest if not *the* greatest series of matches in wrestling history. I attempt to suplex Shelley, who instead drops behind my back and applies a waist lock. I reverse the waist lock before having it reversed by Shelley, then I immediately make a dive for the ropes, bringing Alex along with me for the ride.

When I'd first seen that little sequence — on a videotape (remember them?) custom-made for me by my buddy Brian Hildebrand — it had seemed almost unfathomable, like it was some kind of magic trick being performed. The series of moves took about five seconds to complete. But getting to the bottom of it, trying to figure out how they did it, took several minutes. Not since that brief Phoebe Cates topless scene in *Fast Times at Ridgemont High* had I hit Stop, Rewind, and Play so often.

Unbeknownst to me (at least in theory), Shelley had made a legal tag to Sabin as he was tumbling through the ropes. So when I turned to Sabin, I was hit with a beautiful drop-kick off the apron, sending me flying and depositing my 300 pounds onto the cold, unforgiving concrete with a sickening thud.

Sting later told me that the landing had made him cringe, as it had taken place directly in front of him on the floor. The bump had definitely jarred me, but hadn't seemed especially noteworthy until I watched it later on DVR.

It certainly was a sickening thud, but it was an unusual thud. This wasn't the classic "raw liver falling onto the kitchen tile" type of full body splat. It was more specific. I watched the landing a couple more times before identifying the thud/splat distinction. The difference, I deduced, was that the thud was being caused primarily by the back of my skull bouncing off the concrete, which is not good.

As far as I can remember, I had always kept my chin tucked tightly to my chest during every potentially painful fall. Chin to chest, chin to chest, chin to chest — it's practically beaten into any wrestling recruit by any self-respecting wrestling trainer, until the actions become instinct. And now, at age forty-four, my instincts seemed to be failing me.

At a certain point, Sabin, unable to contain his disdain for the older generation, openly mocked Sting: pounding his chest, Stinger style, before cringing in faux pain, holding his back, and hobbling as if the slightest physical exertion would simply be too much for a man of the Stinger's advanced age to handle.

This raised the ire of the real Stinger, who pulled Sabin down from the ring apron and planted him with a quick Scorpion Death drop on the concrete. One Gun down, one to go. The Sabin thud (not quite as sickening, but certainly impressive) distracted Shelley for just a moment — which happens to be a moment too long when dealing with the catlike reflexes of the Hardcore Legend.

A quick boot to the gut. Double-arm DDT. Here comes Mr. Soc — wait, not sure if I have the copyright to that name, so we'll just refer to it as "a sock with a face drawn on it." I shove Shelley toward the ropes and he tumbles out, leaving me all alone with the sock, which happens to have a smudge of blood on it. Shelley's blood. The devastating sock had simply been too much for Shelley to handle and now, by First Blood rules, I was the winner.

But I didn't feel like a winner. After all, the little smudge of red wasn't exactly what one would think of when carving up a Thanksgiving turkey. Wait, come to think of it, there isn't a whole lot of bloodshed during the Thanksgiving carving. So I may not have used the proper simile/metaphor there — an almost unforgivable wrestling offense.

I walked out to the ringside announcer's desk, grabbing my trusty barbed-wire bat in one hand and a microphone in the other. "This half a thimbleful of blood is not how you win a First Blood match," I yelled into the microphone. "I said someone was going to get busted wide open...and I'm going to make this kid suffer."

Shelley rolled into the ring, oblivious to the barbaric pleasure I was about to indulge in. He's draped over the bottom rope, in perfect position for me to begin the carving process. I lower the bat toward Shelley's head, slowly, carefully. Like so much of wrestling, or life in general, anticipation is such a key to really maximizing potential enjoyment. Far too often, the appetite is not properly whetted for the finer things in life, be it a vintage wine, a decadent dessert, or a barbed-wire bat to the forehead.

So, I let the audience savor the possibilities, slowly placing a single barb on Shelley's head before the Stinger earns a little payback from my chair shot heard around the world. *Bam!* From seemingly nowhere the Stinger has struck the head of the Hardcore Legend with a mighty chair shot. I fall to my butt, roll to my stomach, and come up with half a thimbleful of blood of my own, like a baby chick peeing red down my head.

But it's enough to cost me the match. The referee calls for the bell, and I am the official loser of this First Blood match.

Now it's time to draw some money. The things we have done thus far on the evening's *Impact* — Shelley's challenge, K.C.'s lyrics, the "Tweak It" song, the match itself — are all just reasons to get us to this point.

I hop out to the floor, the warmth of my own blood reassuring me, letting me know that the visual I want is there — the baby chick is peeing a little more freely now. It's not a hideous mask of congealed plasma, like you'd see in way too many matches involving blood. This is more artistic, like a Jackson Pollock done in crimson, if Pollock worked on right sides of faces, instead of boring canvas.

Sting and I converge and throw a barrage of wild haymakers before being pulled apart — really pulled apart by a security force that apparently didn't pass "Pull Aparts 101," which more or less teaches the ancient art of pulling apart while not actually pulling apart. I mean, I'm not asking these guys to be hockey refs and just watch the brawl, but don't be so adamant about breaking it up that the guys can't get their licks in. We don't actually hate each other, you know. Just trying to get people interested.

Hopefully they will be. It's been a good day of television. I'm proud of myself, not just for surviving a match and a pull-apart brawl that was probably pulled apart too soon, but for sending my character out on a limb without a net for the past few weeks of television. Like I wrote earlier, I'm not looking for real heat — just interest. I just want people to care. And I believe that they will. One of the drawbacks of taping our shows in the Impact Zone is that it's difficult to get a true read for what people are buying — and what they're not. The *Impact* crowd is a blend of TNA loyalists and Universal Theme Park guests. Some of these loyalists can't help but feel complacent, as they've been supporting the company so regularly for so long. By now, they've seen it all a bunch of times, and wrestling, no matter how well done, just isn't going to excite them the way it once did.

I heard a similar concern from a respected cameraman in the motion picture industry. Looking for a way to supplement his income, this talented cameraman turned to the world of adult films, brandishing a pseudonym, "Conrad Doughbler" (not to be confused with the legendary NFL player), so as not to stain his legitimate film credentials. I asked Conrad if he found filming the adult stuff to be enjoyable. Alas for the Dough man, the thrill was gone, a casualty of a profession in which DP no longer stands for "director of photography."

Everyone was happy with the match — the Guns, Sting, even me.

The Guns thanked me for letting them get their classic moves in. One of them points to the other and refers to him as Josh. "Who the heck is Josh?" I ask.

"Oh, that's Chris's name," Alex said.

"Really?" I said. "And what's your real name?"

To tell the truth, I can't even remember what he said. Bill or Ted, maybe ... maybe not.

Even after twenty-five years in the business, the name thing can throw a guy just a little bit. Just ask Kip, who wrestled as Billy, but whose name, I believe, is Monte. Or Stinger, who's Steve; or B. G. James, who I think was Brian Armstrong when I met him, before he became the Road Dogg, before he became the Road Dogg Jesse James. It just brings to mind a comedian who many years ago took note of the acting credits in *Hawaii Five-O*, where Kam Fong played Chin Ho, and Zulu played Kono.

Awhile back, I was attempting to leave tickets at the "will call" area of the box office for Frogman LeBlanc, a journeyman wrestler I'd worked with twenty years ago in Texas. The Frog had recently gotten in touch with me through the miracle of MySpace, and I was looking forward to seeing him at the show. Only one problem — I didn't know his real name. I asked around a little, until finally, with a state athletic commissioner and a few local independent wrestlers around me, and with B. G. James/Road Dogg/Brian Armstrong as my witness, the following words were said:

"Hey Silverback, could you get in touch with Slick or Half-squat and see if they know Frogman's real name?"

Only in wrestling, brother — only in wrestling.

ANOTHER DINNER WITH WOLFIE

Yes, I know I detailed a meeting with Wolfowitz previously in *The Hardcore Diaries* in the provocative, erotically charged chapter "My Dinner with Wolfie." No, I'm not rehashing history here. Indeed, this is an altogether different encounter with Wolfie, which took place during the *Diaries'* final editing process.

I was in Washington, D.C., driving an Air Force officer to a Friday night dinner, honoring a wounded warrior on the occasion of the anniversary of the warrior's "alive day" — the date of his injury in Iraq. The officer in my car had been injured in battle as well; in fact I'd met him a few years earlier when he'd been recovering from his injuries at Walter Reed Army Medical Center. The officer knew I wasn't a particularly big fan of Dr. Wolfowitz's, and he warned me that Wolfie/the Wolfmeister/Wolforama might be in attendance at the dinner. Indeed, even after leaving the Pentagon to take up his post as the head of the World Bank, the international financial institution that provides financial and technical assistance to developing countries, Dr. Wolfowitz had remained steadfast in his support for injured service members. Which I admired, even if I did hate the guy's guts . . . and his breath. Especially his breath.

I'd specifically mentioned in *Diaries* that a blast of Wolfowitz's breath would have dropped a lesser man. Ouch! Kind of hard to be friends after a remark like that. I mean, disagreeing on foreign policy is one thing; writing about a man's halitosis is pretty much a non-negotiable nonstarter.

So, during the course of the dinner, I did what I thought was the manly, hardcore, mature thing to do — I hid from Paul Wolfowitz. Hid from Wolfie as if it was my turn to pick up the tab at a Devastation Incorporated reunion dinner.

Finally, after hours of regaling troops injured in real battles with my own exaggerated tales of injuries suffered in make-believe battles, I headed for the door, knowing I had a good three-hundred-mile drive in front of me, thankful I'd been spared any type of incident with the notorious Teen Wolf. (Yes, I know Wolfowitz hasn't technically been a teen wolf since the early sixties, but I'm just about out of Wolf references.)

Suddenly, from across the room, I saw Wolfie's eyes glare at me as he started his move. I was headed for the door and had a sizable lead on him, but Wolfowitz was like a linebacker heading me off at the pass with a precise angle of pursuit. He was going to catch me, interrogate me, breathe on me.

"Excuse me, are you Mick Foley?" he said, not angry, not even a little tired from his journey across the restaurant.

"Yes, sir," I said. "How are you, Dr. Wolfowitz?" Trying to be polite, buying a little time before bolting out the door.

"I just want to thank you for all you do for our troops," Wolfie said, serious, complimentary. Hard to really hate a guy when he's being so nice to you.

"Well, thank you, sir," I said. *Okay*, I thought, *time to leave. Maybe just one polite question, before heading out.* "How is everything at the World Bank, sir?"

"Ughh," Wolfowitz groaned, letting out a blast of breath that was . . . minty fresh? What the heck? I'd expected Nosferatu and gotten Stacy Keibler instead. Because Stacy's breath when I met her was so Doublemint delicious. Stacy once ate a tuna fish sandwich while sitting next to me on a plane (where, I should mention, she specifically asked a passenger if they could move so she and I could hang out), and she even made that smell good. Wait, where was I? Oh yeah, Wolfie, grunting — minty-fresh breath.

"If you thought the Pentagon was full of bureaucrats, you ought to try getting something done at the World Bank," Wolfie explained.

"That must be frustrating, sir."

"Well, it is," he said. "Especially if you're trying to make decisions that could improve millions of lives."

"You know, Dr. Wolfowitz, along with what I do with the troops, world poverty is one of my great passions." Hey, maybe as long as I was talking with one of the most influential men in the world, I could score a couple points.

"Really?" he asked, intrigued.

"Yes, sir, that's true," I said. "I sponsor seven kids around the world with Christian Children's Fund [now ChildFund International]."

"Which countries?" the World Bank head honcho asked.

"Well, I have three kids in Mexico, one in the Philippines, one in Sri Lanka, one in Ethiopia, and I have a wonderful little child in Sierra Leone."

"Sierra Leone," Wolfowitz said. "I sponsor a child there, too."

For the next several minutes, it was just me and him — a battered old wrestler and the president of the World Bank, chatting like old friends, gossiping like schoolgirls, carrying on about things like the illicit diamond smuggling trade in Sierra Leone, child soldiers, amputation by machete — little things like that.

And it dawned on me that none of my friends from home would give a crap about the diamond smuggling trade in Sierra Leone. Wait, check that, John McNulty would. Maybe Steve Zangre, too. But none of the others. Certainly not Imbro, who never seems to tire of personal anecdotes about Christy Canyon, but would shield himself from stories of any emotional depth as if he was Dracula, fending off the first rays of daybreak. Yet here was Wolfie, a guy I claimed to hate, a guy whose very breath I'd cast aspersion on, hanging out with me, trading concerns about the developing world.

I felt like such a phony, like a beauty contestant claiming natural Cs when the slightest feel, the most tender touch, the simplest tweak would have exposed the perfect, impossibly rounded, gravity-defying truth. This talk with Wolfie seemed to be tweaking a nipple of its own: the nipple of my conscience. And was doing it in a less gentle way than I would have found preferable. I just couldn't take it.

"Sir, may I be honest with you?" I said.

"Of course," Wolfie assured me. Okay, do-or-die time here; he really had a grip on that thing, twisting it around metaphorically like he was trying to tune in to the Opry live from Nashville on an AM radio in the old days, all the way from Missouri on a cloudy night.

"Well, sir, I never really liked you."

A hearty laugh from the Wolfmeister, followed by an explanation from the Hardcore Legend and then discussions on the war in Iraq, the care of our wounded veterans, and the benefits of mosquito netting in lands across the world.

Wolfie even offered me a stick of Doublemint gum, noting that my breath smelled like I'd been gargling with a drunk man's balls. Just kidding — he never really specified what kind of balls they were.

I rolled into my driveway around 5 a.m. and was woken by Hugh's predawn declaration — "I'm awake, Dad" — about a half hour later. I felt weary, hungover, though I hadn't had a drop of alcohol.

My wife wandered in, taking note of my precarious perch atop a child's bunk bed.

"Oh man, I feel so guilty," I confided in my wife.

"What did you do, Mick?" Colette said, knowing that from time to time during the course of our marriage I'd sought solace in the arms of bored housewives, grieving widows, adventurous grandmothers, defrocked nuns, and sexy Republican women.*

"Oh, no, it's nothing like that," I assured her. "It's just that I talked to Paul Wolfowitz last night."

"Wolfowitz?" Colette said, shocked. "You hate that guy! But that's nothing to feel guilty about."

"Yes it is," I said. "Because I really enjoyed it."

---

*Author's note: The admission of solace seeking is purely fictional. As, to the best of the author's knowledge, is the rumored existence of sexy Republican women.

COUNTDOWN TO *LOCKDOWN:* 16 DAYS

April 3, 2009
New Orleans, Louisiana

Finally, the end of a long day. A long, long day. It's *WrestleMania* weekend in Houston, site of the event's twenty-fifth anniversary. It has that Super Bowl atmosphere — events all weekend long, wrestling fans making the trek to Houston from states all over the country and countries all over the world. Until a few days ago, I thought I'd miss out on all the fun.

My first *WrestleMania* weekend was 1996 — the first time I saw the grandeur, pomp, and circumstance of the event; families flying in either to bear witness to their loved ones battling it out on their biggest night of the year or, in many cases, families bearing witness to their loved ones' being witness to other families' loved ones battling it out on *their* biggest night of the year. Does that make any sense? Basically, it's a three-day party, a time of great excitement, even for those wrestlers not participating.

My family only came to one *WrestleMania*, back in 2000, for the match that I firmly felt would be the last of my career. The night that my wife said Macaulay Culkin kept checking her out, and the night that I almost called my manager, Barry Bloom, with the sad, untrue news that his tickets weren't available simply because I'd heard that Anna Nicole Smith and her son needed a pair, and there was no pair to be found. Barry later told me that I should have gone ahead and ditched him for Anna Nicole.

In all the years I worked for them, my wife never felt completely comfortable with WWE, dating back to the time in Bangor, Maine, summer of 1996, when a WWE road agent told me my family wasn't allowed backstage and ushered them into a dingy bathroom with an exposed sewage pipe, enabling the pleasant scent of human excrement (referred to as "poopee" and "peepee" at the time) to become part of my family's first collective WWE memory.

In November of that same year, I was specifically told that no family members were allowed backstage at Madison Square Garden for *The Survivor Series*, which my wife and kids had specifically flown in for from Florida. So they stayed at the hotel all day, away from a dad they didn't get to see all that often back then, while the backstage area filled up with fiancées of other wrestlers, girlfriends of other wrestlers, casual romantic flings of other wrestlers, and a host of college buddies/workout partners/guys who knew somebody who used to work security.

A year later, when negotiating a new contract — by myself, before Barry Bloom started making my professional life a lot easier — I brought these issues up with Vince, who gave me his personal guarantee that nothing like that would ever happen again. It didn't, but after hearing Vince compare her to Robin Givens in a radio interview, Colette never felt comfortable at a WWE event again. Maybe that's why nobody in the company has had my home telephone number these past ten or so years. Oddly, I gave the number to TNA owner Dixie Carter the very first time I spoke with her.

Dixie has turned out to be a wonderful boss to work for — warm but wise, understanding but tough, in some ways kind of like an anti-Vince (and that's coming from someone who actually likes Vince). Through what can be seen only as an amazing coincidence or an act of God, Dixie was TNA's original publicist and had the financial means to bail out the fledgling wrestling company when its original sponsor bailed out with little warning. Her decision allowed both wrestlers and wrestling fans an alternative to WWE and has turned out to be the best possible scenario for everyone involved, myself included.

Anyway, I was content to spend the big weekend away from all the action, appearing at a couple of untelevised TNA house shows a few hundred miles away in Louisiana. But I couldn't help but notice a look of sadness on Booker's face at the *Impact* tapings prior to 'Mania weekend. Booker doesn't usually look sad — he's generally an upbeat, funny guy. I've seen him angry a few times, but even then he looks like he's having a good time. I won't go so far as to say he looked distraught, but he was noticeably down.

For months Book and Sharmell had been planning a Legends Convention for Houston, their hometown, for *WrestleMania* weekend. I think WWE looks at any outside event as an intrusion, kind of an invasion of the creative space they carved out for themselves twenty-five years ago. I can understand that. But in truth, fans who travel from around the country and the globe are going to be, inherently, really into wrestling. They're already giving WWE a ton of money. Injecting it into the city of Houston, too. Sure, some of them will want to make their visit a WWE-only event, the same way some Disney fans want to make their Orlando visits Disney only: Disney hotels, Disney parks, Disney restaurants. But a lot of people want to go to Universal, visit Sea World, maybe even take in a feeding at Gatorland. My eight-year-old, Mickey, really wants to visit Holy Land Experience, the religious theme park that re-creates biblical Jerusalem right in the heart of central Florida.

But some fans want more. They want to attend a Ring of Honor show, or watch an Astros game, or attend a Legends Convention whose participants aren't dictated by WWE. Perhaps out there, somewhere, is a child who wants to meet D.D.P., a child for whom the word *legend* doesn't carry too literal an interpretation. Just kidding. Longtime readers of these memoirs will recognize D.D.P. as one of my good buddies, and the guru behind YRG, Yoga for Real Guys.

Within twenty-four hours of posting his Legends lineup on the web, Booker was faced with six cancellations: mysterious phone calls/texts/e-mails citing a cornucopia of cop-out causes. Double bookings, no-compete clauses, family commitments. Just a week out from the convention, Booker was faced with a few more key withdrawals.

I'll let you guys make up your own minds, but I think the truth is that most former WWE wrestlers, no matter how tenuous the nature of their "departure," all secretly (probably not-so-secretly) long for that phone call. That "welcome back, pal" call. That back-in-the-family hug. I can see why, too. Vince is a good hugger — firm but not too constrictive. Christy Canyon once hugged me so hard for so long that I almost had to ask her to stop. Even with the natural double Ds* that had induced so many naughty thoughts squeezed against me, I felt kind of like one of Bruno's old opponents at the Garden, trapped inside the Italian strongman's iron, viselike grip, feeling both the wind

---

*While writing this book, my editor, Ben, and I could not come to agreement as to whether Ms. Canyon's "gifts" were of the D or DD variety. We decided to go right to the source. "Actually, you're both right," Christy informed us. "They fluctuate. If I put on a couple pounds, *boom*, right to my..."

and will to live leave my body. Okay, maybe it wasn't quite so bad. Now that I've written about that hug I probably won't be able to get it off my mind. It was like a two-minute hug, those natural beauties becoming like one with me, her breath hot in my ear, her "I missed you, baby," nearly lost among the sounds a tongue makes when it's flicking in and out of what used to be a guy's ear.

What the hell did this have to do with a phone call from Vince? Oh yeah, very few people want to jeopardize that potential call from Vince — thus the multitude of mysterious cancellations.

I think I just hated to see Booker so down. Especially when I thought I might have the answer to some of his problems. "Hey, Book," I said. "Do you want me to see if I can make the convention?"

"You would do that for me, man?" he said, seemingly unwilling to believe the sacrifice I was willing to make, the courage I was show- ing, the risk I was willing to take, the uncompromising decency that makes up the core of my character. In all honesty, it may have been the Chick-fil-A that swayed me. At each TV taping Booker presents me with a Chick-fil-A chicken sandwich — possibly the best-tasting fast-food chicken sandwich on the planet. Primarily available in the South, they are to chicken sandwiches what Whataburger is to burg- ers — pure fast-food nirvana. Although, come to think of it, Backyard Burgers mesquite chicken with a double coleslaw sandwich might just edge out even the mighty Chick-fil-A. But they're available in only a few states in the South — Tennessee, Arkansas, possibly Mississippi. D.D.P. actually turned me on to them when I lived in Atlanta (maybe there's still a few left in Georgia, I don't really know), singing the praises of the incredible sandwich right down the street from the gym that Sting and Lex Luger owned. I'm not sure exactly what D.D.P. may have said, but I am willing to bet it started with the words, "Bro, I'm telling ya."

So, after arriving home from a night out with the four kids at an Islanders hockey game, I straightened out all my flight details, answered a couple e-mails (that line would have been unthinkable even one year ago), and hit the stationary bike for a little meager workout time. I'd actually been to the gym earlier in the day, returning home to the surprise of my daughter, who couldn't fathom how I'd left, worked out, and returned in less than forty minutes. She seemed so disappointed that I opted not to tell her that I'd also worked a visit to the bank into my forty-minute adventure.

I just keep trying to throw shit at the wall and see what sticks when it comes to these workouts. (I wrote "stuff at the wall" first, but in this case, the bad word really does works better.) That's quite an ironic metaphor, really. Because back when I was a lifeguard for the mentally challenged, in the summer of 1985, there really was a kid who threw shit at the wall. You know, as in his *own* shit. I thought he was a great kid and inquired as to whether he might be granted a two-hour release from the facility to come over to the Foley house for dinner. There was a lot of paperwork involved in these things on all sides, but occasionally these visits would be allowed.

"You know, Mick, that might not be the best idea," I was told.

"Why not?" I said, disappointed, kind of taking it personally.

"Well, Vinnie is a feces thrower."

"A feces thrower," I said, momentarily unable to put the noun and verb together in a way that made visual sense. Don't worry, once the image hit me, it stuck around for a while.

Apparently one of Vinnie's classic gags was to wake up from a "nightmare" screaming, begging for help. A well-meaning but ill-informed worker would charge to the rescue, flicking on the light switch, not knowing that the Vin-man had lathered up the switch with a little gift: a little homemade fudge, a little keepsake from the Hershey factory.

I know a few of my more cynical readers will feel like I included that story just to use the words *Vinnie* and *feces thrower* in the same sentence. They might be right.

But I saw Vinnie the feces thrower just a few years ago, and to the surprise of everyone in attendance I recognized him immediately, even though he was now a man in his early thirties instead of a child.

I have another reunion story from my 1985 lifeguarding days. A few years ago at a book signing, I saw a young man with Down syndrome at the very end of a long line of fans. I mean this line went on forever. In the words of Ricky Morton, "Brother, you never seen so many people, tell 'em, Hoot." A deep drag of his cigarette, take two steps back. If someone sees Chris Jericho or Steve Austin, please show them that line, as it's highly likely that no one else will have any idea what I'm talking about.

Okay, so it wasn't *that* long a line. But it was respectable. And that young man with Down syndrome was at the back of it, which just wasn't going to cut it. Guys like that have probably had it tough enough without waiting in a ten-hour-long, three-thousand-person-strong line. Okay, hour-long, two hundred people. Happy?

So I summoned this young man to the front of the line and imme-diately remembered his smile, his laugh, the kindness in his eyes. "Olaf, Olaf Baez?" I said. And Olaf Baez nearly jumped into my arms, he was so happy to see his old friend. Little did he know that over the last twenty years, without fail, I had mentally changed the words of "Born on the Bayou" to "Born Olaf Baez" every time I heard that Creedence Clearwater Revival song.

"So Olaf," I said. "You're a wrestling fan?"

The woman who was with him, a worker at the home he lived in, quickly cut me off in the nicest way imaginable.

"He's not a fan of yours because you are a wrestler," she said. "He's a fan of yours because you were his lifeguard."

Cool, huh? Let me see, what does any of this have to do with wres-tling? Oh yeah, the stuff on the wall, my workout routine. As you know, I originally wrote *stuff* throughout that whole story, but it just didn't seem that funny without the real S word in there. Which, by the way, is a word I rarely if ever use in real life. It doesn't even have a meaningful action-verb application like the F-bomb does when used correctly and in moderation. Besides, I've seen plenty of PG-13 movies that sprinkle the S word around. But I will do my best to keep this book F-bomb free, regardless of whether or not it's used as a meaningful action verb.

So I put in about twenty minutes on the bike, watching *The Making of Eastbound & Down* on HBO on Demand, probably the best five-dollar monthly expenditure I've ever made. Watching the special got me curious. Were those really April Buchanon's (Katy Mixon's) boobs we saw in the season finale? Or were they stunt boobies?

I figured I could work in a couple hundred hindu squats — deep knee bends without weights, although I don't personally do them deep enough to qualify as such. Still, about twenty-five in, my thighs are burning. Fifty in and I'm really hurting. Wait, there they are, Kenny's unhooking that bad boy, a quick-release, front-loading bra that simply wasn't available back in my clumsy going-for-second-base phase. I don't have too many examples I can mentally cite, but I think the majority — two out of three, maybe three out of four — ended with a female voice saying, "Maybe you'd better just let me do it."

Go, Kenny, go! You can do it! The sparse material gives way and there are April's boobies springing forth like a wire snake from a salted peanut can. Yes, I know I used that exact simile in *Tietam Brown* to describe a similar breast-releasing incident, but that was my book and my simile, and I'll use it however often I want to. And I want to use it now. Because that's what they looked like — a wire snake springing from a salted peanut can. Besides, I've seen the sales figures — not likely many of you actually read *Tietam Brown*. So it's a fresh simile to you.

Wait a second, though. Let me go back, watch it again. I think I saw an edit there. Time for more hindus. Twenty-five, there's the burn. Let's get fifty. Wait, here it is. Medium close-up, that's definitely Katy in her bra. I can see her breasts, heaving, yearning to be set free. Here's Kenny, going for the release. Forget about those hindus, Mick, this is science. There it is, edit. Close-up. Release. *Boing!* Wire snake springing from the can. Hard to tell, almost impossible. Let's get twenty-five more hindus in before doing a before-and-after freeze frame.

I squeeze out twenty-five at 2:30 in the morning. I'll need to leave for the airport at 4:00 a.m. for a 6:30 flight. These hindus are difficult and I'm sweating. I'm going to try to get another fifty, but not before getting to the bottom of this April Buchanon situation. Freeze-frame before photo. Note the faint pattern of freckles and the pendant resting comfortably in the cleavage. There was a time, during the heyday of "the Godfather" in WWE, when I was so inundated with cleavage that I thought I was forever numb to its charms. Apparently, based on this *Countdown to Lockdown* chapter, those days are over.

Edit. Close-up. Are those freckles really the same? The pendant. Wire snake. *Boing!* I review it one more time, like a Super Bowl referee on a critical fumble decision. Is the evidence conclusive? Or does the decision on the field stand?

In the end, it's inconclusive. But I'm leaning toward stunt boobies. Otherwise, why cut at all? Why not just roll tape, show April, pan down, same shot, *boing!* Like a good chair shot with no hands-a-blocking or a Jackie Chan stunt filmed in its entirety, so we know Jackie's still the man. Eventually, I'll get the answer. How? By tracking down Kenny Powers and asking him my question personally.

Until then, I'll accept that those boobies weren't really April's but wish they were. And wonder what they'd feel like if they were crushed against my body during a prolonged hug.

I've got to get to sleep. I'll tell you about that Legends Convention tomorrow. By the way, before I took that shower and got ready for the airport? I reeled off fifty hindus. Bang! That bang's for you, D.D.P.!

COUNTDOWN TO LOCKDOWN:
14 DAYS

April 5, 2009
New Orleans International Airport
New Orleans, Louisiana
11:03 a.m.

Layovers, delays — they're all part of life on the road. My flight to Atlanta is delayed an hour, which is no big deal, but that one-hour delay complicates my flight to Milwaukee, requiring an additional two hours of sitting around. By the time I get to Milwaukee for my prestigious appearance tomorrow at the Potawatomi Bingo Casino, it will be almost seven; time for *WrestleMania*. I may just have to pass on *'Mania* this year in favor of some sleep and for the good of this memoir.

I caught that 6:30 flight on April 3 and did something highly unusual for me: I slept for the entire flight. It's a frustrating thing, not being able to doze at will when so much of this lifestyle involves traveling. Some of the guys are like little cats; they can curl up and catch a napple (my own word for *nap* for the last seven years) just about anywhere; on a plane, a car, a bus, a couch, the floor, during a Jay Lethal match. Hey, I remember Curtis Hughes used to be able to take a nap at ringside while he was playing the role of the menacing enforcer. He'd just close his eyes behind those dark sunglasses he wore and take a little siesta.

Booker had an RV set up outside the convention center, for the guys to hang out in before their appearances. There had to have been ten different events going on at the huge center, most of them simultaneously. There's a Ring of Honor show later on, an 8:00 p.m. bell time, which should result in one of their largest crowds of the year. I still keep in touch with ROH owner Cary Silkin, and though I will not see him on this particular day, he did offer me a ticket to see Leonard Cohen at Radio City on May 17. There's a religious revival taking place, right next to the gun show. Not just any gun show, either, but a "High Caliber" gun show, although I'm not sure if the name is indicative of the type of people or the type of weaponry involved in the show.

Now I don't want to raise the ire of the gun lobby. After all, I was probably treading dangerous waters with the Ted Nugent line, but I've got to think that if we could somehow go back in time to visit little James Madison, the principal framer of our Constitution, and Patrick Henry, the main proponent of the Bill of Rights amendments, and explained the twenty-first century to them, they might just have added a little amendment to that Second Amendment, explaining that rifles with calibers high enough to take an airplane out of the sky might not be such a good thing.

Sorry, guys, but with four police officers gunned down in Pittsburgh yesterday, thirteen killed in Binghamton, New York, two days ago, and, perhaps most shocking of all, eight people senselessly slaughtered at a nursing home in North Carolina just a week ago, my sentiments are going to be with the victims, their families, and all those out there wondering what could possibly be next.

And in this economic environment, with so many losing so much so often, does anyone doubt that there's going to be a next time, or a time after that, or a time after that?

I know there's going to be a vocal minority who will disagree, some vehemently, with any suggestion that might possibly make their quest to procure firearms more inconvenient. But I'd like to see those same people explain their opposition to registration, gun locks, background checks, and legislation to the families of the victims in Pittsburgh, Binghamton, North Carolina, or the town after that, or the town after that.

I stepped into Booker's RV and was met with the unmistakable grin of Stan "the Lariat" Hansen, one of the all-time greats in the business and a veritable legend in Japan. Hansen was a brawler, as realistic as they come, and his matches for All-Japan Wrestling during that promotion's glory days, from the late seventies through the midnineties, are among the hardest hitting and most exciting in the history of the business. Certainly, he was a big influence on me long before I met him, and an even bigger one once I did.

Stan took me under his wing during my one and only tour for All-Japan in 1991 — showing me the ways of the Japanese wrestling world, allowing me to tag along for meals with sponsors that I could have never afforded on my own. He spoke of the joys of fatherhood, the importance of saving money, and offered up the single best piece of advice I've ever heard: "If you're married, nothing good can happen to you in a bar." Think about it, all you married guys, or any of you out there thinking of giving it a shot in the future.

At that time, going out after the show was still the in thing to do; to not go brought on the risks of social isolation and/or downward career momentum. Hey, the bookers, the guys who made the decisions, were often at the forefront of the party environment. Of course, they were going to hook up their buddies from time to time and forget about the faces they seldom saw, except when they were, you know, doing their job in the ring.

I was lucky in a lot of ways, breaking in. I mean, I met a few pricks along the way, but by and large I was largely accepted, if not completely understood, by the boys. I was thought to be a little strange for never smoking pot — never tried it, never inhaled it — but no one ever pressured me to take anything.

Even in ECW, I was blissfully unaware of the copious amount of drug use that was going on all around me. Hell, I didn't even know the Sandman was loaded during our matches until he told me months later. And by the time I got to WWE in 1996, the atmosphere was changing. Guys still went out, but it was no longer a prerequisite for social acceptance. The Internet was becoming big; video games were showing up in wrestlers' suitcases, first in full-console form, later in personal-sized PSPs or Nintendo DSes, sometimes a combination of both. TNA has kind of become like Nerd Central with all the video games, iPods, smart phones, and DVD players. Last night in New Orleans none other than *Eastbound & Down* became the central focus of the conversation, with Jay Lethal — the man of a thousand voices — offering up his imitation of a forlorn Stevie Janowski after being told by Kenny Powers that his personal assistant services would no longer be required:

"I hope we get in a car accident and die right now, so we can live together in heaven."

Hartsfield-Jackson Airport
Atlanta, Georgia
2:53 p.m.

This could take awhile. I'm at the Hartsfield-Jackson Airport. I arrived just as my scheduled flight to Milwaukee was taking off, sending me off to the nearest Delta agent for rebooking. I'm on standby for both the 3:58 and the 6:40 flights before finally having a confirmation at 9:30. In which case I'd only show up in Milwaukee seven and a half hours later than scheduled. I really wonder if this appearance is worth the hassle it's caused. It's already upended my little Williamsburg, Virginia, vacation with Mickey and Noelle, forcing me to book flights for the whole family and three different hotels for what will amount to a couple of days at Busch Gardens and a couple-hour visit to the Colonial Williamsburg attraction, where U.S. history buff Mickey will be in all his glory, observing all the researchers wearing the shirts "with the tissue in the front," his take on colonial attire.

Anyway, Stan and I hit it off, talking family, wrestling, Vince, and baseball until it was time to do the autograph thing for Booker. I was kind of sequestered behind a curtain, visible only to those willing to fork over a little extra money to take a peek behind the curtain for a little face time with the HCL — Hardcore Legend — me.

There wasn't a particularly long line to meet me — I saw maybe sixty or seventy people during my two hours behind the curtain — but man, it was a pretty expensive peek. Granted, all the money was going to Booker's foundation, but I really doubt I would shell out that type of cash to meet someone like me.

Of those sixty or seventy people, I saw maybe ten Americans, tops. The rest of the people I met were like an international coalition, a United Nations security meeting or something. Let me see, in no particular order, I met fans from Ireland, Scotland, England, New Zealand, Belgium, Australia, and France, all in town specifically to meet me...and maybe to watch *WrestleMania*, too.

It was a good time, but unfortunately, my flight time from Houston to New Orleans was so tight that I had to bail right at three, leaving me no chance to say hello to the rest of the boys in attendance — although I did manage to get a note to former WWE Diva Lita, or Amy, as I should probably refer to her these days.

A quick Southwest flight to New Orleans, a rented Dodge Charger, and a seventy-minute drive later, and I am good to go in Thibodaux, Louisiana, home of Frogman LeBlanc. It's a good crowd, maybe three thousand, and enthusiastic in their support from opening bell to the 1, 2, 3 of the main event. I even spotted a fan, too young to know better, cheering on Jay Lethal. Look, I like Jay, I think he's a really good worker, and I find him entertaining as hell. But I've got to pick on someone in these books. And I've decided that for this particular book, Jay is my man. Sure, I don't do an awful lot at these house shows, but I did cut a little promo before the Beer Money tag team match, foreshadowing what might be to come with my ominous line, "Just give me a reason."

So a little later, in the evening's main event, they got involved, thereby "giving me a reason" to get involved as well, which I did, both helping attain a victory for the forces of good (Jeff Jarrett and A. J. Styles) and setting up the main event for Saturday night — a New Orleans street fight pitting the duo of Jeff Jarrett and myself against that dastardly Beer Money — James Storm and Robert Roode.

This will be my first house show match in a long time, at least three years. I did one for promoter Alex Shane in Coventry, England, sometime in 2005 or 2006, as well as a memorial show to honor my good friend Brian Hildebrand in 2005, and I kind of participated in an impromptu tag team, partnering with Jerry "the King" Lawler against Al Snow and Jonathan Coachman — quite possibly the worst teaming of two individuals this side of the duo of Ben Doon and Phil McCracken (go ahead, say it slowly: Ben Doon and Phil McCracken).

But that's pretty much it for my house show history over the past ten years. Why New Orleans, especially in front of what looked to be a weak crowd, maybe a thousand people in a big arena — the same one I battled Vader in at *Halloween Havoc*, October 1993? Really, it's just to shake off some of that ring rust, get me used to being inside the ring so I don't feel so absolutely naked at *Lockdown*, a mere two weeks away. Let's face it, nobody really wants to see me naked out there.

Yet I've just cleared standby and am now aboard Delta Flight 4924, getting ready for takeoff, wedged into a seat — 13D — that was never meant for an ass like mine.

A fun family wrestling story.

A PERFECT WAY TO GO

Look, I know I retired in 2000. I lost a Hell in a Cell to Triple H in Hartford, Connecticut, and even got a royal send-off the next night on *Raw*, courtesy of a tribute video set to Sarah McLachlan's "I Will Remember You," which had to have cost Vince a decent dollar. It even made Stephanie McMahon cry backstage. In my mind, it was the perfect ending to a career that had exceeded my wildest expectations. A tear in my eye, a little blood on the face, one last wave good-bye as I rode off into the sunset — having wrestled my last match ever at the age of thirty-four.

Until six weeks later, that is, when I wrestled again, for the last time ever — my only *WrestleMania* main event.

Until four years after that, in my big comeback match at *WrestleMania XX*, teaming with the Rock in what, ironically, was likely his last wrestling match ever.

Okay, okay, I think you get the point. And since joining TNA in September 2008, I've known that I will wrestle a handful of matches a year. But in January 2008, after completing the six Pay-Per-View matches over a three-year period that my contract with WWE called for, I really had no idea whether I'd wrestle again. So, in a sense, even though I would never have the audacity to announce another "official" retirement match, any match I wrestled at that time could conceivably be considered my last match ever. For about six months, following my June 2007 *Vengeance* Pay-Per View, I at least had the peace of mind of knowing that should I never wrestle again, my last match ever was in a Pay-Per-View main event with four other current or former world champions. Foolishly, in January 2008, I put that peace of mind at risk with the uttering of a few well-intentioned words.

One day earlier, I'd been part of *Raw* in Philadelphia — I think as a judge on "Raw Idol." I'm not really sure, and to tell you the truth, it doesn't really matter. Every once in a while I'd get a call from Brian Gewirtz, *Raw*'s lead writer, asking if I wanted to be part of the show. Usually I would, provided it was a decent idea — which it usually was. I always thought Brian was an exceptionally smart guy, full of good ideas. Plus, he probably deserved some kind of an award, perhaps the Nobel Peace Prize, for being able to coexist with Vince for so many years.

Look, that whole repackaging thing was a bitter pill to swallow — one that took awhile to fully digest. You know, maybe there's still just a tiny fragment of that pill still sitting in my gut, a little sliver of bitterness that might take awhile — a year or two, maybe twenty, to fully, completely digest. But for the most part, I accepted that my days as a big deal with WWE were done.

That night, in January 2008, on my way out of the building in Philly, I happened to see Mr. McMahon and mentioned that I was planning on bringing my kids to the *SmackDown* tapings at Nassau Coliseum the following night. This would be the first time that all four Foley kids would be attending a show together. Dewey and Noelle practically grew up at WWE shows; movie buffs may recall them bawling their eyes out during my 1999 "I Quit" match with the

Rock. Mickey and Hughie had been to a handful of shows several months earlier. But as far as simultaneous show situations go, this would be a first.

The following afternoon, I received a call from WWE. "Vince has something for you on the show," I was told. What did he have? They didn't really know.

So I powered up the Chevy Venture and headed out to the coliseum — a forty-minute ride — to find out what Vince might have for me.

"How about a match?" Vince said when I arrived.

"A match? But Vince, I'm in horrible shape," I said, just in case Vince couldn't grasp the obvious.

"Don't worry, Mick," he said. "This one will be easy."

And so, it came to pass that I wrestled announcer Jonathan Coachman (the Coach) with a leprechaun (Hornswoggle) serving as the guest referee. True to Vince's word, it had been an easy match, just some harmless shenanigans to entertain my hometown fans. Still, as I traveled home along the Northern State Parkway, I couldn't stop thinking that the whole idea had been a huge mistake. The Coach? A leprechaun as guest referee? Yeah, I'd say the whole thing qualified as a huge mistake. I started thinking about some other comeback match I might have left — in me — one last great gasp to erase that Coachman stain on my legacy.

I looked at my children in the rearview mirror. Dewey and Noelle in the third row, listening to their iPods. Like most teenagers they found the thought of traveling forty minutes without some kind of personal entertainment device to be unthinkable. Mickey and Hughie were sound asleep in the second row — their childhood innocence shattered forever by the image of their dad in a black warm-up suit doing battle with the Coach. Forget about those eleven chair shots at the '99 *Rumble* my older kids witnessed — this was real childhood trauma.

Then, I thought about the way the kids had looked when I made my grand entrance for the big match. I quickly spotted them in the second row as I approached the ring; a huge "Did you hear that, Pop," Road Warriors–type reaction accompanying me for this rare *Smack-Down* appearance. At the time, I was almost exclusively a *Raw* guy, having made just one appearance, in December 2005, on *Smack-Down* since leaving full-time wrestling in 2000. Dewey was stoic but proud, holding little Hughie on his lap, who seemed amazed and slightly confused by the fact that fifteen thousand people would care about his dad at all, let alone make loud, appreciative noises at the very sight of him. Noelle was beaming, a big smile on her beautiful face — a far cry (literally) from the little girl with the tears streaming down her face in *Beyond the Mat*. It's funny, because in a way that film has kind of made time stand still. My wife and I (except for the gray in my beard) look largely the same. But for many of the wrestlers and fans, Noelle Foley will always be the five-year-old girl in the little red dress, with the curious choice in favorite words.

And then there was Mickey. How exactly did Mickey greet his beloved dad? With a big thumbs-down, and a hearty "Boo, boo, you're a stinky wrestler."

I broke into a big smile and had to fight to suppress a laugh — a fight I ultimately lost. That image of all my children together at the match for the first time was one I could live with gladly for the rest of my life. If I never wrestled again, this match would be a perfect way to go out. The Coach? A leprechaun? My own son booing me? Absolutely perfect.

The beginning of the end of my WWE days.

A WHOLE NEW CAREER

I sometimes wonder how this whole thing would have played out had I just gone home. I was running late, Colette was out of town, my mom was watching the kids and didn't particularly like playing babysitter after midnight. Still, even as I saw my parking garage approach a couple blocks from the Tribeca Cinemas, I couldn't shake the feeling that just bailing out, avoiding the movie premiere's after-party, would seem somehow...rude, and a little offensive to the McMahons, whose daughter-in-law Marissa had produced the movie.

I had been called about *Anamorph* a couple of years earlier, by Vince himself, who thought I would be perfect in the lead heel role in a movie with a smart, cool script. So I read the script, did indeed find it smart and cool, but didn't see myself in the roll of a heel who can both slip unnoticed into crowds and participate in a chase scene on top of a speeding train. I did mention that I thought there were a few smaller roles I might be effective in. So a few weeks later, I was asked to play a pawnshop owner, no auditioning necessary, just a simple day's work. Sure, why not, I said, then looked over the script again, just to remember my scene. Wow, I'd be doing the scene with Willem Dafoe.

So I showed up around 10:00 a.m., did about twenty takes with one of the best actors in the business, and was on my way home before rush hour. Dafoe was cool, no big-star attitude, and he did a mean Marlon Brando when the talk turned to movies after lunch. I offered up my opinion that *Last Tango in Paris* was the worst movie I'd ever seen, was angry with myself for wasting two hours of my life to watch it, and asked Dafoe if Brando's star had been so big that he was allowed to just make up dialogue as he went along.

"You mean the pig scene," Dafoe said, before breaking into the exact dialogue (in pitch-perfect Brando) I'd been thinking of:

"And I want the pig to vomit in your face and I want you to swallow the vomit. You gonna do that for me? . . . And then you have to go behind and I want you to smell the dying farts of the pig. You gonna do all that for me?"

I'd been a little nervous about meeting Dafoe, simply because I didn't want to show up, say hello, and ask him about playing the Green Goblin in *Spider-Man*, especially given the wealth of diverse work he'd put forth on the screen over the course of his career.

So I took a couple of minutes to study his filmography, and that next morning, by gosh, I was ready.

"Willem, do you mind if I ask about the training you went through for *Triumph of the Spirit*?" I said, in reference to his impressive turn as a concentration camp boxer in Auschwitz.

"Willem, did you need time before takes to really get into character for *Shadow of the Vampire*?" (the eerie drama based on the filming of the classic 1922 film *Nosferatu*, where Dafoe's character may or may not have been a real-life vampire on a set where people mysteriously met unkind fates).

And when the WWE film crew showed up to get a behind-the-scenes look at one of their guys "starring" in a new movie, I was ready.

"Mick, what was your favorite Willem Dafoe role?" I was asked.

"You know, I would have to say that I was very moved by the rivalry between Willem's Sgt. Elias and Tom Berenger's Sgt. Barnes in *Platoon*. I will never forget when Elias dies at Barnes's hand — the death is so tragic, so sad, and almost Christlike in the way Willem's arms are held out during the shooting."

I looked quickly over at Defoe, and could have sworn I saw his lips say *wow*.

The lesson to be learned — if you want an actor, an athlete, a wrestler, et cetera, to enjoy talking to you, don't ask the same questions everyone else does. Don't ask Dafoe about Spidey. Consider, perhaps, asking me about a match other than Hell in a Cell. I mean, I'm proud of the match and I'll talk about it if I have to, but it will kind of be done on autopilot, as there's not a lot more I can add to those conversations I've had hundreds of times. Over the course of the last twelve years, or roughly 4,500 days since that match, I sometimes feel like poor Bill Murray in *Groundhog Day*, reliving the same moments over and over again.

I decided to walk back to the party, figuring my mom would excuse my tardiness long before Vince McMahon would excuse my disrespecting his family. Vince was the first person I ran into when I stepped into the club. I made small talk with the boss for a couple minutes, mentioning that my heel turn in 2006 may have been fun and fairly effective, but ultimately it wasn't what fans wanted to see from me.

Vince looked at me intently, kind of telling me in a nonverbal way that the small-talk session was over; he had something of importance to say.

"Mick, how would you feel about giving announcing a try?"

"I don't know," I said with a laugh. "I've heard about you on those headsets." It was true — I had heard that Vince produced all the announcers from behind the curtains, offering suggestions that weren't really suggestions — more or less demands — and occasionally letting the announcer know in no uncertain terms that he was not pleased with their choice of words. I had done guest commentary for an occasional match a few times over the years, and while I'd never been yelled at, I found the constant stream of suggestions that weren't really suggestions to be disconcerting, and really the antithesis of helpful.

But Vince laughed off my concern. "You know, Mick, I'm getting better at that." Hey, that was good enough for me. I'd been asked about announcing several years before and had dismissed it fairly quickly, thinking that working that closely with Vince could drive me crazy, and knowing I had several options outside wrestling to explore.

By April 2008, I'd been exploring those options for years and had yet to find a legitimate second career. There had been some good, high-paying breaks. *Robot Wars* was a blast, but it was temporary, and despite getting the front page of *USA Today*'s Life section, a piece in *Entertainment Weekly*, an interview with Matt Lauer on the *Today* show, and a weeklong cohosting stint with Jimmy Kimmel, the world had not exactly beaten a path to their local bookstore to track down my first novel, *Tietam Brown*.

I'd long since stopped auditioning for movie roles as a redneck bouncer, or the redneck bodyguard, or the redneck killer, and was beginning to lose count of projects brought to me by legitimate writers and producers who saw me as a potential star of sitcom, drama, sketch comedy, or reality show. *Wrestling My Family* might have opened some doors, but I guess I didn't yell at my wife or kids enough for the reality world's liking.

I now realized that all these projects, failed or otherwise, were like Mick Jagger solo albums — they just weren't what people wanted to see from me. People wanted to see Mick Jagger jam with the Stones. And they wanted to see me involved with a wrestling show.

I'd signed an incredible contract in September 2005, one that allowed me unprecedented freedom outside WWE while calling for only six Pay-Per-View matches over a three-year period. It was known as "the Foley Contract" in wrestling circles, and something tells me we'll never see its like again. I'd completed all the required matches and had five months left on my contract. At that point, I knew it would be highly unlikely that I'd be offered another contract of similar value, but nonetheless I'd made a few inquiries into staying on with WWE in some fashion — maybe in developing new talent in Florida, or in helping with international promotion. I'd even asked former wrestler/ current Sirius Outlaw Country station host Hillbilly Jim if there were jobs within WWE that required as little personal contact with Vince McMahon as possible. For although I respected and genuinely liked Vince (at least most of the time), I had the sneaking suspicion that I wouldn't enjoy such regular exposure to his larger-than-life persona.

After discussing the possibilities with Vince for a few minutes, I agreed to give the announcing thing a try, shook hands with the boss, and headed out into the New York night, hoping my mother wouldn't be too upset with the late arrival of her little boy.

To this day, I'm not sure if the idea of putting me on the *Smack-Down* announce team was one that had been on Vince's mind for months or if it had come to him the moment he saw me. Vince can be a little...spontaneous sometimes.

I went into the WWE studio two days later for a tryout, which really seemed like a mere formality, as my travel itinerary had already been arranged, and two days after that I was calling the matches live on Pay-Per-View...and loving it. I really did love it. I had been concerned about my tendency to become too much of a straight man during commentary, choosing analysis and insight over humor and personality. But Kevin Dunn, Vince's second in command, had assured me that I'd be given time to grow into the role, and they had no doubt that my personality, charm, humor, likability, rugged sexiness, and humility would eventually shine through.

There was a list of mandatory WWE announcing rules that I tried to learn, much of which seemed conducive to good commentary. For example, I saw the logic in doing more than simply telling the viewers exactly what they just saw. Anyone could see that an arm drag was followed by a body slam and a drop-kick. Now explain why the moves were effective, why they hurt. I could also see why the viewer didn't need to hear a constant dialogue during a match; sometimes it was best to lay out and let the action speak for itself.

Some of the other rules seemed slightly less conducive to effective storytelling. For example, Vince hates pronouns. Yeah, pronouns. You know, those pesky little words like *he, she, they, we, it*. Hates them. For example, if play-by-play man Michael Cole were to say, "Wow, Mick, did you see that incredible Swanton by Jeff Hardy?" I could not simply say, "He really nailed that one, Michael," even though it would make perfect sense and was more or less grammatically correct. Although I guess that some could say that using the word *nailed* is morally improper because of its implied sexuality.

So, even though a pronoun is usually the structurally correct way to go once the subject has been identified, in the world of WWE announcers it is all but forbidden.

So although "Wow, Mark Henry is really working on the leg of Batista. Look at him go to work on it," might seem clear and correct, it would be likely to yield a reprimand from the big guy. But "Wow, Mark Henry is really working on the leg of Batista. Look at Mark Henry go to work on Batista's leg" would be just fine. No pronouns! Got it!

A belt is never a belt. It is the "WWE Championship" or the "World Heavyweight Championship." During one episode, a championship was up for grabs, and that championship belt was placed in a display case so that everyone competing for it (the World Heavyweight Championship — don't want to use a pronoun there) could get a good look at what was on the line.

"Finlay is really taking a good look at that belt," I said, before quickly trying to correct the serious mistake I'd made. "Yes, that belt, which is representative of being the World Heavyweight Champion."

"Dammit, it's not a belt!" Vince helpfully reminded me.

So after coming to TNA, I have made it a point to call a belt a belt whenever I can. I've even called it a strap a time or two, which might be a fineable, even fireable offense at the WWE announcer's table.

Don't even *think* about calling Taker "Taker." He's the Undertaker. Period.

Nonetheless, despite some pronoun problems and an occasional belt-related belittling, I really enjoyed my first few days on the job, and I also enjoyed the feedback from the guys in the dressing room, who seemed to appreciate that I took my job seriously, tried to do research to tell the stories as best I could, and never tried to put myself over at the expense of the guys in the ring. I knew I didn't appreciate that type of announcing when I was a wrestler; trying to make things happen in the ring, working hard, enduring punishment, only to watch the match and hear an announcer whose priority was clearly himself.

The *SmackDown* main event on that first night's Pay-Per-View was Edge versus Taker — sorry, Undertaker. The Undertaker, a true legend in the business, and a guy who was invaluable in the direction of my career, has been able to stay vital and valuable for twenty years by constantly tweaking (one of my favorite words) his image and his repertoire. As an avid mixed martial arts (MMA) enthusiast, he had worked a Brazilian jujitsu choke into his game. But the hold, known as a gogoplata, was having trouble gaining a real foothold in the minds of WWE fans, who had never seen this type of move in the Undertaker's arsenal.

Part of the problem, I thought, was that fans could simply not appreciate how painful such a hold could be. I'm not talking about "punch in the face" pain, "broken ankle" pain, or even good old-fashioned "Gitmo implementation of torture" type of pain. I'm talking about that hideous, nauseating, hurts-too-much-to-move, hoping-just-to-die type of pain that most human beings will thankfully never know.

For better or worse, however, I did know that type of pain, courtesy of "Exotic" Adrian Street, who, back in 1989, at my own request, had put me in a couple of holds that made me hope and pray that death would come to my little apartment in Montgomery, Alabama, and take me quickly, away from the unimaginable agony that I was being subjected to.

That was the type of pain I tried to explain to WWE fans. So I told the story of that night in Montgomery when the five-foot-six, 180-pound Street, a flamboyant Welsh painter, sculptor, singer, writer, and expert in the ways of pain, opened up my mind to the possibility of fates worse than death. And I think it was effective.

A few days later, I read that I'd gotten my own story wrong; that the incident with Adrian Street had taken place in Philadelphia and involved a simple wrist crank at one of Joel Goodhart's old TNA shows. So how do I address this charge? Well, I guess I would have to ask the guy who witnessed the wrist crank in Philadelphia if he ever examined the possibility that Adrian Street had stretched (caused intense pain with wrestling holds) me on more than one occasion. That maybe Adrian was capable of stretching me just about every time he saw me, whether it was at my own request or not.

Actually, one of my career regrets is that I didn't try to learn more of that stuff from Adrian, especially when I moved to the Florida panhandle and saw Adrian and his wife, Miss Linda, regularly, like a few times a week. They'd work out at our gym, and I'd stop by and help him train some wrestling students now and then, but I never did inquire about hooking and shooting (other synonyms for stretching) again.

Anyway, for those first several weeks, I was ecstatic, thinking I'd found a viable new career — something I could do for the next ten years, maybe more. I had tentatively signed on for a lucrative independent tour of Ireland, but had canceled at WWE's insistence (giving the promoter about four months' notice to find a replacement) as they didn't want me to miss even one episode of *SmackDown*.

Michael Cole was a huge help, and he and I developed a good

on-air chemistry. After a month or so, I felt like we were really on a roll. Michael was a legitimate journalist, having served as a radio correspondent for several years, covering the horrible 1994 genocide in Rwanda and the war in Serbia, as well as the 1993 siege in Waco, Texas, and the 1995 Oklahoma City bombing. Sometimes his abilities are disregarded by fans who tend to use Jim Ross as a yardstick by which to judge all other wrestling announcers. Which is kind of like using Babe Ruth or Lou Gehrig as the yardstick for judging all Yankee outfielders.

I even gave Cole a gift, a way of showing thanks for teaching me the *SmackDown* ropes. "Watch this," I told Triple H, who I'd been talking to around ringside several hours before the doors opened — a good time to hang out and relax before the stress of taping *Smack-Down*, where guys and girls mill around, work on a new move, talk to a road agent about an upcoming match, or just complain in general, since it's the time-honored thing to do.

"I've got a present for Michael Cole," I said. "He's either going to think it's the greatest thing in the world, or he'll fart on it so hard it will sound like the bombing of Baghdad."

"What is it?" Triple H asked.

"Well, it's a harmonica that Bruce Springsteen used onstage at MSG — a friend of his gave it to me."

I walked up to Cole and handed him the gift. Initially, he thought it was a joke. As he gradually realized it wasn't, he broke out into a huge smile, taking out the harmonica and turning it over in his palms.

"Wow," Michael said. "It's even got Bruce's lip marks on it."

Indeed it did. Bruce's…or Hughie's…or Mickey's…or mine. But I guess Bruce's lip marks were on there somewhere.

Chris Jericho asked me about the announcing job one time. "Oh man, I love it," I said. "You know, I used to walk around all the time, thinking of promos I could do — ways to talk about myself. Now I walk around thinking of things I can say about the other boys."

Yeah, I really did love the announcing gig, and I even took to carrying notebooks around with me, jotting down ideas for different wrestlers. I would talk to the guys before their matches, asking about a potential big move to look for, or some type of story they were trying to get across in their match. For years, during my full-time wrestling days, I would seek out the announcers, trying to explain the story I wanted to convey. Sometimes I got the distinct feeling I was bothering them. Personally, as an announcer, I *wanted* the feedback — I wanted to be on the same page as the guys in the match. I wanted them to feel comfortable approaching me, talking to me about their characters or their opponents. I was usually treated with the utmost respect by the wrestlers, both old and young, and I tried my best to treat everyone with respect, whether they were a main event superstar or just a rookie trying to catch a break.

On one occasion, at the end of May, I was onboard a cross-country flight, doing some work in preparation for our June 1 Pay-Per-View in San Diego. It was an experience I was especially looking forward to because of two big matchups that Cole and I would have the opportunity to broadcast: Batista and Shawn Michaels in a stretcher match, and the Undertaker and Edge in a TLC (Tables, Ladders, and Chairs) extravaganza. The majority of the Pay-Per-Views seemed to lean to the *Raw* brand in terms of marquee matches. The *Raw* broadcast team of Jim Ross and Jerry "the King" Lawler was practically a Monday night institution — they'd been a tandem for almost twelve years, and their teamwork and instincts were second to none in the business. But this particular show seemed to have a *SmackDown* flavor, and I was intent on showing what I could do with a big, well-built matchup. On this night, I'd have two of them to work with.

Colette and my two little guys would be joining me out in California a day later — in fact, they would be landing in San Diego while the show was in progress and would be waiting for me at the hotel when I got back. Surely this was going to be a big occasion for me, as I could bask in the glow of my broadcast performance, have a day off with the kids at Legoland on Monday, kick some serious butt on *SmackDown* in Los Angeles on Tuesday, then finish the trip in style — walking in Walt's footsteps for three days at Disneyland.

I noticed that the passenger seated next to me had four daily newspapers and about five weekly newsmagazines: the *Economist*, *Time*, *Newsweek*, and a couple others too exclusive and obscure to recall.

"You've either got to be in the news business or in politics," I said early in the flight.

"No," the man said. "I just like to be well informed."

I didn't believe him — no one likes to be *that* well informed, but I respected his implied wish to be left alone. It's not like I hadn't avoided a question or two about my vocation over the years. In fact, if someone doesn't know what I do or who I am, they darn near have to play twenty questions to figure out exactly what my job is.

About three hours into the flight, the man, who had been discreetly observing me at work, asked a work-related question of his own.

"Excuse me," he said. "Are you a college professor?"

"A college professor?" I said, laughing. "No, definitely not. Why do you ask?" I mean, I'd been accused of being a lot of things over the years, but "college professor" was a new one.

"Well," the man said, "I couldn't help but notice that you've been writing nonstop for a long time. And you look somewhat professorial."

"I do?" The man who asked the question was well dressed, well groomed. If I had to guess, I'd say he had money, lots of it.

Usually I play twenty questions, but this fruit was just too ripe not to pick. "No, actually I'm a professional wrestling announcer. And I'm taking notes for an upcoming show."

"You must really believe in preparation," the well-dressed man said.

"Yes sir, I do," I said. "And you *are* in news or politics, aren't you?"

He shook my hand and gave me a business card. Lewis Eisenberg, John McCain's finance committee cochair.

I told Mr. Eisenberg that I wasn't likely to vote for his guy, but that I liked and respected Senator McCain, and I had actually had a brief, pleasant conversation with the senator about a year earlier. I spoke with Mr. Eisenberg for the next couple of hours, enjoying an in-depth discussion on politics and the news of the day.

Looking back on it now, it's somewhat ironic that Mr. Eisenberg thought I was a college professor, based on my prodigious note-taking tendencies. Because following the San Diego show, I never made another announcing note.

Use your imagination.

THE MAGIC HEADSETS

My wife heard the distinctive sound of alcohol bottles clinking together as I walked through the door of our San Diego hotel room. Knowing I'm not much of a drinker — usually utilizing my famed two-drink tolerance to make a happy occasion a little happier — Colette broke into a big grin at the very sound of the clinking. Obviously, I was in the mind to celebrate.

"Oh, it went that well?" she asked.

I shook my head. "No, it went that bad."

Look, I know this is where some people expect to hear every word spoken to me, every magical F-bomb thrown my way. Those people are going to be disappointed. When I left WWE, I was asked to sign a paper stating that I would never speak disparagingly of the McMahon family. Now I never signed that paper because the word *disparaging* is really open to interpretation. In a sense, I'd be placed on a lifetime gag order, to more or less never speak of the McMahons again. I'd already spoken and written freely (some might say disparagingly) of Vince McMahon in the past, especially in books that WWE themselves published. I thought I should have the right to continue to do so.

Nonetheless, I'd like the actual content of the headphone head games to be left between Vince and myself, and between you and your imaginations. The way Hitchcock did with horror films. Just imagine it's a horror story and the language used was more horrible than the most horrible language you've ever experienced. Or better yet, imagine it's a fantasy movie, and the hero of this movie puts on a special set of "magic" headsets. Yes, they are magic, because from the very instant our hero places them on his head, all the respect he thought he'd earned over the course of twelve years working for Mr. McMagical simply disappeared. After twelve years, it was gone in an instant; like the respect itself had been a mere speck of dust swept away by the winds of change.

Our hero just sat at that table wondering how that respect could have disappeared so quickly and so suddenly. Surely, he was still the same man who had slayed dragons in the past at the bequest of Mr. McMagical. He had so enjoyed Mr. McMagical's respect, acceptance, possibly even friendship back then. He really enjoyed the money, too, to be perfectly honest. Still, our hero wondered how he could have lost Mr. McMagical's respect simply because he now sat at a desk and told of how others slew dragons, instead of he.

At one point, after Mr. McMagical used the magic headsets to transmit his unhappiness to our hero for about the fifth time in one evening, the hero began wondering why he still remained at the table at all. Certainly, his pride told him to flee the offensive table — to throw down the magic headsets and leave this arena where previously he had been the hero.

For a long time, our hero would be angry with himself for not displaying the fortitude necessary to flee that evil table and tell Mr. McMagical in no uncertain terms that he would not tolerate that type of tyrannical treatment.

Alas, it was not to be. The best our hero could do was muster the thimbleful of fortitude needed to make his feelings known to Mr. McMagical via an incredible device known as a cellamaphone. Yes, while heading to the land of giant Legos, also known as Legoland, in the town of Carlsbad, the state of California, our hero made his feelings known.

To tell the truth, our hero really just expected to hear a recording of Mr. McMagical's voice on the cellamaphone — for he thought Mr. McMagical would be far too busy to actually answer the incredible device himself. At which point, our hero would leave a recording of his own voice that Mr. McMagical could listen to at a later time. Even though our hero had performed great acts of courage throughout the period of his employment with Mr. McMagical — being hurled off large structures, dueling large dragons while being thrown into piles of shiny, sharp objects — he nonetheless would have preferred not to speak to Mr. McMagical directly. For that required more fortitude than our hero's testicles could provide at that point.

"Hello, this is Mr. McMagical."

Drat. What was our hero to do? He had his princess and two of his offspring with him, and they were only a few miles from the land of the giant Legos.

"Hello, Mr. McMagical, this is McFoley [a heroic Irish name if ever there was one] and, um, I just want you to know that I can't remember the last time I was spoken to so disrespectfully, and if this job involves being spoken to that way, I think you should find someone else to do it."

Whoa! Wow! Looks like quite a bit of fortitude had sprung forth from our hero's balls! Mr. McMagical was momentarily silent. Surely, he was not used to displays of such insolence surging from the mouths of his subjects, be they former dragon slayers or not. Be they scribes of towering number one best sellers or not.

"You know, McFoley," Mr. McMagical said slowly and most unmagically, "I apologize for that. I was having a bad night and I took it out on you. Just give me a chance to make it up to you, and we'll just chalk it up to having a bad night."

Well, our hero thought, that seemed fair. After all, everyone has bad nights, and Mr. McMagical's position of all-powerful but benevolent ruler of his people surely was a stressful one. Plus, our hero McFoley was well versed in Freud's theory of transference. Once in a while, our hero would have a bad day and, upon returning to his lair, would complain about the size of his princess's Majestic Express bill, even though the bills themselves were not the cause of the hero's bad day. Yes, our hero could live with that. We would indeed just chalk it up to having a bad day.

"Thank you, Mr. McMagical," our hero said. "You just have to understand that I'm taking my kids to Disneyland in two days, and I won't let anyone ruin a trip to Disneyland, not even you."

Our hero's princess later said that our hero sounded psychotic when he said that thing about Disneyland to Mr. McMagical.

For a while — three weeks, maybe four, things were fine. Then came the day the magic headphones once again stung our hero's ears — once more a victim of Mr. McMagical's verbal venom. The venom started spewing forth more regularly, almost weekly at some points, leaving our hero once again wondering why he remained at the table at all.

Our hero spoke to Mr. McMagical a time or two about the magic headsets and how bad the venom stung. But by now our hero realized that all who sat at the table and wore the magic headsets were subject to the venom.

Our hero was faced with a difficult choice: to stay inside Mr. McMagical's magical kingdom, or to venture out into the great unknown.

COUNTDOWN TO LOCKDOWN: 13 DAYS

April 6, 2009
Milwaukee, Wisconsin
2:11 p.m.

Just two hours and forty-nine minutes until showtime — my big appearance at the Potawatomi Bingo Casino. The big time. I'm sure it will be fun, and the truth is, I would rather deal with casinos, whose checks aren't likely to bounce, than with all but a few independent promoters. I'm going to put my booking information out there on the

Web in a few days, and I will probably be the only guy whose info comes with a warning: "Don't book me unless you really, really know what you're doing" — especially because a promoter could book a few quality wrestlers, guys who can wrestle a good, entertaining match, for the same price I get to show up and sign autographs.

But following my tag match in New Orleans, I actually began to rethink my "no wrestling except for Pay-Per-View" policy. The match went so well, and Beer Money — Robert Roode and James Storm — were so much fun to work with that I started to think about participating in a few more matches. Certainly TNA would welcome it. I even found myself openly talking with friends about possibly teaming up with Al Snow for a Best Friends Ten-Year Reunion tour. You know, as long as Al did most of the work and I got top billing. Kind of like this:

MICK FOLEY
AL SNOW
10-YEAR TAG TEAM REUNION

I had last worked the Lakefront Arena in New Orleans in October 1993, battling the 400-pound colossus known as Vader at *Halloween Havoc*. Man, that was a brutal and bloody affair; hard fought, a Pay-Per-View main event to be proud of. I found myself comparing my life, what I'd gained, what I'd lost during the near sixteen years since then.

In a way, it could have felt like returning in front of a smaller crowd in a far different type of match was a setback, a step down. After all, there were five or six thousand fans on hand that night in '93, compared to maybe a thousand two nights ago. I gave that *Havoc* match almost everything I had, including a sickening bump on the wooden entrance ramp that I literally hoped would end my career. A career-ending injury would have meant a $120,000 payoff from my Lloyd's of London disability policy, enabling me to bail out on a business I'd grown tired of and frustrated with, and that I really thought offered me little hope for the future. At one point in the match, after hitting Vader with a fan's camera and looking at the crowd, setting off a wave of reaction, I sensed that I was simultaneously seeing the highest and the lowest points of my career. The highest because I had never been able to command that type of reaction before. The lowest because I felt like I'd never hit that high again.

Fortunately, I was wrong. I got a little higher than *Halloween Havoc* over the next several years.

But back to two nights ago. How did that compare? In terms of dignity and prestige I think I've become a little more sensitive to that type of analysis since *The Wrestler*, where even glowing reviews regularly pointed to Mickey Rourke's character's regression from Madison Square Garden to VFW halls or dingy gymnasiums as the ultimate sign of his fall from grace. Maybe it was. But I think that no matter the venue or the size of the crowd, there is something to be said for the pride one takes in their work and in how they carry themselves.

In 1981, I was a major Kinks fan, buying all their albums, taking the Long Island Railroad into the Garden to watch them on their Give the People What They Want tour. After hitting it big as part of the midsixties British Invasion with such classic rock staples as "You Really Got Me" and "All Day and All of the Night," the Kinks had fallen into midseventies obscurity, releasing critically acclaimed but little-noticed concept albums and seeing their massive fan base dissipate. They were even banned from touring in the United States for an extended period, for reasons I could never fully comprehend.

Given all this, it would have seemed logical for the group to see their early eighties return to prominence as the ultimate comeback story: selling out hockey arenas, moving millions of albums.

So it was with great surprise that I heard lead singer Ray Davies downplay the importance of these huge events, talking instead about the importance of "seeing faces in the crowd." As long as he could see faces, Davies said, he was fulfilled. The size of the crowd didn't matter. Just as long as he saw faces.

That was a little disappointing to me back then, especially as an avid WWF fan who thought of wrestling at MSG as not only the pinnacle of wrestling success but the standard of it as well. It wasn't until four years later, setting up rings for promoter Tommy Dee in small venues throughout the five boroughs of New York, that I learned that not every wrestling show pulled in twenty thousand people. Most of those Tommy Dee shows drew several hundred fans, sometimes a thousand. I mean, I remember going to Nassau Coliseum shows in '82 and '83, seeing a crowd of thirteen thousand, and thinking it was a lousy house.

I saw Ray Davies several months ago on a solo tour, at the Hammerstein Ballroom right across the street from the Garden. I thought it was awesome; the guy sounded great and I knew the words to every song but one. I don't think a single fan in attendance thought any less of Davies just because he was playing across the street from the Garden instead of in it, to a crowd of 2,500 instead of 20,000. They probably enjoyed the show even more.

Ironically, the Hammerstein is the venue where the finale for *The Wrestler* was filmed, during a Ring of Honor show — one of the best-attended shows in company history. But many reviewers, not understanding the nature of the wrestling business, saw the Hammerstein setting as a sad indicator of just how far Mickey Rourke's character, Ram, had fallen.

(Hold on. I just sent a text to Chris Jericho, wondering why there was no Ram Jam at last night's *WrestleMania*. I caught only half of *'Mania*, as it had been a long, draining day by the time I arrived in Milwaukee. I was a little disappointed with the show overall. Jericho and Steamboat were great, but the show seemed to peak with an incredible Undertaker versus Michaels match and never quite refound itself. Still a very good show, but I think WWE should have seen the possibility of that particular problem coming and avoided it.)

It just seems like that perception is part of the challenge facing wrestlers, even the most successful ones. How do you find dignity in a post-Garden world, when so many onlookers see success in the wrestling business as an all-or-nothing proposition?

So, maybe there were only a thousand people in New Orleans two nights ago. At least I got to look at them, really take a good look at their faces. And they were happy.

Now if only *Lockdown* were as simple. People in Philadelphia don't smile anyway, not unless someone gets hurt. Those are some pretty ruthless SOBs in the City of Brotherly Love. And I will try to give them a match they can appreciate and remember. If only my legs will cooperate.

COUNTDOWN TO *LOCKDOWN:* 11 DAYS

April 8, 2009
Williamsburg, Virginia
10:26 p.m.

I'm two days into what is quite possibly the worst vacation of my life. Do you have any idea how sick I have to feel in order to bail out on a Busch Gardens visit? Passing up on Alpengeist, the Big Bad Wolf, and Apollo's Chariot? Something up in Milwaukee must have really disagreed with me — something far worse than promoter Dave Hero's constant disapproval of the recent TNA product. I've known and liked Dave for years, and he's picked up many a dinner tab over the years, but man, talk about a downer.

It's not as if he didn't have valid points, even if some of them were nit-picking. This close to match time — less than two weeks — I try to keep everything positive, blocking out anything negative, no matter how valid that feedback might be. I don't check the Internet, look at newsletters, ask for opinions — nothing. I'm just happy living in a little bubble of contentment, not really caring which side of that self-confidence/self-delusion line I fall on. At least not until *Lockdown* is over. Ultimately, the ratings and buy rate will let me know how well I did, as well as a number of other factors; where TNA goes from *Lockdown*, how well Sting is positioned, whether or not I'm still in a good position to help the company advance.

I spent fifteen hours lying in bed yesterday, getting up only long enough for spirited sprints to the bathroom, if you know what I mean. I was a little better today, though far from good. I couldn't make it to Busch Gardens, but I was able to keep a little food down — my first success in two full days. I had hoped to really work on my conditioning for the next several days, planning to ease up about three or four days before the big event for some light cardio work. I'm afraid this stomach bug or whatever is going to set me back quite a way.

Maybe walking up and down the rolling hills of Busch Gardens, or climbing up several flights of stairs at the indoor water park at Great Wolf Lodge will be just what I need.

Self-explanatory.

GOOD-BYE, VINCE

Being far too frugal with my money to valet-park, I was heading from the remote lot at the Disneyland Hotel when I got the message, "Mick, this is Scott Fishman. Give me a call. We may have a unique opportunity for you at Spike TV."

Hmm. Spike TV. Home of TNA — Total Nonstop Action — the place I'd almost called home three years earlier, before Vince McMahon had made me an offer I couldn't refuse. I had worked for Fishman (or Fish, as we'll now refer to him) several years earlier, as the host of *Robot Wars*, back when Spike was The New TNN. Perhaps in life, you sometimes really do reap what you sow, as I had thoroughly enjoyed my time at the *Robot* helm and had apparently been easy to work with. Word has it that several of the crew members enjoyed my unique perspectives on life — made over the course of several days when I didn't know my microphone was still on.

I wonder, still really sometimes wonder, what I would have said to Fish if that call had come just a few days earlier. I believe it would have been a simple and friendly "Thanks, but no thanks," before heading back to the job I loved, the job I honestly felt would be mine for the next several years.

But that was before Sunday, before having F-bombs of the "shock and awe" variety dropped on me. As far as the initial barrage was concerned, it had come as a complete surprise — truly, I had never seen it coming.

When I was a kid, I remember sleeping over at Jack Donohue's Friendship Farm Basketball Camp in upstate New York. I was about three or four years old, and I very vaguely remember seeing a tall, gangly figure playing on those outdoor courts; a seven-foot-plus silhouette looming larger than life — if only in my memory.

Jack Donohue had been my father's best friend, and was perhaps best known as the high school basketball coach of Lew Alcindor, later known as Kareem Abdul-Jabbar, one of the all-time greats in the game of basketball. My mom remembers the teenage Alcindor at Donohue's wedding — knees practically up to his chest in the church pew, before he succumbed to food poisoning and was pulled from the cockpit, sporting his trademark goggles, and his basketball shorts. Oh, wait, that last part happened in the first *Airplane* movie.

But Donohue, later the coach of the Canadian national basketball team, had been a huge influence on Abdul-Jabbar — a fact I read about in detail in Abdul-Jabbar's 1987 autobiography *Giant Steps*. Kareem was full of praise for my dad's best friend, until one pivotal game in Power High School's 1965 season, where Coach Donohue had been unhappy with Alcindor's first-half performance and let him know it. "You're playing like a nigger," he told Alcindor, referring to a type of flashy play that was popular on New York City playgrounds, which catered to a largely African-American clientele. He never actually called Lew the N word — not technically — but for Alcindor it was a turning point in his relationship with Donohue; a point from which the relationship would never be the same.

Abdul-Jabbar's reaction had struck me as harsh back then. How, I wondered, could that one comment have forever changed a relationship that had been forged over such a long period of time, that had seen them both accomplish so much?

In San Diego, I finally got it. Even as I sat at that table, doing my best to call the match at hand, I thought of Alcindor and Donohue, and really felt that my relationship with Vince McMahon had changed forever. It wasn't just the F-bombs. Those I could live with. It was instead the total disdain that accompanied them. I didn't let Vince McMahon ruin my Disneyland trip, but I did wonder why I had let *anyone*, even a larger-than-life billionaire, speak to me in a way that was simply unacceptable. Even during early morning Magic Kingdom Matterhorn Mountain coaster runs, or while rocketing through Space Mountain, I was visualizing the way things should have been — removing my headset in the middle of the match, calmly walking up that ramp, getting closer to that man behind the curtain with each step. Then stepping through that curtain, calmly looking at the shocked billionaire and saying, "You'll never talk to me that way again," before exiting to an ovation not seen since Richard Gere came back to the factory to literally sweep Debra Winger off her feet in *An Officer and a Gentleman* — an ending so thick with good old-fashioned love syrup that even finding out Gere and Winger couldn't stand each other in real life didn't diminish the taste of the treat.

So, I didn't do it. At least I thought about it, seriously thought about it. Besides, such an act would never be cheered by the guys — at least not outwardly.

Still, those few days in Disneyland weren't all preoccupied by images of the great walk-off. I was also giving great thought to the opportunity at Spike. What could it be? I had returned Fish's call and agreed to a meeting, but was told nothing else, except that it was a big deal.

About a week later, I walked into the Spike offices in New York and met with the network's president, Kevin Kay, and its senior vice president of sports and specials, Brian Diamond. In all my years at WWE, I'd never met with any type of television executive. Then again, unlike many top WWE stars, I'd never even been invited to the McMahon house. Kevin Kay gave me a one-sentence synopsis of their plans. True to Fish's word, it *was* a big deal. Done right, this idea could be huge.*

I spoke with TNA founder Jeff Jarrett and Fishman on conference phone and assured them I was interested. I told them that I knew they probably felt that I'd played TNA and WWE off each other three years earlier, and that they'd probably been right. Things would be different this time, I assured them.

I told them if we arrived at a deal we were happy with, I'd take it, provided the WWE atmosphere didn't magically improve.

Actually, for a while, the atmosphere did improve. I had yet to be paid for announcing, and so I had no idea how to gauge how they valued my work, but from all indications they were happy with my contributions as a broadcaster. Besides, I was told, being yelled at in demeaning fashion by Vince was apparently no big deal. Everyone went through it. It was just the way Vince did things.

For a while, those F-bomb clouds disappeared. Look at the rainbow, Mick. I only had to work one day a week, not including the two travel days to get to and from work. I no longer took notes or talked to the guys as much about their matches, but it didn't seem to hurt; I knew the business and could ad-lib my way through just about anything. Plus, Vince would always offer suggestions (which weren't really suggestions), some of them more helpful than others. And there was always the chance that a big, fat announcing check was going to show up at my house and make me feel foolish for ever finding Vince's big bowl of bile so unappetizing.

A few weeks had gone by with no further word from TNA. Maybe

---

*It still might. The idea was put on hold until the TNA brand could become better known.

I would just stay put with WWE. This was my home, after all. And those F-bombs weren't really *that* bad, were they? I didn't get hit with them *that* often, did I? So what if he didn't say he was sorry — a few weeks later, when it happened a second time. It wouldn't happen *that* much, would it?

Even then, I realized I sounded something like an abused spouse, rationalizing the behavior of the abuser, accepting it, condoning it.

June 23, 2008, was the big draft — the yearly extravaganza where all three WWE brands (*Raw, SmackDown*, ECW) had their rosters shaken up. This year, we were told, even the announcers would be eligible for rebranding. I began joking with Michael Cole regularly, talking about what an honor it would be to work with Jim Ross, neither of us thinking for a moment that Vince would mess with the Monday night institution that J.R. and Lawler had become.

At one point, I thanked Cole for all his help, noting that even if we were to part ways, I still considered the opportunity to work with him to be one of the greatest of my life. "Thanks, Mick," Cole said — waiting, I think, for the zinger that never came. Even then, the remark was more of a possible good-bye to broadcasting than it was a good-bye to *SmackDown*. For with or without TNA, I had come to the realization that this broadcasting thing just wasn't for me.

Oddly, WWE did make a big move at the draft, sending J.R. to *SmackDown* and sending Michael Cole to *Raw*, effectively shaking the foundations of the shows in a way that none of us had anticipated. We were all in something like shock when the switch was made. None of us knew, or else we certainly would have been animated in our surprise — maybe not to the point of popping classic J.B. "Furley" eyes, but certainly doing more than just sitting like mourners at a funeral, the broadcast tables our own unique pews.

J.R. was livid afterward, thinking that the switch had been made just to mess with him, which in my opinion has been the impetus for many an on-air decision over the years. In retrospect, I really think that WWE was showing great faith in the *SmackDown* brand. Unlike most draft years, in which *Raw* cleans up on these talent exchanges, *SmackDown* had really had a banner evening, picking up Triple H, Rey Mysterio, and Batista, as well as good ol' J.R. behind the desk. A lot of people saw it as a sign of faith in me as well — that WWE saw great potential in a J.R./Mick Foley announce team.

But for me, on that night, I was looking at the move as my ticket out. "Listen, J.R.," I said after the show, "the announcing really isn't for me. I don't know how much longer I'm going to do it. If you want to walk out now, I'll go with you."

J.R. thanked me for the offer but told me not to worry. He was going to cool off for a while before making any kind of decision.

He was back at work the next day, emotionally hurt but professionally unfazed, the consummate wrestling announcer, just doing what he does better than anyone else.

Would it really have taken so much away from the element of surprise for Vince to have sat J.R. down and explained the reasons why he *might* be moved to *SmackDown*?

So it was me and J.R. on *SmackDown* — a team that drew immediate praise from wrestlers and fans alike. If my heart had been into it, I have no doubt that we really could have been good. But I no longer did the research; I no longer thought of things to say when I was on my own time. I just tuned it out Wednesday through Monday, did the best I could on Tuesday, and upon completion of the show, dealt with the most profound feeling of emptiness. Profound emptiness — like announcing was the least important thing I'd ever been involved with.

At one point, I received a call from Kevin Dunn, asking how I liked the job, wondering if I wanted to commit to it, past the expiration of my contract on September 1.

"Kevin, I like it, but I don't love it," I said, before suggesting that we try a one-year contract.

That type of talk should have raised a red flag (and probably did). In a business where everybody aims for the longest possible contract, aimed at generating the maximum amount of dollars, someone looking for a one-year deal would be something of an anomaly, practically an abomination.

Even so, I regretted my answer to Kevin, knowing it was a whopper of Pinocchio-sized proportions. Because I definitely did not *like* announcing.

A few days later, while waiting at WWE's Stamford headquarters (I was several minutes early for a voice-over session), I asked if I could speak to one of WWE's top producers, a woman I'd been friends with for several years, even talked literature with every now and then.

"You know a few days ago, Kevin asked me how I liked announcing, and I told him that I liked it, but didn't love it," I said.

She nodded.

"I think it would be closer to the truth to say I don't like it and sometimes I *really* don't like it."

At our next *SmackDown*, I spoke to Kevin Dunn, and we agreed to part ways amicably when my contract expired.

"I want to leave while I've still got all of my good memories," I told Kevin. "I want to look back and laugh at the idea of Vince yelling at me over the headsets, not worry about it happening every week."

I told Kevin that I would be open to doing some kind of big angle to explain my departure — some way of building up one of the wrestlers for his upcoming match at *SummerSlam*. Something memorable.

On July 10, 2008, I broadcast my last WWE Pay-Per-View, *The Great American Bash*, at the Nassau Coliseum, forty minutes from my home. With all four of my kids looking on from the second row, I turned in what I thought was my top announcing performance. I hadn't seen Vince McMahon at all and was more than happy to keep it that way, even after the show went off the air. I was easing my way out of the backstage area when little Mickey spotted several boxes of cereal at the craft services table — the go-to place for junk food and quick pick-me-ups in just about every form of entertainment — television, movies, news, wrestling, opera, politics.

Yeah, if only Mickey hadn't needed, absolutely *needed*, those Cheerios, I'd have escaped Vince-free. But as it happened, craft services was directly in front of Vince's office, and when Vince walked out, he essentially walked right into me.

"I know you're not happy with me," Vince said. "But I want you to know that the last match you called with J.R. [Triple H versus Edge] was as good a call as I've ever heard."

"Well thank you, Vince," I said. "I thought it was good, too, but the problem is, I never know when you're going to —"

"Jump your shit?" Vince interjected. Not the way I would have phrased it, but eerily accurate.

We talked for about twenty minutes, the conversation intense but never heated, until I implied that WWE hadn't treated J.R. with the respect I thought they should have.

"You think I've treated him bad?" Vince said.

"Vince, I think you've made his life a lot more difficult than it's needed to be," I said, holding my ground in the face of a guy who's fairly difficult to hold one's ground with.

And that was pretty much the end of any attempt at broadcast reconciliation. My older kids never said anything about it, but I think they were proud of me for the way I handled myself in the wake of the bellicose billionaire.

Meanwhile, the numbers were lining up nicely at TNA. I had told them that if the deal was right, I wouldn't play TNA's offer off of WWE's, but in the end, there was no need. WWE never once spoke to me about any potential role I might want to pursue outside of broadcasting. I'd been performing my announcing duties in good faith for thirteen weeks and had still not been paid.

On August 1, 2008, I took part in my last WWE show, doing a big angle with Edge to explain my exit from the broadcast position. I hadn't given a real honest-to-goodness promo in almost eighteen months. And I think I made the most of it. In fact, I think the back-and-forth with Edge was one of the best promos I'd ever been a part of. In the end, I was speared into a set of stairs and put through a table, which merited a unique last moment in the company; a stretcher ride through the curtain, content with the knowledge that my last night with WWE had also been of my favorites.

I finally did get paid for my announcing duties. John Laurinaitis was given the duty of explaining to me that since I had only recently started as an announcer, I would be paid what starting announcers got. I wish they would have let me know earlier — it would have saved everyone a lot of trouble. It's too bad Vince didn't tell me about the starting announcer's money when he offered me the job; I never would have taken it. It's too bad I didn't get paid after the first week; I would have given two weeks' notice immediately and left before the first F-bomb landed. In the end, I broadcast fifteen episodes of *Smack-Down* and five Pay-Per-View shows, and made less than I would have for that one-week tour of Ireland.

Looking back, however, I believe Vince McMahon did me a favor. Because I still think I would have made the move to TNA. Less days on the road, considerably more money, and the opportunity to once again make a difference.

But I may have felt guilty about it. My experience as an announcer, and the money that accompanied it, made the move guilt free. Absolutely, positively, guilt free.

COUNTDOWN TO LOCKDOWN: 10 DAYS

April 9, 2009
Williamsburg, Virginia
11:25 p.m.

It would have been so cool to see *Impact* tonight, with Hughie (or at least his photo) making his big national debut. But alas, the Great Wolf Lodge only gets twenty or so stations, so we carried on as best we could, watching *Paul Blart: Mall Cop* on PPV to cushion us from the disappointment of the missing Spike channel.

I know I name-dropped Kevin James a couple of times in *Hardcore Diaries,* but this *Mall Cop* thing was so huge that I figure I might as well get a little more mileage out of my high school and college association with the man who breathed life into Paul Blart.

My son Dewey asked me what Kevin was like back in high school, wondering if he was a lot like the hapless but likable losers he plays so well on-screen.

I laughed. "Actually, he was kind of a stud back then," I said. "He was the star of the football team, and only one of two guys who could bench-press three hundred pounds in high school."

Just in case you were wondering, I was *not* the other guy. Definitely not.

Which actually got me thinking about my high school wrestling days, including the question: What the heck was I thinking going out for a team on which Kevin, the guy with the 300-pound bench, was already penciled in as the top heavyweight?

Actually, I think Kevin was going to be our go-to guy at 275, one of the guys who could wrestle at 215, but put away some big meals later in the season to go into the county tournament at the higher weight. Sometimes a really good athlete could do very well for themselves at 275, making up for lack of experience with power and attitude.

So I went out for the team on a whim, convinced by my buddy John McNulty that I could get in better shape for lacrosse — my real sport — by wrestling, as opposed to embarrassing myself at Winter Track.

I immediately became the number three heavyweight behind Kevin and Gus Johnson, the only other kid at Ward Melville High School with a tattoo on his bicep, this one some kind of lion. Back then, tattoos on a high schooler were so rare that their appearance alone could sometimes provide a distinct psychological edge on the mat. Of course, a tattoo hidden on a hip, inked solely to impress Diane Bentley, provided no advantage whatsoever.

By the second or third meet of the season, Johnson was history, after a practice-halting F-bomb directed at Patriots coach Jim McGonigle. Coach McGonigle, having dealt leukemia a serious butt kicking in 1978, wasn't about to let some punk kid with a tattoo drop an unanswered F-bomb in his gym. So, McGonigle, with his classic New England accent, dropped one of his own, and we all got back to practice as if nothing had changed. Oh, but something had changed. I was no longer the third-string heavyweight. Nope, now I was the second-string heavyweight.

A mere week or two later, Kevin James went down with a season-ending back injury, and bingo, Foley gets the slot. As Kenny Powers might just say, "You're f'n out, I'm f'n in." And so it went, one of sports' great success stories, from third-string heavyweight all the way to the state championship.

Wait, what's that, you say? I wasn't a state champion? Not even close?

Okay, okay, I'll admit it. After winning a couple matches by pinfall in the county tournament, I lost a heartbreaker, and failed to advance past the quarterfinals.

Sometimes things have a way of working themselves out. I went on to do pretty well for myself: got thrown off a cell by the Undertaker, was interviewed (twice) by Katie Couric, and got a hug from Tori Amos. One of my former high school wrestling opponents was arrested for tying up a woman and making her watch as he danced naked to the "Eye of the Tiger." Hey, I couldn't make something like that up.

I saw Coach McGonigle in Las Vegas about a year ago, where he has lived since retiring from teaching. He took me out to eat at a casino, and while we waited for a table I dropped a quick twenty dollars on blackjack — the first time I had ever gambled with anything other than my own body.

I told Coach that I had recently uncovered a few of my old wrestling clippings. After my two dynamic pinfall victories at the county meet, Coach McGonigle was quoted as saying, "Mickey Foley is on the verge of becoming a respectable heavyweight."

That was as good as it got for me. I may have never actually become a respectable heavyweight, but at one time I was right on the verge.

So, who, you may ask, was the better high school wrestler, Kevin or me? You know what, it was pretty darn close. We were both spectacularly mediocre. Neither of us actually respectable. But both of us right on the verge.

Every book needs a scoop or two, something provocative to get people talking, generate some buzz. In past memoirs, it's been the old kiss-and-tell, unveiling the curtain on my superhuman sexual performances with celebrities both large and small, literally and figuratively, from years gone by. Wait, what's that you say? That wasn't my book? I've never delivered a superhuman sexual performance with any celebrity, big or small? Or any type of sexual performance with a celebrity for that matter? You say that was Geraldo's memoir, *Exposing Myself*, a best seller in 1991? Oh, sorry.

Anyway, here's a *Countdown* exclusive. Ready? Here goes. I once scripted a wrestling match! Good, got it out, feel a lot better now. A wrestler admitting to scripting a match isn't such a big deal anymore, right? Randy "the Ram" Robinson showed how it was done in *The Wrestler*. Oh yeah, but what if I told you that the match I scripted was back in the winter of 1982 inside the Ward Melville High School wrestling gym? And that the guy I scripted it with was none other than the "King of Queens," Kevin James?

That's right, the secret's out, and now I can finally shed some light on the whole sordid affair. Keep in mind the Ward Melville wrestling gym was in the bowels of the building, a stifling hot slice of hell on earth assigned to the team years earlier by the school's sadistic athletic director, Dr. Jack Foley, also known as, um, you know, my dad. So, anyway this sadistic Foley guy had the team locked inside this sweltering sauna, a place so vile that even a callous Gitmo guard might likely tap McGonigle on the shoulder and say, "Hey, Coach, maybe you should take it easy on these kids."

So Kevin and I, both around 215 (although he looked likely to kick some ass in his green Melville singlet, and I really didn't), are watching these poor guys — all of them except us trying to drop weight — sweating their balls off. Literally, sweating their balls off. Don't believe me? Go ahead, check the balls of any former Melville wrestler. Not there. Gone.

The two of us figured there had to be a better way. To this day, I don't know who first made the suggestion. The "single leg" suggestion. Or who first said, "Sit out and switch." But, my goodness, we started doing impressive stuff in that godforsaken gym. Takedowns, reversals, escapes, the sock, the worm. And boy, did we earn the admiration of Coach McGonigle. "Good work!" "That's the way!" "What the hell are you doing with that sock on your hand?"

And then Kevin had to ruin it with that back injury. But I learned a valuable lesson. Wrestling sure is a lot more fun with someone helping you look good.

You know who won't like this story? Coach McGonigle, who will feel a certain sense of betrayal upon learning that not all of my actions in that ball-melting furnace he called a gym were done in the true spirit of competition. But at least he'll understand why I could never hit a Granby roll in competition.

You know who will like it even less? Kurt Angle, who will see it as a betrayal to everything he's stood for, lived for, breathed for.

Actually, I think Coach McGonigle might get a kick out of it all these years (twenty-seven of them) later. Kurt? Not so much.

Eight parts wrestling, two parts sadness.

KURT ANGLE, THE SENSITIVE OLYMPIAN

As long as I'm on the subject of Kurt Angle, let me share a touching story with you, designed not only to enlighten and entertain, but also to illustrate some of the emotional burdens that go hand in hand with an almost superhuman drive to be the very best.

In January 2009, I took part in a two-week TNA tour of the United Kingdom — England, Scotland, Ireland. I was hobbling pretty bad, having lacked the judgment at our January Pay-Per-View to remove my leg from underneath a table when A. J. Styles and Kip James came crashing through it. So my main goal on the tour was to entertain; telling the fans in Birmingham that it was an honor to be in the city that was the cradle of the Civil Rights Movement — before being informed by J.B. that we weren't in *that* Birmingham. *That* was Alabama. *This* was England. Oops. Each night was an attempt to outdo the night before, to raise the tomfoolery to previously unthinkable levels.

Our little band of traveling entertainers arose early one morning, around 6:00 a.m., for a 9:00 a.m. flight out of Dublin. We showed up at the Dublin Airport weary, looking much the worse for wear. I was exhausted, having spent the better part of three days writing the Tori Amos chapter that I hope you enjoyed. I'd finished writing somewhere around 5:00–5:30 a.m., and knowing it would be fruitless to lie down for thirty minutes, and with Jim Croce's "Time in a Bottle" still in my head, passed the remaining time until departure by reimagining the song as a Jim Croce/Hulk Hogan composition entitled "Time in a Bottle Brother." Sample lyric:

I've looked around enough to know
That you're the one I want to show
My twenty-three-inch pythons to, brother.

The airport was full of UFC guys, as their company had held a huge show in Dublin the night before. There were a couple of pretty impressive black eyes and other assorted bruises among the fighters; apparently there'd been a couple of world-class slobber-knockers on the card.

I felt a hand on my back and heard the hoarse whisper of a voice. "Hey brother," it said.

I turned and was met with a big smile peering out of the most hideously battered visage I'd ever been witness to. I had no idea who the guy was; his features were so swollen, he could have been anyone. He looked almost antlike, the way his cheekbones were swollen in almost perfectly symmetrical fashion; as if his opponent had been thoughtful enough to bludgeon him in a most nonexclusionary way.

"Brother, it's Mark Coleman."

Mark Coleman! Holy crap! I mean, he was just unrecognizable. I'd met Mark once, in Japan in 2004, and I had told him that he'd seemed unstoppable, like an impenetrable monster, back in his days as UFC Champion in 1997. The guy had just destroyed Don Frye, one of the great MMA fighters of all time, and seemed poised to rule the MMA roost for years to come.

But that was 1997. A lot had changed since then. The head butt, Coleman's main offensive weapon, was now barred, part of an overall attempt to clean up the sport, which was dismissed even in the halls of Congress as "human cockfighting." In retrospect, the rule changes were a great idea and helped lead to a rebirth of UFC, but they also served to sweep old-school gladiators like Coleman to the wayside. Back then, Coleman, an All-American wrestler at Ohio State, could simply manhandle overmatched martial artists and nail them on the ground.

By 2009, slowed by age and injuries, Coleman was happy just to be in the game, noting that he'd gotten a bonus for "best fight" the previous night, a slugfest with Antonio Rodrigo Nogueira that had been stopped with only fifteen seconds left, after the referee decided Mark had simply had enough.

Kurt Angle walked by, said hello to me, and briefly shook Coleman's hand, obviously not recognizing the battered brawler in front of him.

"Kurt, it's Mark Coleman," he said as Kurt began to walk away.

"Mark?" Kurt said, turning, surprised. "Oh my God, Mark."

It was really quite a touching scene — a big hug in the Dublin airport by two men who'd known each other for almost twenty years, having been among the world's wrestling elite for several simultaneous years.

"We wrestled each other eight times," Mark said.

"That's right," Kurt said, nodding. "I won four and you won four."

"That's right," Coleman said. His eyes actually kind of twinkled beneath all that swelling. "I beat you at the '92 Nationals and then the next year you beat me, and I said, take it, brother, it's all yours."

Kurt smiled and said a quick good-bye, noting that he had a plane to catch. Which, in retrospect, should have seemed odd, given that we still had plenty of time, probably an hour, before boarding.

Besides, I had other things to think about. Like that "Time in a Bottle Brother" song I had going for me. I was walking around with my lyrics, regaling whichever guys I thought I could get a chuckle out of with my Croce/Hulkster tune.

> *There never seems to be enough time*
> *to say your prayers, take vitamins*
> *and pump iron, brother.*

Granted, over the past few days not everyone in our crew had written a life-changing tribute to their favorite performer or had gloriously reimagined a favorite song from their youth. But everyone seemed happy, or at least mildly content. The tour was going well, and our final show, in London, was set to break TNA's all-time attendance record.

But not everyone seemed happy. Kurt Angle mysteriously seemed sullen, somber, morose, like his childhood pet had been put down, or worse.

"Kurt, are you okay?" I asked.

"Something's bothering me, but don't worry about it."

"Are you sure?"

"Yeah."

"Okay, then... hey, J.B., listen to this line..."

Several minutes later, right before boarding, I checked on Kurt again.

"Kurt, are you going to be all right?"

"Yeah." What a liar. The guy looked terrible, like he'd just found out his wife was dating his best friend.

"Are you sure?"

"I just can't believe he said that."

"Said what? Who?"

"Mark."

"Coleman?"

"What did he say?" I was really confused. I'd been privy to their entire conversation and hadn't heard anything even slightly disrespectful or confrontational, or even mildly controversial.

"He said he beat me at the '92 Nationals."

"So?"

"I beat *him* at the '92 Nationals."

"You're kidding, right?" I really thought he might be kidding.

"Look, I may not have much," Kurt said. "But don't try to take my amateur career from me." Obviously, I'd been mistaken about Kurt kidding.

Passengers were starting to board. I had to try to get through to this guy, before he killed off my writer's buzz.

"Kurt, listen... how many times did you two wrestle?"

"Eight times."

"Okay, how many did you win?"

"Four."

"So you won four and he won four?"

"Yeah."

"Well isn't it possible that he just made a mistake, you know, that he got his dates mixed up?"

"No, he knew," Kurt said, his eyes beginning to water.

This was crazy. It was like the guy needed an intervention from the three Dans — Hodge, Gable and Severn — to get him out of this funk. Sadly, all he had was me, but I would do the best I could — one last appeal for sanity before getting on the plane.

"Listen, Kurt, I'm going to do the best I can here to help you out, okay?"

He just stared.

"Look, you saw Mark's face, right? Kurt, he had the crap beaten out of him last night. I think he'd been up all night, probably had a couple drinks. And it was seventeen years ago! Let it go, Kurt, let it... go."

"I can't believe he said that," was all the Gold Medalist could say.

Skip it if you like, but we'll no longer be friends.

A SPONSOR FOR ALIMANY

"Did that kid just yell my name?" I was on a dilapidated back road in the Bombali area of the West African country of Sierra Leone, and I thought I'd just heard a young child on the street call my name as our vehicle lurched by.

I remember riding in an Army Humvee, visiting soldiers on peacetime maneuvers in the Kuwaiti desert in the fall of 1997. Our driver continually took the Humvee off road, up little banks, or down into gulleys, to avoid the perilous potholes that pockmarked our desert road.

The road, the driver explained, had been built by Saddam Hussein to advance his tanks from Iraq into Kuwait during the Iraqi invasion that resulted in Desert Storm in 1990. Because the road had been Saddam's handiwork, the Kuwaitis had vowed never to repair it, leaving U.S. vehicles the hefty task of dodging the huge craters that were the residue of war and neglect.

At that point in my life, that Kuwaiti road was the worst I'd ever seen. Eleven years later, Saddam's road seemed like the German autobahn compared to this dirt road in Sierra Leone — the one I thought I'd heard my name shouted out from.

Sierra Leone is one of the poorest nations in the world — second poorest, by some standards. Its infrastructure was ravaged by a vicious civil war lasting from 1992 to 2001, which killed tens of thousands and displaced more than two million — a staggering third of the country's population. Over 1,200 schools had been destroyed in the war, leaving a good portion of school-age children with nowhere to learn.

Which I guess is where I came into the picture, having agreed to finance the construction of a handful of small, community schools in small villages in Bombali. In November 2008, after a couple of false starts (a passport problem, postelection violence), I returned to Africa after a twenty-one-year absence.

I'd been a part of three separate African wrestling tours in 1987 — two to Nigeria, one to Burkina Faso — and had left with a wealth of experiences and stories but with an emptiness of the pocket, having amassed a grand sum of $480 for my combined six weeks of African wrestling work.

But over the years, especially as I got a little older — old enough at least to see that the world didn't revolve around me — I kind of felt the continent calling out to me, beckoning me to return. I began reading about Africa in earnest after the 1994 genocide in Rwanda — eight hundred thousand lives lost in less than ninety days, while the outside world sat on its collective hands. I read and saw photos of the horrible atrocities in Sierra Leone — mass amputations by machete as an instrument of terror, the indoctrination of child soldiers as a main method of warfare. I saw photos of Angelina Jolie visiting with refugees — thankfully bringing a little much-needed media attention to the largely forgotten and little-known war.

For several years I'd thought about returning, but wanted to do it in a way that might have some impact — meaning I thought I would visit a country familiar with WWE programming. Don't laugh — many

African countries are familiar with wrestling, none more so than Nigeria, where wrestling tradition runs deep, and where I learned the hard way that fans take their wrestling seriously. A good rule of thumb for those interested in the Nigerian mat scene: don't use a foreign object on the Nigerian champion when you're the lone white man in a crowd of thousands, especially when that particular country hasn't caught on to the "entertainment" aspect of wrestling.

I paid for that little lapse in judgment with about ten stitches in my head — the result of a little ringside riot — administered without benefit of anesthetic, using sewing thread for the stitching, in a chemist's office with a dirt floor. The chemist's office was the place to be stitched, according to the Nigerian wrestlers. The hospital, apparently, was not to be trusted.

I almost went back to Nigeria a few years ago, for a wrestling reunion tour promoted by Mr. Haitti, the man who had booked me way back in 1987. Of all the wrestlers who had worked in Nigeria, he said, I turned out to be the most famous, and having me there would be incredibly big.

Two things changed my mind. First and foremost was the religious tension caused by the Miss World competition in the capital city of Lagos, started when a Nigerian newspaper columnist suggested that the prophet Muhammad might possibly have dated a Miss World contestant if he'd been offered the chance during his lifetime.

The comment sparked rioting throughout the country, killing at least one hundred and wounding hundreds more.

Second, but still important to me, I happened to see a photo of then Nigerian president Olusegun Obasanjo in my copy of *BBC Focus on Africa*, my bimonthly window into the African world. I thought I recognized the guy standing next to the president, apparently his right-hand man, trusted advisor, or personal bodyguard. It was Power Uti, that Nigerian champion I just mentioned — the one I probably shouldn't have used the foreign object on. I hadn't exactly heaped praise on Power Uti in my first book, *Have a Nice Day!*, as a wrestler or as a person. I couldn't go to Nigeria — I'd never make it back out! This whole invitation was merely a ploy to get me to Nigeria so that Power Uti could exact his revenge! I only half-jokingly thought my body might be hacked to pieces and used to fertilize a mango tree outside Obasanjo's presidential palace.

So my African plans were put on indefinite hold. At least until I made my first visit to ChildFund International (then known as Christian Children's Fund) headquarters in Richmond, Virginia, in 2005. I'd been a ChildFund sponsor since 1992, but kind of a lazy one; my checks were always late, I didn't write to my child too often. And my checks for special projects were certainly nothing to brag about; even during my prime earning years, I would routinely respond to famine, disease, or some natural disaster with a whopping ten or twenty extra big ones.

But in 2004, I interpreted the coincidence that an early childhood education center in the Philippines cost almost exactly what I would earn for my children's book *Tales from Wrescal Lane* as some kind of sign from God, and made the big phone call, explaining in a slightly shaky delivery that I was Mick Foley, I had a children's book coming out, and I wanted to help build that center.

And with that one phone call, a relationship was born, or at least greatly strengthened. I was no longer the estranged distant cousin with the late checks and the extra twenty bucks to spend. I really became part of the family, and I even made the shocking, previously unthinkable discovery that in some isolated cases it really might be better to give than to receive.

So when I showed up in Richmond in 2005, it was as an official "major sponsor" — I even have a little plaque on my wall designating me as such. I was invited to address the staff before receiving a tour of the facility, during which I first spotted a photo of Alimany, the two-year-old boy who would hasten my return to the continent.

"I have to sponsor that child," I said.

For my wife, Alimany's photo inspired instant feelings of motherly love. "Can we adopt him?" she said, showing just a slight misunderstanding of what the sponsorship program is all about. She was so taken with the little guy that the adoption subject was not fully dropped for a couple of years.

Sadly, Sierra Leone was not on my official list of African countries where wrestling was broadcast. Not that it would have really mattered too much. As I was to find out, televisions were something of a rarity in the Bombali area — not a whole lot of flat-screens gracing the walls of the mud huts that most villagers called home. Villagers were aware of what a television *was*, but thought of them as a special attraction, an event they might pay for once a year, when a man with a generator came into town and fired up a movie or two.

But as I embarked on my trip, Freetown by way of London — two seven-hour trips (with an eight-hour layover between), crammed into coach, my 300-pound frame squeezed into seats never designed for bodies like mine — I did so knowing I'd be entering a land where I'd be completely unknown.

If the flight from London to Freetown solidified my feeling of anonymity, the next day's ferry trip from the airport area to Freetown proper cast it in stone. Seven hundred people jammed onto that ferry — poor but proud people heading out to the city for long hours spent hawking their wares, be they fruit or cookies, or nuts or native woodwork. Seven hundred people...and not a single soul knew me. Sure, they stared quite a bit. Other than Gary Duncan and Renee Monroe, the two ChildFund staff members who were with me, I was the only Caucasian on the ferry. And Gary and Renee resembled what most might describe as "normal" white people. Me...not so much. So, sure, I got quite a few looks, but not a soul in Sierra Leone knew who I was.

At least not until I heard that kid by the side of that Bombali road. "Mick Foley." I could have sworn he'd said my name. But perhaps I was wrong.

"Mick Foley, Mick Foley." Two other kids. That time I was sure.

What were the odds that these two little kids had seen wrestling somewhere?

As our vehicle approached a bridge, our driver, Uzmam (who later in the trip would quite literally give me the shirt off his back), continued to show off an expert's skill in navigating these stretches of very bad road. Children were lined up on each side of the bridge, singing in unison — some song they all knew.

What could they be singing about? "Welcome, welcome, Mick Foley. Welcome, welcome, Mick Foley." Hey, they were singing about me!

"What is going on," I said aloud, feeling as if I was in a strange new episode of *The Twilight Zone* or *Punked*, the "Ashton in Africa" edition.

I knew I would be meeting Alimany, the little boy who'd started me on this long journey. I wondered what this beautiful child might look like now — no longer a cherubic baby, but a little boy instead. Hughie's age. Indeed, the night before my trip, realizing I'd lacked the foresight to buy a gift, I'd hurriedly packed a unique assortment of goodies for Alimany — a copy of *Mick Foley's Halloween Hijinx*, a Mick Foley action figure, and Hughie's stuffed Pluto (which he pronounced "Cluto") figure. Hughie has enough things, I thought. Surely he'd never miss it.

When it came to things, little Alimany had few. I knew of his plight from the letters his father wrote. The family slept on the floor of a tiny mud hut, eating one meal a day, living largely off rice and the faraway hope of a better tomorrow.

I had offered to help several months earlier. "Find out what they need and I'll get it for them," I said. A similar offer to a child in the United States would probably yield a giant scroll of must-have items: cell phone, iPod, computer, video games, a Mick Foley action figure.

Alimany's list was a little lower tech: a mattress, a mosquito net, used clothes, a sack of rice.

A few months later, I received a photo of Alimany sitting on the family's new mattress, his wish-list gifts splayed out in front of him — the mosquito net, the used clothes, the sack of rice. He had the broad, beaming smile of a child on Christmas morning.

Arriving in Alimany's village, we were greeted by a cast of hundreds, dancing in the street, singing, pounding traditional drums. "The strangers are here, the strangers are here," people yelled in the street.

I would meet Alimany later, I was told. But first, I would watch from my special table as the children from the village displayed their talents through traditional African song and dance. The sports coat I had brought for the trip was soaked through with sweat, and once removed, it would see no further duty on our African tour. I was thirsty and tired, hungry and hot, but nonetheless happy, looking at the joy in the eyes of the children.

This was apparently a big deal for this village, which had turned out en masse to witness the songs and dances of its children.

A boy walked out, eight or nine years old, a handsome little kid with obvious charisma, and a commanding voice he was about to display.

"Tonight, we celebrate the friendship of two individuals," he said. "Two individuals who will meet for the first time."

Cool, I thought. *Who are these two people?*

"Two individuals who, until tonight, knew each other only through letters."

That was when it finally dawned on me. I turned to Renee, seated next to me at the table. "Are they talking about me?" I asked.

Actually, they were. Alimany was brought out, and our public embrace brought a huge ovation, an outpouring of joy from the village at large.

"Mick, you have to understand," Gary Duncan from ChildFund told me. "This is their first sponsor visit in sixteen years, since before the war started. This is a very big deal to them."

For a long time, after returning back to the States, I wondered if my thoughts of this trip might sound crazy to some. After all, I'd been blessed to take part in some wonderful things during the course of my career. So why did I keep coming back to the thought that my week in this country had been the best week of my life? But wait, I reasoned. Hadn't several WWE guys spoken of visiting our troops overseas in Iraq or Afghanistan as the best trip of their lives? No one thought *they* were crazy.

I'd been on two of those trips — one to Iraq, one to Afghanistan. They were great ones, no doubt. But the WWE's first Tribute to the Troops tour had taken place without me. I'd been along for the second and third trips in 2004 and 2005. Then the trips resumed without me. WWE does one each year, and each year the trips are a huge success, with or without my participation.

Sierra Leone felt different. It felt like *my* trip. Like I had personally made a big difference. Some other stars had been there before, much bigger stars. Angelina Jolie, President Clinton. I read just last week that Salma Hayek had visited recently and managed to do one thing I never will. Holding a hungry infant, and realizing that she was with milk of her own, Salma Hayek, one of Hollywood's biggest, most beautiful stars, nursed a hungry child in Sierra Leone. How cool is that?

Still, I've come to think of those three or four Bombali villages all lying along that stretch of horrible road as my little corner of the world to nurture and care for. A small dot on life's map where I can make a visible difference. Where a little compassion and a little more money can go such a long way.

I've got so many great memories of my time in that land. Like that first visit with Alimany, and each visit after, when the tiny African child with the movie-star looks would lay his head on my leg and fall fast asleep.

Or meeting the SEFAFU (Sealing the Past, Facing the Future) girls — the victims of rape during that country's cruel war. Looking into the eyes of each one and letting them know that I'd never forget them. Seeing these brave young women caring for the children of rape, realizing they'd been children themselves when forced into motherhood.

I saw the United States presidential election in Sierra Leone — watching as African men freely shed tears at 5:00 a.m. local time, when the results finally arrived: Barack Obama had been elected the next president of the United States. Our hotel in Maceny was the hotspot that night for foreign-aid workers and journalists, who all ventured out from their self-imposed exiles from modern civilization. Young, talented, caring people choosing to forgo life's luxuries — for months, a year, sometimes even longer — so that they might help others.

My wake-up call came early, way too early, later that same morning — about an hour and ten minutes later, to be exact. I really didn't want to move — I just wanted to lie there for a while, another eight or ten hours, right about the time the hotel's daily ten-hour allotment of electricity would kick in.

Besides, my knee was swollen and throbbing, the result of a most untimely fall down a hill at the SEFAFU project a day earlier, when my left leg slipped on the dusty steep slope and my entire weight came crashing down on my right knee, which was pinned at a precarious angle beneath me.

The last MRI of my right knee, taken two years earlier, hadn't been pretty: three partial ligament tears. I accepted that one day a ligament might go, maybe a second, maybe a third — but not all at once, which was certainly my fear when I first fell. And not in Sierra Leone, the home of one doctor for every two hundred thousand people. And not in front of the poor SEFAFU girls, who'd already been through quite enough in their young lives.

The singing never quite stopped, it just got considerably softer; the pounding of traditional drums softened, too.

Eventually, realizing there was no good option, I struggled to my feet. A loud cheer went up and the singing and playing resumed at normal volume.

I was tired and sore, just longing for sleep, but nonetheless woke up after a few minutes of insistent knocking, and hobbled sleepily to our vehicle.

This was, after all, an important day: the dedication of the schools. Until about a month earlier, I'd had no idea that my money had funded the schools. I thought my donation had been used to purchase school materials — desks, textbooks, library books, teacher training manuals for other, previously built schools. It wasn't until I received a booklet, detailing the five "Mick Foley Schools," that I even found out. My wife had come to me teary-eyed, having read the booklet, and said, "Why didn't you tell me you'd built these schools?"

"Because I really didn't know."

I was still in a light stage of rest, my head leaning on the vehicle door, eyes closed but not really sleeping, when I heard the voices of children singing, off in the distance. I rubbed my eyes, then looked up at the sunrise coming over a mountain. My eyes panned down to the source of the singing. Children, beautiful children, singing their hearts out in front of their school.

Remember the Whos? Those adorable figments of Dr. Seuss's incredible imagination who sang with such joy despite the Grinch's best efforts to stop Christmas from coming?

That's what these children reminded me of. For as we lurched closer along that rough road, then started our ascent up the hill to the school, I could see the joy and hope in the eyes of those children. Singing with such pride in front of one of the Mick Foley Schools. It wasn't really a school as we know them. Just some walls and a ceiling — three little classrooms with tiny desks and some chairs. My children would have laughed at the prospect of learning there — most U.S. children would. Then again, my older kids shudder in fear at the prospect of being seen by their friends while riding in their dad's minivan.

Come to think of it, I don't think my four kids would feel much like singing if they awoke Christmas morning and saw that everything — pop guns, pampoolers, pantookers and drums, check-erboards, bisselbinks, popcorn and plums — had been stuffed up the chimbley.

I guess it's just a matter of expectations. For these kids, who'd been learning their lessons under a tree, the Mick Foley Schools, as humble as they may have been, were pretty good places to learn.

We visited all the little schools that day, each visit accompanied by the songs of children and that look of hope and joy that had become synonymous with my time in this desperately poor country. Hope and joy. We don't hear much about these words in the limited attention the twenty-four-hour news channels begrudgingly give to Africa. Usually it's famine, genocide, civil war, natural disasters. To be sure, those are part of Africa's story — a large part. But there are other stories waiting to be told, if only more people would be willing to look.

Perhaps my week's most distinct memory took place on the last stop of the day, the last official stop on my trip. We visited a ChildFund International health clinic — a basic thatched-roof structure that had helped bring a marked improvement to the community. "Our children still die," the village chieftain told me. "But not as often as before."

The village now had one nurse to look after the needs of an entire community. One nurse instead of none, one birthing bed instead of none. Children still died here, but not as often as before. None of this would be acceptable in the United States. It shouldn't be acceptable in Sierra Leone. Yet, it was so much more than they had before — and they were thankful just to have it.

I spoke with the chieftain before I left, and he made a list of requests for things his community was in need of. A new primary school. A new junior secondary school. A paved road connecting the villages to the highway. Water projects, sanitation projects, more health clinics for the surrounding villages. As he spoke, I got the distinct feeling he thought I was doing a lot better financially than I actually was.

"But most of all," he said, "the children need sponsors."

"Really?" I said.

"Yes," he assured me. "The children need sponsors. Very few have them and it's so important to them."

In my last book, I wrote of ChildFund International's work and gave their contact information for anyone interested in helping. Over time several dozen children found sponsors as a result of the book. Several dozen children from all over the world.

I'd like to try something a little different with this book. Contact ChildFund International and let them know you're specifically looking to sponsor a child from the Bombali area in Sierra Leone. I know I wrote of this little dot on the map as *my* corner of the world to nurture and care for — but maybe some of you could nurture it with me. Tell them Mick Foley sent you.

Contact info: 800-776-6767
www.childfund.org

When I was much younger, I dreamed about wrestling in Madison Square Garden, performing feats of skill and great daring, in front of twenty thousand cheering fans. Fortunately, I got a chance to live out that dream — several times. It was great, too — everything I had dreamed it might be.

Just not as great as the response I received in an impoverished land, from children and chieftains, mothers and fathers, teachers and students, singers and dancers, none of whom had any idea what I did for a living. To them, I was just Mick Foley, the guy who helped build the schools.

I arrived home weary but happy, bearing gifts of traditional African attire for every member of my family — none of which would ever be worn.

Amid the many smiling faces of my family, I saw one of some concern. "Hughie, are you all right?" I said.

"Dad, have you seen Cluto?"

Oops.

COUNTDOWN TO LOCKDOWN:
8 DAYS

April 11, 2009
Long Island, New York
11:41 p.m.

It's just a few minutes until Easter, and my challenge for the evening is to outwait Mickey, who has his heart set on catching the *Eastern* Bunny (Hughie's name for the floppy-eared Easter icon). The idea was originally Hughie's, who had set up a sleeping bag in the living room, intent not only on catching the furry little guy but on killing him as well, all part of a sinister plot to confiscate and hoard goodies meant for an entire world of good boys and girls.

Fortunately, Hugh nodded off right at the end of *Nim's Island*, one of his favorite movies, and a very good choice for family movie night, even if it can't top *Stealing Home* on my list of all-time favorite Jodie Foster movies. *Stealing Home*, you may ask? Yeah, *Stealing Home*, the movie I saw all by myself back in August 1988, on a rare evening off in the old Memphis territory, after hearing of the death of my beloved cat, Sunny, my faithful companion for some sixteen years.

But then this *Nim's Island* Jodie made me think of the *Stealing Home* Jodie, which made me think of Sunny — which made me think of this poor cat I saw a few miles from my home, a most unfortunate example of excessive roadkill.

Man, I know I'm showing my wimpy side here, but that cat just kind of tugged at my conscience, the way it lay there in the rain, fur all matted down, its body nearly flat from numerous postmortem impacts.

Somewhere, I kept thinking, even as I ran my errands — the post office, the bank, the library — there's a little child who loves that cat. And that little child will be devastated, not only because his beloved pet is gone but because no one cared enough to pull him out of the road.

No one but me, I guess. My brother and his wife had once seen me moving the dead carcass of a raccoon out of the road and thought it was borderline psychotic behavior. After all, it wasn't as if it was any-one's pet. Oh yeah? Well apparently, they hadn't met Jeff Hardy, who did indeed once have a pet raccoon.

That cat was in rough shape. Its head was crushed, its brains splayed out on the wet pavement. I wished I'd stopped when I first saw the cat, instead of waiting that extra hour. I put a couple plastic bags over my hand and lifted the poor thing by its hind feet. A few hours earlier, it might have been playing with a ball, some yarn, maybe freaking out with some catnip. A night before it might have been curled up next to its owner, the small kid I imagined finding it in this battered state. Well, at least he'd find it beneath a tree, on the grass by the side of the road.

Wow, thanks for opening up that wound, Jodie Foster. And no, I never had a pet named Sable, Ivory, or Chyna.

I've been thinking a lot about this match at *Lockdown*. Thinking of ways to make this thing work. And I do believe I'm onto something, courtesy of the Undertaker and Shawn Michaels at *WrestleMania*. As I watched that classic contest unfold last Sunday night, I realized how much they were getting out of each big move. How they maximized the emotional impact of their saga by making sure each big move really meant something. Even while Gino, and Wynn, whose home we were in, and the other guy whose name I can't quite recall, were *ooh*ing and *aah*ing, I was busy absorbing, thinking to myself, *I can do that.*

So, if conditioning is my weakness, I'll make sure to stay away from the type of match that will more readily expose it: I'll play to my strengths, which may seem like a challenge, since I have so few of them left. But one of my goals in this match is to create one magic moment, a lasting impression that wrestling fans can keep with them for a while, maybe even share with a friend or pass down to their heirs. And one thing I learned from this horrible Virginia vacation is that impressions are relative.

Busch Gardens was a disaster — one of my worst theme-park failures. Sure, I wasn't granted an optimal hand to play with, as a radio call-in to Bubba the Love Sponge took me to five minutes until ten, only five minutes to official park opening. Bubba had been on hand in Orlando for the taping where I'd conducted an interview with myself (don't worry, I'll explain later). He seemed quite impressed with it, noting several times that he thought I was the only guy who could pull off a promo that would have seemed ridiculous in the hands of a more reasonable, mentally balanced man.

Actually, the feedback I'm getting from both nights of tapings has been really good, including the buildup and match with the Machine Guns. I don't know the rating and won't unless someone tells me, but I hope that it did well enough for the Guns to get another try in a big angle.

Dixie Carter has been very pleased with the way things have been unfolding. I have previously told her that I am having more fun in the wrestling business than I've had in nine years, since I was the WWE commissioner and could kind of just make things up as I went. But in these past few weeks, I also feel that I am as valuable to the direction of a company as I've ever been. And it's all been relatively easy.

Sure, there was a part of me that enjoyed the give-and-take with Vince McMahon. But this has been more like give-and-give. I give Russo and Jeff Jarrett a few suggestions, and more often than not those suggestions get done. Maybe not exactly as I'd laid them out, but close enough to give me creative fulfillment.

For example, I had suggested making Kurt Angle the guest referee for my match with Sting. Russo and Jeff both looked perplexed. Why would you want to do that? they asked.

"Because I think the idea of the executive shareholder making unreasonable, selfish decisions might lead to a lot of intrigue as to who really has the power in the company."

So, maybe the Kurt-as-referee idea didn't make the final cut, but the suggestion of a little tension between the founder and the shareholder has become a big part of the show. And there's room to grow.

A few weeks ago, when I gave my initial rationale for my actions toward Sting — the chair shot heard round the world — I had made the conscious decision to sit in the founder's chair, a place where no one but Jeff had dared to reside. And over the course of the next few shows, I continued to sit there, thinking the chair would be symbolic of a greater struggle for ultimate control of the company.

Before one segment, Jeff threw out a suggestion: "If you really want to look like you're moving in, why don't you hold my guitar." Yes, the guitar! The guitar was like Orson Welles's Rosebud, Linus's blanket,

Flavor Flav's clock, and Davy Crockett's rifle Old Betsy all rolled into one.

Right before filming I had to fight to suppress a laugh.

"Oh, no," Jeff said. "What have you got going on?"

"Nothing," I lied. "But if I happen to start singing, try not to laugh."

And that's how the "Tweak It" song was born: "Tweak it, just tweak it."

So I feel really good about where my character has gone. I'm not rehashing old material, and thankfully, I'm not going into our go-home week with that homogenized "Look, brother, I respect you, but when that cage door slams shut, I only know one way to wrestle" promo that I had really thought could have been my best approach just a few weeks ago.

So what does any of this have to do with my vacation? Plenty. Even though Bubba the Love Sponge had blown me off my "arrive half an hour before official park opening" schedule, even though I had to wait in a forty-minute line just to get into the parking lot, and even though my son Mickey absolutely, positively would not hear about riding the Big Bad Wolf until he'd done a water ride, I still had high hopes for a successful day of theme-park touring. After all, the counterintuitive strategy of hitting water rides on fifty-degree spring mornings is a virtual guarantee of procuring multiple thrills without the hassle of long lines, *if* you plan ahead:

1. Lawn and leaf bags, the effective economic way to repel most water thrown your way? Check!
2. A change of clothes in a backpack? Check!
3. An extra pair of shoes? Oops! Kind of forgot that one.

What a rookie mistake. You always bring an extra pair of shoes for the water rides. Flip-flops, beach shoes, old Chuck Taylors. Something. Alas, it was not to be. The Raging Roman Rapids so thoroughly saturated their sneakers that no rationalizing, no apologizing, no promise of buying flip-flops at the park was going to work. Our day was shot. This certainly was going to be the worst vacation ever.

But it wasn't. Until that desperate point, I hadn't realized that I'd been avoiding my obvious vacation strength. It wasn't Colonial Williamsburg. It wasn't Busch Gardens. It was the water park! Jeez, there was a water park in our hotel. And doggone it, I was going to use it.

We went to that water park when we returned from Busch Gardens. We returned three hours later and stayed until closing; challenging the wave pool, cascading down the slides, navigating the lazy river. By the way, what is it about the name "Lazy River" that so many teenagers don't seem to understand? It's a *lazy* river, guys, not a *raucous* river. Not a *crazy* river. A *lazy* river.

Couldn't there be some type of prerequisite for entry onto the river? An ID bracelet showing that one is either under twelve, over twenty-four, or certified "not an asshole" by some type of officially sanctioned authority?

We even returned the next morning for one last hour of water-park madness before heading home.

I decided to test out my vacation/*Lockdown* metaphor on the way to the airport. By focusing on the strengths of the vacation — the water park — I felt that my children would believe they had just had an awesome vacation experience.

"Hey guys," I said, a little Clark Griswold sparkle in my eyes, "wasn't that the best vacation ever?" My eyes would sparkle all the time, too, if I got the chance to nail Beverly D'Angelo, even in a fictional setting.

"Yes," Mickey yelled. Exactly what I thought. A few big moves, each one providing maximum emotional impact, and my legacy at *Lockdown* will be secure.

"No," Hughie said, his definitive tone cutting off my enthusiasm like an early morning wake-up call snuffing out a carnal dream.

"What do you mean, buddy? We had a great time."

But Hughie wasn't buying into my optimism. "No we didn't," he said. "Busch Gardens was bad. *Mall Cop* wasn't even funny. And you were in bed for two days."

I swear, sometimes I think that kid is too smart for his own good. Maybe he's more of a Bryan Danielson–Nigel McGuinness type of fan (now known as a Daniel Bryan–Desmond Wolfe type of fan); a guy who wants his wrestling pure, from lock-up to pinfall. For that type of fan, nothing I do in Philadelphia is going to suffice. My hope, then, is that there will be far more Mickeys than Hughies as we head into *Lockdown*.

It's now 3:05 a.m., Easter morning. If you'll excuse me, I have some eggs to hide.

COUNTDOWN TO LOCKDOWN:
7 DAYS

April 12, 2009
Long Island, New York
10:25 p.m.

Maybe I should have gone to bed a little earlier. By the time I hid the eggs, filled the Easter baskets, and wrapped a couple gifts, it was a little past four. Then it was off to bed, where, try as I might, I couldn't get my match with Sting out of my mind. Which is good. It means this thing is coming together in my mind — just one step away from actually making it happen in the ring. I was always pretty good at visualizing my matches, seeing them in my mind, making them feel so real that I just had to physically make the action come to life come bell time.

When I was a kid, maybe eleven or twelve, I attended a town-run summer basketball camp for three hours every morning. Every year, Coach Stan Kellner would come lecture about "basketball cybernetics," a unique brand of goal-based visualizations that he had pioneered. To this day, I remember Coach Kellner's rules for success:

1. See the picture.
2. Think the picture.
3. Be the picture.
4. Don't be afraid to make mistakes.

Coach Kellner would ask some random kid in the crowd what his goal was. "Jump higher," the kid might say.

Then Coach Kellner would bring the kid out and ask him to jump as high as he could. In one case, the kid could barely skim the bottom of the backboard. But after a few minutes of Coach Kellner's cybernetic guidance — of seeing, thinking, being the picture, and not being afraid to make mistakes, the kid would give that jump another try. And I'll be darned if that kid didn't jump almost a foot higher, hitting the rim with his palm, to the amazement of all — the kid himself being the most shocked of all.

Maybe basketball cybernetics weren't going to springboard a slow white kid with absolutely no spring in his step to basketball stardom, but for about fifteen years in the wrestling world (1985–2000), I certainly saw, thought, and became the picture a lot of times, and as just about anyone who's caught my matches might have guessed, I really wasn't afraid to make mistakes. Especially if mistakes had the potential to look even better on tape than successes. Kind of like a classic Reggie Jackson home-run swing — it was even more exciting when he missed. So, kind of like Reggie, whether it was a clout or an out, I wanted to make sure the fans saw a show.

I was thinking a few days ago about the last time I actually practiced a move before a match. And I kept coming back to Philadelphia in September 1996, my "Mind Games" match with Shawn Michaels. For years, it was my favorite match, twenty-six minutes of pulse-pounding, innovative action, and to this day it's probably in my top three. Shawn once told me that the match had gone a long way in helping fans see him in a different, more hardcore light, and I know it did a great deal for me as well. On that day, I practiced one move, just making sure I could do it safely, as I kind of had the guy's life in my hands.

Some guys have a style much more intricate than mine — out of necessity, they're going to need to practice a few more things, work on timing, make sure their opponent is safe. But for me, the lessons I'd learned from Stan Kellner were enough to see me through.

Unfortunately, seeing the picture, thinking the picture, and being the picture at 4:00 a.m. doesn't leave a whole lot of time for sleeping, especially with children who are intent on catching the *Eastern* Bunny. It was officially 6:02 a.m. when I heard Hughie's voice, talking about presents he'd already unwrapped, and asking his brother Mickey if they needed to wake up Mom and Dad before heading out for the big *Eastern* egg hunt.

The little guys seemed thrilled with their presents, too — a lineup that on paper looked to be the worst assemblage of gifts ever presented under the Foley roof on a major holiday. Two 99¢ gliders, a $1.99 kite, four Burger King value-meal Hulk toys, a couple DVDs left over from Christmas, and three stuffed animals I found in an old box a few days before Easter. Oh yeah, my wife had also bought them a couple of "green" coloring books, complete with helpful pointers on reducing one's carbon footprint.

Sometimes my wife can drive me crazy with all her green talk and seemingly radical ideas about getting off the grid and living on the coast in some Central American country. But I think she's onto something when it comes to the food we eat and the amount of chemicals and preservatives we willingly pour into our bodies.

So I've been trying to eat healthy, even organic, trying to flush some of that bad stuff out of my system before *Lockdown*. Sure, I ate a little junk for Easter, but not too much, especially by my junk-food standards. But that gives me one full week to try to get things right, so I will be at my absolute healthiest right before deliberately putting myself in some mighty unhealthy situations at *Lockdown*.

In no particular order, these are some of the steps I've been taking in preparation for this match:

1. Drink more water. I've been told I may need to drink as much as one ounce of water for every two pounds of body weight per day. Which seems a little excessive, especially if you don't want to spend most of your day in the urinary position. But I am drinking more.

2. Eliminate caffeine. Caffeine started out high on my list of possible suspects in my extreme case of the dry mouth. By now I've deduced that the main culprit is the FX fog at the Impact Zone, but even so, like millions of people out there, I'd become a little too dependent on the world's most popular drug to get me up for the day. So long, coffee. So long, soda. Hello, herbal teas and organic carrot juice.

3. Organic cleanse. By now, everyone's heard these horror stories of people walking around with up to thirty pounds of undigested fecal matter sticking to their intestinal walls. Wow, that's a lot of poop. I don't know whether I buy it, but clearly there's some stuff sticking around that I don't need, so I'll give these pills a try. My good friend, the actress Sandi Taylor, one of the world's most beautiful women, recommended the Master Cleanse to me, but without mentioning the ten-day fast that is part of the program. So I may give it a try down the line, but I'll probably need a little more energy at *Lockdown* than the Master Cleanse can provide. I'm sure Sandi will love being mentioned in the same paragraph as the words *fecal matter*.

4. Adrenal support. Dixie Carter's personal nutritionist checked me out and felt that my slow metabolism and constant fatigue were the result of sluggish adrenal glands. So I need to take some supplements (which are on their way), and adjust the way I eat. Rethink it, really. From the time I was fifteen I've had the importance of a high-protein diet drummed into my head. Some guys I know would force down over one gram of protein per pound of body weight per day — yeah, I'm talking about you, Kane. This new way of thinking would see a whole lot less of that type of thing. More fresh fruits and vegetables. Less protein. Don't I need that protein? I asked. Yes, Mick, I was told, you would...if you were twenty-five and in the gym two hours every day. Which, come to think of it, I'm not...and I'm not.

5. Massage. Flush all those toxins out of the system.

6. Stretching. I was told this might be adding to my leg fatigue. I might not become RVD, who stretches more than any man I've ever seen, but it sure wouldn't hurt to be a little more flexible. Which has got me thinking — maybe D.D.P.'s *Yoga for Real Guys* is the answer to my problems.

7. Secrets of the Kama Sutra. These ancient sexual techniques may actually be the fountain of youth Ponce de León searched for in his life-time. All right, I made up number seven, and probably couldn't reveal a secret of the Kama Sutra if our nation's future depended on it.

I don't know if all of it, some of it, or any of it will actually work, but in a business where so much of success is psychological, it certainly couldn't hurt.

Speaking of hurting, I had to abandon my hindu squat program in its infancy, after noting a direct correlation between the onset of the hindus and the onset of extreme lower back pain. Maybe it had something to do with my technique, which was kind of hideous when I observed it with the help of a full-length mirror at the Doubletree in Orlando. Granted, most of my experiences involving full-length mirrors could be accurately described as hideous, but this was different. I'm not sure my legs really even bent all that much. My back bent. My butt stuck out. But that was about it. I'm not sure how hindu squats even got their name. Ever check out the quads on Gandhi? Not much of a leg guy.

COUNTDOWN TO LOCKDOWN: 6 DAYS

April 13, 2009
Long Island, New York
11:57 p.m.

Eleven fifty-seven p.m. Probably not the best time to start writing, especially when my back is kind of crying out for a rest. But maybe I'll put in an hour or so with the pen — see if anything interesting comes out of it.

I went to the circus at Madison Square Garden today — my first time at the circus in three years and my first time at MSG since the *Royal Rumble* last January. It was a good time, maybe even great; taking in the death-defying acts, even getting to see the animals up close at intermission. Unfortunately, I kept thinking of the untimely demise of poor Chuckles the Clown on the old *Mary Tyler Moore Show* — the one where a rogue elephant mistook Chuckles (who was in the guise of Peter Peanut) for a real peanut and tried to shell him. I had no real way of knowing if such an incident were possible but thought it best to err on the side of caution.

I kept *seeing* the picture, though. *Thinking* the picture, too. I haven't *become* the picture just yet, as that's a trick best pulled off in Philly, on the night of the actual show. But I can really see this thing happening now.

Of all the conceivable roadblocks that could pop up, wardrobe would seem not to be of major concern. After all, I kind of wrestle in my street clothes — cutoff flannel, Cactus T-shirt, black sweats, sneakers. Except this coming Thursday, three days from now, just three days before the big match, I kind of make it a point to talk about getting out of the sweatpants and putting on the classic Cactus Jack black and white. And the classic Cactus faux-leopard boots, too. What, all this time you thought it was real leopard skin? It sure sounded good when I said it, and the promo I cut — the one where I get the heat on myself and feed my own comeback — is getting a lot of buzz. At least that's what I hear. I'm not going to look into the buzz myself. No, I'm going to keep myself firmly ensconced in the bubble I'm in, shutting out feedback, negative or positive, from the world outside. I'm like former president Bush on the eve of war, hearing only what I want to hear.

Turns out I'm promising something I don't actually have. No Cactus Jack tights to be found, classic or otherwise. And time is getting tight. So, I did what every hardcore, one-eared survivor of countless Japanese Death matches would likely do — went shopping with my daughter for plus-sized ladies' tights. In case you didn't guess, those tights aren't for my daughter, who's five eleven and weighs in around a buck twenty. Lane Bryant? No luck. Danskin dancing apparel? No dice. Dick's Sporting Goods? Don't even think about it.

I'll look for men's black thermal underwear tomorrow.

My son Dewey actually had a date tonight. On the way to the theater, I offered up a couple of suggestions, time-tested secrets, really, on how to ensure a little in-theater physical contact. You know what I'm talking about, right? Yawn, stretch, out goes the arm, contact. Dewey had a better idea. "How about the popcorn trick, Dad?"

"What's the popcorn trick?" Noelle asked, her interest apparently piqued at the mere mention of the move Mickey Rourke first made famous in the 1982 film *Diner.*

Dewey proceeded to give Noelle a slightly more descriptive definition than I would have preferred, explaining how Rourke had slipped his...member through the bottom of a popcorn box, giving his date a little more than she had bargained for when she reached down for a handful.

"Oh, that's gross," Noelle said. "Like, what did she do when she found out? Did she, like, scream, or hit him?"

"Oh no," I said, not particularly caring for where the accusation was heading. "Actually, he managed to convince her it was an accident, like an honest mistake."

"Well, how could that be a mistake?" Noelle asked.

I actually weighed the pros and cons of continuing this conversation with my daughter before opting for a slightly more conservative approach.

"You know, honey, I'm not really comfortable discussing this type of thing with you."

"Okay," she said, laughing.

"Maybe you'd better talk to Mom about it."

"Okay."

COUNTDOWN TO LOCKDOWN:
5 DAYS

April 14, 2009
Long Island, New York
9:45 p.m.

"Oh fuuuuuuuudge!" Remember when little Ralphie said these words, after losing his hubcap full of lugnuts while his old man tried to fix a flat tire in record time in *A Christmas Story*? Except he used a different word than *fudge*? Well that was kind of how I felt this evening, about two hours ago, after finding out that all these great visualizations I'd had would be of no help to me at *Lockdown*.

You see, all of my visualization had revolved around a special cage I'd been told would be built for the show. Hell, I'd even sat down with the engineer, working out the specifics and dimensions, trying to customize the cage to fit my strengths and hide my weaknesses. Now it's gone. The beautiful blue steel bars? Gone. The easy climbing access? Gone. The three-foot walking section at the top of the structure, perfect for exchanging high-altitude punches or for dropping a dramatic elbow? Gone, gone, all gone. My dreams, hopes, and aspirations? Those too are gone, gone, all gone.

I was told it was a dollars-and-cents issue. That close to a million dollars for the new structure might be a little too high a tab to pay to disguise the fact that Mick Foley can't climb. Sure, they didn't put it quite like that, but I think that was essentially what the decision came down to.

In truth, most of the guys in TNA are more than athletic enough to take care of the creative opportunities a standard steel-mesh cage provides. When I first heard about TNA's annual all-cage match show a few years ago, I couldn't help but feel skeptical. After all, when I was growing up, a cage was the match of last resort. It was the place where feuds went to be settled. Bruno and Koloff. Snuka and Muraco. Oz and Kazmaier. I just couldn't quite grasp what an all-cage match show might look like, or how it could possibly work. But TNA has made it work for the past four years. Then again, those shows didn't have me in their main event. No wonder they worked.

I really had *seen* that picture involving that sinister blue steel structure. I had *thought* the picture, too. Was this close (thumb and forefinger maybe an inch apart) to *being* the picture. Certainly, I wasn't going to be afraid to make mistakes.

But now the picture's been changed dramatically, and I'm not sure I'll be able to psychologically adjust in time for *Lockdown*. It seems like an awful lot to ask me to adapt only five days out. Like asking

Tiger Woods to win a tournament before his knee has had sufficient time to heal. Like asking Santa to fly around the world with only seven reindeer. Sorry, without that extra reindeer, no way he visits billions of kids in a single night. It's like asking Barry Bonds to crack seventy-three homers in a single season without the proper nutrition and training.

I considered myself an average cage-match wrestler at best. And that was in my prime. Sure, I had some pretty good cage matches along the way, but back in those days I could at least count on a couple of the old standbys to see me through the tough times. You know, throwing your opponent into the cage, raking his face against the mesh. As long as I had those two life vests in my boat, I could pretty much save any match from a stagnant pool of mediocrity. Something tells me that our fans will need a little more than the throw and rake in the *Lockdown* main event. Too bad I've got nothing else to offer, at least for now. Let's see if a new picture materializes in the next five days.

At least I'll have some help, having pored over the famous Foley CD selection for some time-tested tunes that will hopefully provide a well-needed jolt of inspiration as I travel the roads from Long Island to Elmira, New York; to Scranton, Pennsylvania; to Philadelphia; to Honesdale, Pennsylvania; and back to Philadelphia for *Lockdown*. A total of around seven hundred miles — and I think I'll need every one of them.

Here's some of the CDs I've hand-selected for the task. Sometimes I'll listen to the whole thing, sometimes just a song or two. Sometimes I'll listen to one song several times in a row. So I'll mention each CD and then a song or two from each that's given me a goose bump or two over the years. Maybe you can give a few of them a try sometime.

David Allan Coe — *16 Biggest Hits*: "The Ride" still does it for me after all these years. Coe singing, "Boy can you make folks feel what you feel inside? 'Cause if you're big star bound, let me warn you it's a long hard ride," brings me back to all those weekend trips from my college in Cortland, New York, to DeNucci's wrestling school in Freedom, Pennsylvania.

Sheryl Crow — *The Very Best of Sheryl Crow*: I dig Sheryl; from her remake of "The First Cut Is the Deepest" through her better-known hits, this is one of those CDs I can listen to from start to finish. Wait, check that. I do skip the duet with Kid Rock, and that's no knock on the Kid, but I just can't buy "a different girl every night at the hotel" as an accurate description of "living my life in a slow hell."

Blackfoot — *Rattlesnake Rock 'n' Roll: The Best of Blackfoot*: Rickey Medlocke's primal scream and a soaring guitar solo make "Diary of a Workingman" one of the most motivational, depressing songs ever recorded.

Warren Zevon — *I'll Sleep When I'm Dead (An Anthology)*, *Volume II*: For some reason, I can listen to "Suzie Lightning" over and over, despite the fact that I have no idea what it's about. Coincidentally, the song always makes me think of a girl I kissed in 1987 while another Zevon tune, "Sentimental Hygiene," played on MTV in the background.

Eclectic Sampler 1: A student at Vincennes Junior College in Indiana gave this to me after I spoke at the school. There's some cool stuff on it, but I picked it for the Johnny Cash version of "Hurt." Over the years I've been given a lot of cool stuff by my fans.

Gillian Welch — *Soul Journey*: This disc was given to me by Michael "Mad Dog" Tearson, who now hosts *Classic Vinyl* on Sirius satellite radio. "Look at Miss Ohio" and "Wrecking Ball" were two of my tunes of choice when I was getting ready for Randy Orton in 2004.

Bruce Springsteen and the E Street Band — *Live in New York City*: "Youngstown" contains my all-time favorite guitar solo. I spoke with E Street guitarist Nils Lofgren at considerable length about the solo, telling him it reminded me of a great wrestling match, constantly building, ultimately concluding in a breathtaking fashion.

Sinead O'Connor — *The Lion and the Cobra*: Yeah, I know, Sinead kind of put the boots to her career when she tore up a photo of the pope on live TV back in 1992. But "Just Like U Said It Would B" is a little treasure from 1987 I discovered just a few years ago. I really feed off the emotion at the end of the song.

John Mellencamp — *Human Wheels*: I'll listen to "Sweet Evening Breeze" and "What If I Came Knocking" back-to-back about four times in a row. "Sweet Evening Breeze," a sad but nostalgic look back at a short-term romance, isn't on any of his greatest-hits compilations, but it's probably my favorite Mellencamp tune.

Kenny Loggins — "Danger Zone": Yes, I'm still kidding about that one.

Julie Miller — *Broken Things*: I once listed "All My Tears" as one of the songs I'd take with me to a deserted island. It's probably been a good three years since I've listened to it, so it may get a few consecutive listens on this road trip.

Hole — *Live Through This*: I know Courtney Love has some issues, which is probably what makes a line like "someday you will ache like I ache" in "Doll Parts" feel so raw and real.

Steve Earle — *Transcendental Blues*: Maybe I really am a glutton for punishment, but I just love "Lonelier Than This," one of the saddest songs I've ever heard. I've been a huge Steve Earle fan for over twenty years, but he's been out of the rotation for a while. Glad to have him back in.

Drive-By Truckers — *Southern Rock Opera, Act 1*: Another disc I haven't listened to in a while. These guys pay tribute to their seventies Southern rock heroes on kick-ass tunes like "Ronnie and Neil" and "Birmingham."

Dire Straits — *Making Movies*: I used to play this CD to death — both on my radio show in college and on all those road trips to DeNucci's school. "Tunnel of Love," "Expresso Love," "Romeo and Juliet," and "Skateaway" — one of my all-time favorite discs.

The White Stripes — *Icky Thump*: A couple listens of the title track at high volume might be just what I need.

Tori Amos — *Little Earthquakes* and *Live at Montreux*: Come on, you didn't think I'd take a road trip leading to my biggest match in years without "Winter," did you? The 1991 version from *Live at Montreux* may be my favorite of all. But asking Tori Amos to salvage my match at *Lockdown* may be too much to ask of anyone.

I'm not sure what, if anything, I'll listen to right before my match. But this selection of songs should at least get me into the building, if not inside the cage itself. Once there, it will be up to me to really *be* the picture. Provided I can *see* the picture first. I've still got five days to look.

One of the worst days in my career.

A BAD DAY IN JUNE

Let me state for the record that I hated the June 2007 WWE story line that featured the car-bomb explosion and possible death of Vince McMahon. Absolutely hated it.

Especially when I watched *SmackDown* a few days after the initial *Raw* explosion and saw the announcers treating the feigned death like it was a real one. There's a certain tone of sincerity WWE announcers have when tragedy has struck; a tone that lets the viewers know that what they are seeing is no longer a show, that something very real has taken place. When done in the wake of a real-life tragedy, such as the in-ring death of Owen Hart in 1999 or the death of Eddie Guerrero in 2005, that tone can be of great comfort. In those cases the announce team serves almost as trusted friends helping millions of viewers through an emotionally trying time. In the case of the McMahon fake car-bomb death, the announce team was being asked to duplicate that same legitimate emotion for a completely bogus angle. In the process, I think we greatly violated that trust.

I hate to use the word *hate* too often. *Hate* is a strong word when used correctly and infrequently. So, I'm going to go with it here and hope that it's the right choice to properly convey my dislike, disbelief, and disgust with what I saw on the television screen later in that same show.

I hated, absolutely hated, the television segment that saw dozens of WWE wrestlers walk out onto the entrance ramp to pay "tribute" to the memory of Vince McMahon, who was alive and well behind the curtain, pulling the strings to the world's largest puppet show — a cast of barely willing participants, doing their best to appear sad at the make-believe loss of their employer, but with an occasional legitimate "I can't believe I'm doing this" look betraying their faux sadness.

This entrance-ramp tribute was the exact way the WWE had paid tribute to the very real deaths of Owen and Eddie, and I found the replication of those tributes for the sake of a completely fabricated death to be of almost impossibly bad taste.

I returned to *Raw* a week later to promote the *Vengeance* main event I'd been so subtly repackaged for, and felt an instant sickening in my stomach and an inexplicable tightening of my back when given dialogue that would have me expressing similar forlorn sadness at the fake fate of Mr. McMahon.

Several wrestlers had told me of their feelings of disgust and shame while standing on that ramp, but unlike me they weren't just occasional visitors to the WWE playground. They more or less needed to keep their relationship with the boss as harmonious as possible, which from time to time meant having to do little things like hiding their shame and disgust.

I simply couldn't take it, and I asked Vince if I might have a few words with him concerning my dialogue on that evening's show.

A few words turned into a contentious forty-minute conversation. I wish I could say that I delivered a well-reasoned, well-structured dissertation on the tastelessness of this story line, but in truth it was more of a rambling outpouring of pent-up frustration, throwing in things like the rescinding of my dress code waiver, the lack of promotion for *The Hardcore Diaries*, and the whole need for repackaging Mick.

There were, however, some highlights to the rambling dialogue.

For one, Vince had found the very idea of my objection to the angle to be objectionable.

"Vince McMahon didn't die, Mick," Vince said. "Mr. McMahon died."

Excuse me? What? Actually, I don't think I said anything. I think I let my open-jawed look of disbelief do all my talking for me. Apparently Vince McMahon is a real person who was still alive and well. Mr. McMahon was a television character. He was the dead guy. So, Vince said, there was no need for my concern.

I picked up my open jaw long enough to ask if he was sure our fans knew the difference.

"Of course they do, Mick," he said.

Apparently, all this time I'd been the only one too dumb to make that obvious distinction.

I had hoped to approach this discussion as something of a linguistic pugilist, dissecting Mr. McMah — oops, I mean Vince McMahon with razor-sharp verbal jabs. Instead, I'd resorted to throwing wild ideological haymakers, most of them either missing by a mile or easily dodged or deflected by a wily Mr. McMah — oops, Vince McMahon.

But before retreating from the fray, I landed one solid verbal blow.

"Vince, what will happen if, God forbid, one of our guys really dies? How will our fans ever trust us again?"

This whole *Vengeance* main event thing had come about pretty suddenly. One day I'm at home, wondering how to go about reconnecting with the fans. The next — I'm in the main event.

I had already committed to attending the opening dedication ceremony for an early childhood education center I'd helped fund in the southwest Mexican state of Michoacán and didn't want to miss it. After all, this was the center I'd worked hand in hand with the Dalai

Lama on, and it was very special to me. Okay, so maybe we hadn't really worked together, and maybe I didn't actually even know the Dalai Lama personally, but we really were the two biggest donors on the project. Pretty cool.

Fortunately, the *Vengeance* show was in Houston, where I would connect for my flight to Michoacán anyway, so the trip for the dedication was possible, if not completely advisable. Door to door, from my home in Long Island, it was a seventeen-hour trip. Plus a four-hour drive to Mexico City after the dedication. Then a simple three-hour flight to Houston the next morning. Looking back at it now, I guess twenty-one hours of travel in the thirty-six hours before a big Pay-Per-View event was probably a mistake. But it's a mistake I'm glad I made and hopefully would make all over again.

The education center was beautiful and will no doubt be a place of great importance in its small village for decades to come. More important, I had a chance to meet Rosita, one of the children I sponsor through ChildFund International. I had been to Michoacán about a year earlier on a ChildFund study trip, and I had returned home with a plan to help out with the funding of the center and to sponsor a few more children.

Rosita was one of those children, and she had become my steady pen pal over the following months, a thoughtful writer with a wisdom that belied her eleven years.

I hoped I would get a chance to meet her on this trip. But, man, it was hard to tell. All the girls I saw looked almost identical, with long, dark hair and traditional dresses for the festive occasion.

One of the girls said hello. Actually, I think she said *hola*, since, you know, we were in Mexico.

"*Como se lama*," I said — "How are you?" — utilizing my extensive knowledge of Spanish, which consists of two or three dozen words.

"Rosita," the girl said.

"Rosita," I said, before it dawned on me. "My Rosita?"

And with that, my Rosita gave me the biggest hug her little arms were capable of, instantly making the seventeen hours spent traveling seem like a very small price to pay for such a special moment.

Sure, I'd be a little tired for my main event match in Houston, but I felt like I had taken part in something very good in that little village in the Mexican state of Michoacán.

Meanwhile, unbeknownst to any of us, back in the United States, another event involving a wrestler was simultaneously taking place. Something very, very bad.

Vengeance turned out fine. The main event match, the five-way for the WWE Championship, was a good match, and my participation had not been a source of embarrassment. Just as I'd hoped, the number of wrestlers involved had afforded me the chance to take a few much-needed rests, a chance to catch my breath while other guys took turns as the focal points of the match. Plus, I finally had a new answer for all those kids who always wanted to know if I'd ever "versed" John Cena.

Oddly, Chris Benoit had not made it to Houston for his match — staying home, rumor said, because of a case of food poisoning.

"It must be pretty bad for Chris not to make it," I'd said out loud in the dressing room earlier that night.

Yes, for Chris Benoit, among the most dedicated wrestlers I'd ever met, to miss any show, let alone a Pay-Per-View match, something pretty bad must have happened.

My flight into Corpus Christi was delayed for two hours the next morning, and upon arriving at the arena I was told that my services would not be needed at that evening's show. Which was fine with me, as I had no desire to take part in the elaborately planned funeral for Mr. (not Vince) McMahon. All of the wrestlers had been told to bring their best attire for the solemn occasion, which was scheduled to include, among other things, a gospel choir honoring Mr. McMahon's memory with a rendition of "Amazing Grace."

I was glad to be heading home, despite the threatening skies, which had all flights out of Corpus delayed for an unknown period of time.

That unknown period of time just kept getting longer. An hour, then two, then four, finally eight before we took off. All the while, I was forging ahead through *Children at War*, quite possibly the most depressing book I'd ever read. I'd visited places of great historical suffering over the years — the Dachau concentration camp in Germany, the Hiroshima Peace Memorial Park in Japan, the Nanking massacre monument in China — but the depictions of brutality I read in this book were almost unfathomable.

The weather that had delayed the Corpus flights had hit much of the country hard, causing delays and cancellations of flights on a massive scale. When my flight landed in Atlanta, it was almost midnight, and I had no chance of catching my connection to New York until the following day. Thousands of travelers found themselves in similar situations, scrambling to find last-minute hotel rooms in a city whose every hotel was seemingly booked to capacity.

I tried every number I could — as a frequent traveler, I've got a lot of contact information — before finally finding an EconoLodge with one extra room in a pretty shady part of town. The hotel shuttle buses were overwhelmed, and lines for taxis stretched hundreds of yards. I've done quite a bit of traveling since 1985, and this was without a doubt the worst debacle of its kind I'd ever endured. I managed to hop on board a hotel shuttle bus whose list of hotels serviced didn't include mine. The driver did the best he could, dropping me off about a mile from my hotel.

Slowly, I trudged toward the EconoLodge in the bad part of town, a pro wrestler with a rolling bag making his way past pawnshops and a couple of nefarious street deals.

With the exception of the fifteen minutes I'd been in the arena in Corpus Christi, I'd been driving, waiting, flying, and walking for sixteen straight hours, during which I'd started and finished *Children at War*, a truly disturbing and enlightening work.

Two days earlier I'd been on hand for the dedication of the early childhood education center I'd played a big part in, and met my sponsored child, Rosita, the girl from Michoacán whose letters mean so much to me.

The night before, I'd been respectable in the main event of a big Pay-Per-View show.

But this day, June 24, 2007, had been a disaster, probably one of the worst days of my year, possibly even my life.

And that was before the phone call.

"Hi, Mick, it's Colette."

"Yes?" Right away I knew something was wrong.

"Did you hear about Chris Benoit?"

"No, what is it?"

"Chris, his wife, and child were all killed in their home in Atlanta."

Mandatory for every wrestler.

AN OPEN LETTER

Of course, as it turned out, there was far more to the Benoit deaths than originally thought. For reasons that may never be completely known, Chris Benoit murdered his wife and child before taking his own life. This series of events shook the foundations of the wrestling world, and for a long time — weeks, months — it made me feel self-conscious and even ashamed to be part of the business. There had been brief moments of time over the course of my career where I might have wondered just what I was doing in a business that can be occasionally heartless and uncaring, but for the first few weeks follow-ing those previously unthinkable actions, I actually felt ill at ease just walking around, thinking I would be looked at, pointed to, and talked about as "one of them."

The press didn't help much. It seemed for the most part that they were interested only in ratings and information that fit into their two-word sound-bite explanation: "'roid rage." I'm not really into bashing the mainstream media, but it would certainly seem that with so many hours to fill on cable news, there should have been more room for some nuanced reporting and actual investigation instead of a parade of talking heads and a grand rush to judgment. I almost became one of those talking heads, after agreeing to do *The O'Reilly Factor*, before a friend at ChildFund International convinced me to reconsider. "You've done so much to help people," she said. "Are you sure you want to jeopardize all that to be on his show?"

"I think we could have a good conversation," I said.

"Yes, Mick, you could...but that's really his choice. Do you want to trust him to make that choice for you?"

Not really. Which was probably a good decision, especially after seeing Bill tee off on one of his wrestling guests (I can't honestly remember who — there were so many of them for a few weeks) for no real reason, and then present cherry-picked information on the famous Lionel Tate murder case without ever mentioning that the judge and jury had unanimously rejected the Tate defense team's bogus "wrestling defense." (They had attempted to blame the murder of a little girl on Tate's imitating moves he had seen on pro-wrestling television shows.) I'm not really bashing O'Reilly, either; he was no worse than anybody else out there, even if his reporting on the Tate case was a pretty good case of putting a little misleading spin into the "no-spin zone."

But there was part of me that really wanted to talk. I felt like the wrestling business was being unfairly blamed for the heinous Benoit deaths, and I wanted to defend it. But so many of the guys in the wrestling business came off poorly — even Kevin Nash, one of the smartest guys in the business, wasn't allowed to make valid points without enduring constant interruption on *Hannity & Colmes*. Really, only Chris Jericho and Bret Hart came across truly well — in Jericho's case, because he was smart enough to agree to appear only if he wasn't part of a panel of guests, where arguing and yelling are seemingly encouraged.

I wanted to have my say, but I came to the conclusion that it would be better to do so after the smoke had cleared and the scramble for ratings had dissipated. I felt like this issue would be with us in the wrestling business for a long time to come, and eventually I would have a chance to make some sort of sense out of it. I even thought about writing a novel, *Letters to Eddie,* attempting to get into Chris Benoit's head during those last few months of his life and explain the frustration, rage, and fear that he may have expressed through his journals to his deceased best friend, Eddie Guerrero. I had so many ideas running through my head during those first few weeks, and I was looking for some way to get them out. I absolutely knew that it wasn't as simple as the 'roid rage the press was attempting to pin the blame on, or, later, the head injuries that Chris's father was placing all of his faith in as an explanation. Of course, Benoit's history of steroid use may have been one *part* of the problem, as may have been a history of possible concussions. But I believe *each* of these was just a simple ingredient in a complex stew of factors, stirred and seasoned over time and circumstance, eventually bubbling forth at the worst possible time and in the worst possible way.

I think it's entirely possible (perhaps even probable) that Benoit would have never gotten a series of big career breaks had he not had the impressive physique that anabolic steroids helped make possible. But at a certain point, when he had been a big star for many years, I think the only person who thought Chris Benoit still needed steroids to maintain his career was Chris himself. Apparently Chris was so psychologically dependent on maintaining his look that he didn't cycle off steroids even when recuperating from neck surgery, when he wouldn't be in the public eye for several months. So there is a chance that his longtime usage may have played a contributory role, but the idea of the guy just "snapping" due to steroid use struck me as highly unlikely, especially given the drawn-out nature of the murders/ suicide.

I completely understand the emphasis that Chris Benoit's father has placed on his son's head injuries as an attempt to explain the unexplainable; living with the tragedy and the knowledge that his son was responsible for these deaths is a burden too great for me to even imagine. I heard Mr. Benoit on a television show, talking about the severity of the blows Chris had taken over the years from chairs, tables, garbage cans — all the stuff that I'm pretty closely associated with. To be sure, Chris had some experience with those types of matches, but I think that it's more likely that his traumatic brain injuries were a result of a hard-hitting style that really never relented over the course of time. Everything he did was just so intense; every forearm, every suplex, every one of those diving head butts from the top rope. I thought he might come back from his neck surgery with a slightly more relaxed style; certainly I thought he'd take the top-rope head butt out of his repertoire of regular moves.

As a matter of necessity, most guys who wrestle in a physically demanding style will eventually find a way to ease up, to change their style, to incorporate a little levity into their character if they want to continue wrestling past the point where Mother Nature starts suggesting they slow down. Just about everyone who has had a long run in a top spot has found a way. I know I did, practically turning a 180 and becoming a comedic character with a sock puppet after so many years of doing all that hardcore stuff. But Benoit never changed. He was still pretty much full tilt every night, with very little in the way of comedy or even promos to take the pressure off his body, especially when it came to absorbing some type of punishment to the head on an almost nightly basis.

I'm not trying to sell the gravity of the concussion crisis in the wrestling business short, either. Believe me, I think about it every single day, wondering if I took too many head shots for too long, and what type of price I may eventually pay for doing so. I think there was some argument to make years ago that taking unprotected chair shots to the head was the right thing to do for business. I mean it looked so convincing on camera, back in the day when people still could be emotionally swayed by that type of image. Now, it's a ridiculous argument to even have. Barring some huge angle, where a chair shot absolutely, positively, has to look devastating on camera (and even *then* it's questionable), every wrestler needs to get those hands up when a chair is headed their way.

A few months ago, after a couple years of persistence on the part of my friend Chris Nowinski, I agreed to contribute posthumous samples of my brain to the Sports Legacy Institute, the group that Nowinski cofounded after his own pro-wrestling career was cut short due to a history of concussions. It's not like I find the image of a drill burring its way into my brain after death to be a real comforting one. But after doing some studying on all the problems associated with concussions in football, hockey, wrestling, and just about any contact sport, I do realize the great importance of this type of science, and I hope that my life and career can be of some use to others after I'm gone.

A few months after the Benoit deaths, I asked WWE if I could speak to the wrestlers in their two developmental territories, Ohio Valley Wrestling and Florida Championship Wrestling, and pass on whatever knowledge or advice I could in order to possibly prevent any further tragedy in the future. In truth, the Benoit situation was probably some kind of perfect horrible storm, the likes of which our business will never see again, but one need only look at the ever-expanding list of wrestler deaths to see that certain mistakes keep being made over and over again. It was my intent to arm those young wrestlers with as much information as possible so they could make the best possible decisions for themselves. I don't pretend to have all the answers, but at the very least I hoped that my experiences and advice would add another voice to a much-needed conversation about life and death in the world of professional wrestling. Maybe it could even act as food for thought, which the younger guys could feel free to digest and absorb, or eliminate from their systems as quickly as possible.

I thought the talks were very effective — and who knows, maybe some of it even sank in. I spoke to a total of maybe one hundred men and women, all wrestlers that WWE had thought enough of to have in their developmental program. These men and women were set to become the stars of tomorrow — some of them already have. But there are thousands of professional wrestlers out there, and no possible way to talk to them all. So I'm going to use this chapter as a means of hopefully reaching a few more. Again, I'm not going to pretend to have all of the answers, or that listening to me is going to have a profound effect on many lives. But I am hoping to get through to a few. And though I usually try my best not to be preachy, in this case, I probably do know more than almost any of you. So I'm going to do my best to share my feelings/knowledge/advice, in what I would like to think of as an open letter to every wrestler: past, present, and future.

I'm going to start out by acknowledging this incredibly sobering list of young wrestlers' deaths. In 2001, when *Foley Is Good* was published, I had a list of only four wrestlers whose deaths may have been attributed in part to problems with prescription drugs, which was then, and still is, the biggest problem concerning these deaths in the wrestling business. Maybe I didn't have all the facts, or maybe I just had my head in the sand, because the problem was surely bigger than I described it then, and has gotten far worse since that time. I know there are all kinds of different lists concerning wrestlers' deaths out there, with all different types of criteria, but for the sake of this book I looked at wrestlers who died at fifty or younger in the last twenty years and whose deaths might possibly be seen as unnatural. So I didn't include people like Brian Hildebrand, one of my very best friends, who died of stomach cancer, or others whose deaths, however tragic, could not be linked to wrestling in any realistic way.

There are sixty-six names on my list; it's far from complete, as I have chosen only the names of wrestlers who had some type of regional or national success. If I were to include all the deaths involving young, independent wrestlers, I know the list would be far more extensive. Still, sixty-six wrestlers is an incredible number. Out of those sixty-six, I knew forty-nine. Out of those forty-nine, I considered myself friendly with thirty of them. *Thirty* human beings I knew well and liked — gone before age fifty.

These losses used to devastate me. But in the last several years, there have just been so many, so often, that I've almost built up an immunity to it; it's like I can no longer mourn deaths that I almost expect to occur. And that is a pretty sad statement. It makes me feel somehow less human, and in truth it probably offers some explanation as to why I am no longer close with many guys in the business. I think it's almost a defense mechanism to protect myself from the inevitable sadness of losing even more friends in the future. I would most likely be deceiving myself to think that the news of my own death would be much news at all...and that's a sad statement, too.

Okay, enough of the sad statements. Let's see what we can do about it.

When I was a kid, maybe eight or nine, I read a statistic claiming that NFL football players had a life expectancy of forty-two. For the life of me, I can't find that statistic now — at least not with my limited web-surfing skills, but I can almost swear to its existence; most likely in *Sports Illustrated*, *Sport*, or *Sporting News*, as those were my three go-to magazines when I was that age. So, even though I can't find that statistic or prove it, I'd like all of you to accept it, at least long enough for me to explain it as it pertains to pro wrestling. Now, when I was a kid, that statistic baffled me — a forty-two-year life expectancy. How could that possibly be? But my mother explained it in a way that made a little more sense of it. "Mickey, people who are drawn to pro football are going to be more likely to be drawn to other things in life that are going to be dangerous. They will be more likely to drive fast, live fast, and die fast."

Like the statistic itself, my mother's explanation can't be proven, but it made perfect sense to me then. As I became involved with pro wrestling, I saw my mother's explanation in action. The guys I met lived lives filled with risks both inside and outside the ring. Wrestling is really not a profession likely to draw from those who have done a careful analysis of risk and reward, because anyone who weighs such things carefully would stay far away from a business like ours. The chances of making a decent living are small, the chances of ending up broke are good, and the chances of living the rest of your life in some degree of pain because of the foolishness of pursuing this dream are almost guaranteed.

NBC did an intriguing story during its 2010 Winter Olympics coverage, asking whether some of the Olympians drawn to the more potentially dangerous events might actually have a different genetic makeup than those who avoid such things as half-pipes, ski jumps, moguls, and the adrenaline rush of world-class downhill speed.

From what I could tell (including a couple of hours of follow-up research), the answers were inconclusive, but I think it's a question worthy of asking and scientifically researching. I know during the course of my career I may have struck many as something of a thrill seeker; a guy who needed a fix of danger every now and then. I guess that's the way I struck the producers of the *Dr. Phil* show, as I was recently asked (and declined) to be on an episode about "adrenaline junkies," or something of that nature. In truth, I just didn't think I accurately fit the bill. I just can't envision myself on a motorcycle, a snowboard, skis (water or snow), or any number of commonly accepted adventurer apparatuses without wiping out and getting badly injured. So common sense tells me to stay far away from those types of things. I weigh the risk/reward ratio for such activities and overwhelmingly err on the side of caution. I don't even drive particularly fast.

But for some reason, pro wrestling has historically been the one area of my life where caution has repeatedly been thrown to the wind, and where that risk/reward ratio has sometimes been thrown away completely. I vividly recall being told how dangerous the Murtala Muhammed International Airport in Lagos, Nigeria, was before flying there twice in 1987. For many years, I remember seeing signs at *every* international airport I flew out of, stating that the Lagos airport did not meet international safety standards. The Federal Aviation Administration even suspended service between Lagos and the United States in 1993. Yet such knowledge wasn't even a *consideration* when I was given the chance to wrestle in Nigeria. Even when I was given a one-way ticket to Lagos. Even when I handed my passport to a man who bypassed customs and immigration — and kept the passport with him for the duration of the trip.

It wasn't as if I was stupid. I was a recent college graduate and had even received an award for being an outstanding student in my major. But in 1987 (and for many years after), I just didn't consider the possible risks when it came to the decision-making process in so many aspects of professional wrestling. I made it to shows no matter what. If a flight was canceled because of weather, I got in my car and drove. On occasions when my car broke down, I left it on the side of the road and hitchhiked. That's just the way it was when I broke in and, in many ways, the way it still is for people who choose to pursue dreams that often don't coincide with logical thought processes.

Obviously, there is an upside to the realization of those illogical dream pursuits. But there is a heck of a price to pay for those who willingly go through life with blinders on — even when those dreams come true.

So the people who are drawn to pro wrestling are likely to ignore the risks not only of being pummeled on a nightly basis, but of just about every other facet of life as well: driving fast, drinking hard, driving fast while drinking hard, and living life itself in that proverbial fast lane. We've got some extreme personalities in our world; guys who seem bigger than life in the ring often don't know how to turn off that persona once they leave the ring. The best wrestling characters are usually just natural extensions of a performer's real self — with the volume turned up. And throughout the decades, torrid tales of the wrestling lifestyle have filled dressing rooms from Portland, Maine, to Portland, Oregon. But those lifestyles — more alcohol, more drugs, more women, more cars, more money — come with a price. And that price quite often includes a shortened life. So many of the lives on that list of sixty-six names were ended by heart attacks — almost half of them, by my count. Some have links to use (and possible abuse) of prescription drugs, some to steroid abuse, some to the cocaine heyday of the 1980s. In so many cases, wrestlers have just attempted to pack too many excesses into too few years.

I think things are changing for the better, even if some of the changes have been slow in coming and sometimes were forced from the outside world. Guys take better care of their bodies now, and there is not nearly as much pressure to conform to a late-night-party atmosphere in order to gain acceptance among one's peers. Sure, instances of late-night debauchery still take place, but not on such a regular basis.

Drug testing has certainly helped. For years I wondered how wrestlers could travel from city to city, collecting prescriptions from doctors across the country, treating the world as one giant pharmacy. In *Foley Is Good* I wondered about some type of national database and whether the lack of such a thing was financially motivated — because in the end everything seems to come down to money. I don't know if such a database currently exists, but I know WWE and TNA are doing their best to ensure that no wrestler has more than one physician. Now that doesn't mean that guys won't find ways to cheat the system or won't find doctors willing to overprescribe legal medications, but I think this step has been a highly effective one in limiting the potential misuse of prescription drugs.

Every wrestler has got to accept that pain is going to be part of the lifestyle, and that the things we do to entertain and to follow our dream are going to lead to a certain amount of discomfort for the rest of our lives. Accept it. Deal with it. Don't mask it with pills. I'm not saying there is never a need for pain medication. No matter how tough the guy or how strong the will, there will most likely be a time (hopefully a very temporary time) in every wrestler's life when the pain simply becomes unbearable. And during those certain times, prescribed pain medication certainly can be of great help. For example, while vacationing with my two younger children at Dutch Wonderland in Lancaster, Pennsylvania, I was slightly dismayed to find that my kneecap had become dislocated during the course of navigating a children's raft ride. Hey, these things occasionally happen when one has taken so many chances with his body for so many years. I managed to get the kneecap back into its groove, but the area swelled almost instantly and made movement painful and difficult. With the entire vacation in jeopardy, I made the call to go to the pill bottle (kind of like a baseball manager going to his closer) and was able to return to the park and get through the day with the help of half a Vicodin (or the generic equivalent). There are certainly times when pain medicine can be of great use in a pro wrestler's life, but the abuse of such medicine is a good way to ruin a career…and cut short a life.

I have heard it said that the pro-wrestling lifestyle doesn't necessarily create personal weaknesses, but it will exploit any weaknesses that an individual might bring with him (or her) into the business. Unlike other sports teams, which travel to venues as a group aboard buses and planes, much of the travel in pro wrestling is done in a personal automobile or rental car. Traveling in such a way, the world can kind of seem like one's own personal playground, beckoning to each individual to follow his or her heart's desire. If one has a fondness or a weakness for anything, it's pretty easy to find it while cruising down life's highway. If one has a fondness/weakness for alcohol, there's a favorite bar in every city. Likewise, a fondness/weakness for other substances can be easily exploited. For me, the constant calling from late-night restaurants was almost impossible to resist. I'm one of those guys who uses food as both a reward and a consolation, and I did plenty of both at plenty of late-night diners and fast-food haunts over the years.

And if the drug of choice is women? Well, for so many of the guys throughout pro wrestling's history, that drug is an awfully tough one to resist.

The title character in my novel *Tietam Brown* was an amalgamation of several of the wrestlers I had seen over the years, who had let their insatiable need for women dominate and eventually destroy their lives. It's like a sickness, as real as any addiction I've ever seen and probably equally damaging both emotionally and financially. It's not like I'm immune to that sickness, either; being the kid who never could get the girls, transformed into some kind of star with the very real possibility of attracting women, occasionally has me feeling like that proverbial kid in the candy store. It's like a veritable recipe for disaster — so I just do my very best to stay out of the candy store at all times.

For many years (even decades, from what I've heard), the wrestling business seemed to encourage, even nurture, a certain atmosphere of disrespect from its wrestlers toward their female audience. As odd as it sounds now, I think it actually had something to do with perpetuating the legitimacy of good guys and bad guys; a "bad guy" certainly couldn't have word getting around that he was nice to women ... or, even worse, that he'd been a gentle, sensitive lover! So guys were encouraged to be kind of crummy to the girls, even if they weren't being blatantly mean. I even had my job threatened one night in 1988, by a booker who had seen me talking to a girl in a wheelchair after the matches in Evansville, Indiana. The girl, Terri DePriest, had Duchenne muscular dystrophy, and thus a limited time to live, but in the interest of remaining a "bad guy," I was told not to let anyone see me speaking to her again. I may have really needed that job, but fortunately that was one order I deliberately disobeyed.

For the most part, much of that type of mentality has gone the way of the Burgermeister Meisterburger's laws concerning Kris Kringle in the Rankin-Bass Claymation classic *Santa Claus Is Comin' to Town*. Most of the guys in the business realize that it's a new day and that most of those old philosophies regarding women no longer pertain to them. Still, there's this subtle sense of disrespect for women that occasionally rears its ugly head, and it's almost always the wrestler who pays the ultimate price in the end (whether they realize it or not).

I don't claim to know everything about successful relationships (even though, at twenty years, my relationship has to be some sort of pro-wrestling record), but I can advise any prospective wrestler not to fall into the trap of disrespecting women that has led to so many failed relationships with dire financial and emotional consequences.

It bothers me to hear any wrestler still talking about female fans in a derogatory fashion (the common names are *ring rat*, *arena rat*, or just plain *rat*) just because someone had the poor judgment to physically associate with them. Guys should be flattered that women would want to watch them, let alone sleep with them. In so many cases, wrestlers who break into the business without learning to respect women end up lonely, miserable, and destitute, and I'm pretty sure there is a cor-relation. And, if I hear of any wrestler messing around with Rohypnol (roofies — the date rape drug), I will do whatever is in my power to make sure they never get booked again.

Look, I know that wrestlers are targets: for women, for fights, for lawsuits. Just try to remember that as a wrestler you are a public per-sonality with a bull's-eye on your back. Check IDs, never assume that no means yes, and try to stay out of places where drunk people hang out. I know that seems difficult, and kind of uncool, but unless you have this real need to spend time in court, watching your hard-earned money go to some drunk in a bar who probably deserved the beating he got, find a new hobby. There's nothing wrong with being a nerd these days. Hey, half the TNA crew stays in their hotel rooms with their video games, or tweeting, or texting, or possibly even reading. If I could recommend one specific talent to a wrestler who wants to hold on to some of the money he (or she) has made, it would be "enjoy the act of doing nothing." Enjoy being by yourself in a hotel room, or on a beach, or in front of a computer screen watching, um, movies...in moderation, of course. You know, if I was sure I could do it without getting busted by my children, I just might do it, too.

No matter what we get paid, wrestlers work hard for their money. There is a physical and emotional toll for everything we do in the ring. No one gets out of the business without paying some kind of price. So do yourselves a favor and save as much money as you can. As much as you can, whenever you can, for as long as you can. No

matter how good you might think you are, or how much you might
think you'll make, everyone is just one wrong move, one bad bump,
one missed step, from being out of a job. No one should think of the
wrestling business as a lifetime job or a right to make a good living.
With TNA in the picture more wrestlers of different looks can get
a fair shot. But there are still only fifty or so really good jobs for the
thousands that want them, and most of those thousands are going to
be putting an awful lot of faith in one man's whim. I used to sit in
on production meetings when I did some announcing for that man's
company. And that man I'm making reference to, Vince McMahon,
well, he kind of changes his mind for any reason he wants, or for no
reason at all. So a wrestler, no matter how good, or how popular, or
how filled with potential, should probably not rest all his financial
dreams, professional hopes, and sense of personal self on the whims
of a somewhat impulsive billionaire.

The wrestling business is filled with lists of guys who *made* a fortune, and guys who are *worth* a fortune...and it's *not* the same list.
Believe me, there are some big spenders in the business, guys who
believe that the good times are never going to end, who have very
little, if anything, to show for a lifetime of hard work. On the other
hand, there are wrestlers who made steady but never really big money,
who nonetheless get to call their own shots in life because they were
smart enough to save and invest the money they made, and realized
that the business might not always be there to take care of them.

Speaking of being smart — the real world can be a tough place, and
you may eventually need every brain cell you can spare. Get as much
of an education as you can, so that you'll have something to fall back
on in the event that your life doesn't work out exactly as you would
have booked it.

On one of the last days of my WWE stay, when few outside of
the front office staff knew of my imminent departure, I asked if I
could address the wrestlers in one of the regular talent meetings, held
every few weeks. I'm sure there were a couple of anxious moments

for the front office staff on hand as I made my way to the front of the
room.

"Look, I don't know how many of you follow the stock market,
but it's down right now, and it might be a good time to start thinking
about funding your own retirement."

I had asked the developmental wrestlers in Ohio Valley and Florida
a year earlier if any of them had heard of a Simplified Employee Pension plan. Two or three wrestlers in each place had heard of such a
thing. A total of one replied that he had started funding his own retirement through an SEP. I explained that it might seem like it was way
too soon to start thinking about retirement, but that no one gets out
of the business without paying a price, and the very least they owed
themselves was the hope of a dignified retirement and the chance of
passing some money down to their heirs.

WWE Hall of Famer Gerald Brisco later remarked that it had been
the most important thing said all day. I laughed and said, "Do you
think anyone listened?"

"Well, Mick, if just one person listened, it would be worth it."

Something tells me he was giving our wrestlers way too much credit.
Something tells me that very few of them have — but that somewhere
down the line, most of them will complain that there is no retirement
or pension plan for wrestlers. Look, it would be really nice if a retirement fairy or an insurance fairy floated down and started bestowing
nice things like that on us. But it's not likely to happen. And until it
does, it's really up to you to take the initiative and do the right thing
when you're young enough for it to matter.

I think that wrestlers in general have trouble believing in their
own mortality, or in the eventuality of their own decline. Wrestling
is objective, and rare is the worker I have met who isn't convinced
they've still got it. In baseball, it's so much easier; if you can't get
around on a fastball, you and everyone else is going to know. Wrestling is full of dreamers and the easily confused; guys who perform
in front of a symphony of silence and then come back to the dressing

room, claiming to have had that "silent heat." We don't tend to draw those guys who look to get health insurance when they are young and healthy, and insurance is relatively cheap. Although even "relatively cheap" is all relative these days. We don't draw too many guys who get into the business thinking about compounding interest on their SEP plans when they're twenty years old. Because if we all thought logically about the future, we'd never get involved in a business like wrestling.

I once talked to Dennis Knight (WCW's Tex Slazenger, WWE's Mideon — one of my favorite guys in the business) about saving some money, putting a little away each week, paying his taxes on time, funding his retirement. A few days later, he came up to me, saying my talk had changed his life. "So you started saving?" I said.

"Well, I'm going to . . . right after I buy Barry's bike." Like they say, you can lead a horse to water . . . but you can't make him drink.

Retirement can be especially tough on a wrestler, even if it's not a true retirement, but just a retirement from the big time. Life can be tough on a guy who goes from being an action figure on the shelf next to Spider-Man to being unemployed in a day's time. If a guy has a name, he can make some money on the independent circuit, but that's a tough row to hoe, and fame can be fleeting. The Mickey Rourke movie *The Wrestler* did an incredible job of showing the pitfalls of a career in steep decline — a subject I got a little closer to than I'd planned when reviewing the film for a respected website, Slate .com. A writer from *Sports Illustrated* who met me at the media screening pretty much depicted me in his article as a real-life Randy "the Ram" Robinson ("Finding dignity in retirement can be difficult," the *SI* piece said of me) because I had the audacity to appear as Santa Claus later that night at the Twisted Sister holiday show. The writer later claimed he didn't know that I was doing the show for free, that I was a good friend of lead singer Dee Snider, or that I was a huge Santa fanatic.

Here's the big question, not only for that writer, but for the retired wrestlers as well as the fans: what exactly is a dignified retirement? What job would have been sufficient for that writer... or for our wrestling fans? What if I really had been being paid to be Santa... for just one show, or as a full-time job? Would that really be undignified? Or would it be a pretty cool job for anyone, be they a former wrestler or not? Putting smiles on kids' faces — undignified? Not to me.

I'm not saying that there haven't been moments where I've wrestled with the dignity, or the lack thereof, that certain situations have presented. For every college lecture at an MIT or a Notre Dame that I've been fortunate to give, there's been a handful of minor-league baseball mascots to clothesline, or that occasional personal appearance that the world forgot to attend. But no way am I pleading guilty in the case of the Twisted Sister Santa.

How about being a chef at a restaurant? Justin Credible (former ECW champion) does just that at an Olive Garden, and gets taunted by fans because of it. For doing something he enjoys, that he trained for, that he wanted to do. I don't want to single out wrestling fans as being particularly cruel, especially after having heard the worst that baseball and football fans have to offer. But some of our fans who read the Internet sites, who are familiar with some of the inside sheets, assume that their knowledge is some kind of license to be hurtful or insensitive or mean.

What exactly is an acceptable postwrestling job? Governor? Yes, we've had one of those. A member of the Japanese diet (equivalent of a U.S. senator)? We've had a couple of those. A *New York Times* number one best-selling author? Yes, that sounds dignified — unless, of course, that author is wearing a Santa Claus suit. Look, there is no real answer to the question, but to this wrestler, at least, any job done with pride is a dignified job. I recently did a comedy show in Worcester, Massachusetts, that only sixteen people showed up for. Sixteen! I know, because I counted them. I guess I could have seen it as an undignified experience, but I did my very best to entertain the few who were on hand. I left with a definite feeling of accomplishment, because I knew I'd taken pride in the work I'd done, despite the small crowd.

And if you never hit the big time, and don't have occasion to save a lot of money — so so what? Have fun anyway; just be reasonable with your goals. Give yourself a realistic timeline for success and stick to it. I gave myself until I was twenty-six to start making a decent living, and hope I would have been brave enough to push the fantasy world of pro wrestling aside if that time had arrived and I was still living week to week. Some of the happiest wrestlers I know are guys who realized their time was up and entered the real world full-time, while still playing superhero a couple of weekends a month. They're not waiting every day for that phone to ring, or that e-mail to arrive, or that text to come, or whatever method guys hope and pray their break will come by these days. For your sake, I hope it does. But it's always best to have a Plan B in life.

I sometimes look back on my adventures in the world of pro wrestling the way Dorothy described her journey in *The Wizard of Oz* — some of it was horrible, but most of it was beautiful. Even though I agree partially with her sentiment that "there's no place like home," I wonder how long Dorothy herself would have felt that way. Would she really have been content to confine herself to a mundane existence on a Kansas farm? Maybe for a while. But something tells me that after that while, Dorothy would have started yearning for another journey over the rainbow.

Pro wrestling, even on its smallest scale, is about as close to that journey as I can imagine. Good guys, bad guys, costumes, fakers, treachery, joy, heartbreak, beauty, friendship. Even in my early days — the ten-dollar payoffs, the nights sleeping in the car — there was no experience that could even come close, even after encountering more than a few men who seemed to lack brains and/or hearts. I know how lucky I am that I never truly had to leave it; that I can jump between that "no place like home" feeling and that yellow brick road any time I want.

Most wrestlers don't have that luxury. For many, the transition from fictional battles with in-ring foes to real-life battles with grocery bills and mortgage payments is a difficult one. For some, it's heartbreaking and unbearable, especially when maintaining the belief (however right or wrong) that the business didn't treat them right. The baggage one accumulates along the way — bad habits, addictions, long-term injuries (including repetitive concussions) — can make that transition feel almost impossible. Depression is frequent — and more than a few of the men on that list of wrestlers who died too young decided that no life at all was better than the one they had remaining.

I wish I had a simple solution to all of the challenges the pro-wrestling business faces. Or all of the challenges that confront every wrestler — past, present, and future. I can't say for sure how I would have reacted, or how life would have worked out for me, if a couple of important people hadn't seen *something* in me, or if a couple of lucky breaks hadn't worked out my way. But I hope I would have had the wisdom and sense to leave the business better in some way than I found it. Stone Cold Steve Austin caught some flak when he was rumored to have said something along the lines of "Stop dying; you're making the business look bad" at a WWE talent meeting a few years ago — but I think there's something to that sentiment. There are all kinds of possible *excuses* but no legitimate *reasons* for the staggering list of deaths I've tried to address. We've all got to realize that as horrible as it can sometimes be, and as beautiful as it often is, this wrestling business of ours is not worth dying over.

There you go — thousands of words of advice from a guy with a history of head injuries. I don't expect anything I've written to have too much of an effect on anyone, but in the words of Gerald Brisco, "If one person listened, it would be worth it."

Substantial wrestling stuff.

A SUBSTANCE PROBLEM

Remember another scene in *The Wizard of Oz* — where Dorothy is making her way to the Emerald City and comes to that fork in the yellow brick road? Faced with no real answer, and with her entire trip to see the Wizard in great jeopardy, Dorothy is fortunate indeed to have a scarecrow come to life to not only help her reach a decision, but treat her to an elaborately choreographed song and a dance routine as well.

Well, about twenty-five years ago, I was at a similar crossroads— although mine was metaphorical—concerning the decision to partake in substances that might just make me look and feel better and perform at a higher level. I was driving a former top wrestling star to an independent show in the New York area, and the star asked me if I'd ever considered taking steroids.

"I've thought about that," I said. "But I heard they were bad for you." At the time I was six foot four, about 230 pounds, and working out hard with very little to show for it.

The wrestler smiled. "Son, all drugs are made to help you, if you use them correctly."

I specifically remember him mentioning the drug Anavar as something that might be good for me, and I gave the matter a great deal of thought before ultimately deciding to take another route at that great crossroads of life.

My route turned out to be the right one for me, although getting to the finish line meant encountering obstacles along the way; barbed wire, thumbtacks, fire, steel chairs, a two-man kayak (handed to me for use as a weapon at the ECW Arena). Fortunately, there weren't too many people on my path, so I stood out a little, and I even managed to pick up some valuable skills—ring psychology, public speaking, a certain likability—along the way.

So many of those guys who took the other path looked alike—muscular, handsome, tanned, toned, shaved, rocking the mullet—that standing out with a completely different look among that crowd turned out to be a good thing.

Yes, I took a slightly different path to wrestling stardom, which was ultimately the right decision for me. But that doesn't mean it would have been the right decision for everybody. Over the years, when asked about steroids, I've tried hard not to frame the issue as a moral one. I've never really referred to anyone as a cheater, as Congress seems fond of doing—nor have I seen it as a decidedly medical one, especially because I would be hard-pressed to point to my body of work and offer it up as a safe alternative to steroids. I would guess that most doctors, given just a cursory look at a three-minute Mick Foley career-highlights video, would reach the same conclusion.

A couple of years ago, I voluntarily responded to a letter from Congressman Henry Waxman, who was looking at holding hearings concerning the use of anabolic steroids in professional wrestling. I knew that Waxman's phone lines were most likely not lighting up with the voluntary calls of the wrestling community, but felt like I might have something to contribute to the proceedings.

I told Waxman's aides that I had never been offered, given, nor told to take anabolic steroids, nor had I felt any pressure to take any drug of any kind. I knew there was some use of steroids in the business, but I didn't think it was as widespread as had been occasionally reported, and I hadn't actually seen a wrestler take steroids in close to twenty years. I acknowledged that I probably wouldn't be privy to much of the talks or behavior regarding steroid use, as I was never really in the loop as far as all of that training and nutritional stuff went.

But I think the most important information I contributed to the congressional process was my belief that wrestlers had developed a deep mistrust of medical science as it pertained to the findings and studies of performance-enhancing substances.

I told them of my fairly extensive reading in the mid-1980s on the subject, and how so much of the science claimed that steroids didn't actually work, that the supposed increases in size were merely due to increased water retention. Increases in strength were said to be minimal or psychological. A quick look around any decent gym or any independent wrestling show revealed these findings to be ludicrous. Guys who got on the gas got bigger and stronger, usually quicker. Guys who didn't...didn't.

Of course, there were the health warnings—liver damage, testicular atrophication, etc.—but to many of the wrestlers, these medical science guys were like the witnesses at a trial who have been caught in a lie; once a single *part* of the testimony is declared invalid, the *whole* story is invalid. As far as most of the wrestlers were concerned, these so-called experts had no validity whatsoever.

As I said earlier, wrestlers don't tend to do all that well when it comes to belief in their own mortality. Many of them decided they could live with a little back acne—the rest of those threats could be dealt with at a later time.

Of course, some of those threats were real, and I have no doubt that the long-term abuse of anabolic steroids has been a contributory factor to some of those wrestling deaths I wrote of earlier. I wish guys could have been given all the facts, but in a sense, so many of them were finding out the facts as they went, more or less human guinea pigs in their own experiments—and they were reaching different conclusions than the experts were.

I believe we may well be at another crossroads of sorts when it comes to so much of modern-day sports medicine and science. I am not an expert of any sort in this field, and have made the decision not to pore over an endless array of information, looking only for facts that might support one viewpoint or another. Instead, with an eye on the past and some serious questions about the future, I just want to inject a few cc's of perspective and a couple of earnest questions into the body of this debate.

Have you seen that occasional movie actor who looks better in his fifties than he did thirty years earlier? Maybe even an actor in his early sixties, doing shirtless scenes, with sculpted abs and amazingly little body fat? How exactly did that actor manage to get that way—through diet and exercise alone? Or did he perhaps have a little pharmaceutical advantage?

How about the skinny actor who packs on twenty pounds of muscle for a role? I can think of four or five movies off the top of my head. Big movie roles, too. I seriously doubt that a potentially huge motion picture would be put in a position to live or die based on a single actor's nutritional program, exercise routine, or genetics—and I am pretty sure that their guy will be allowed to do whatever he needs to do to look as good as possible on the big screen.

I have no real proof, but circumstantial evidence, a little bit of knowledge, and some common sense certainly lead me to believe that some of the key actors in Hollywood are on the gas—or at least some human growth hormone. Why shouldn't they be? Something that makes them look and feel younger, stronger, healthier, more energetic, more virile? Who wouldn't want to sign up for that?

I saw a famous singer from the 1980s in a television comeback concert recently. In his prime, this singer appeared gaunt, skinny, almost sickly. Twenty-five years later, in his fifties, at an age where normal human beings—even regularly active ones—start to sag and loosen, this singer was ripped, pumped, sporting the type of muscularity you just don't get naturally.

Cast aside the potential health benefits of human growth hormone for just a moment. Some scientists tout HGH as a modern-day fountain of youth, though others say studies are inconclusive. Forget, for now, that HGH could possibly improve the lives of ailing seniors and allow them to live a life with less pain, and possibly even save untold billions of dollars in agonizing (and agonizingly expensive) end-of-life care. Forget also that the use of HGH without proper monitoring has possible side effects (enlarged bone structure, enlarged organs, death) of its own. Just push all that to the side.

Instead, I want to ask about what kind of pressure those athletic actors in their fifties, pumped punk rockers, and even ripped rappers put on guys in our business who are supposed to look better, much better, than the average guy out there.

Like I wrote in the last chapter, our action figures are on the rack right next to Spider-Man's, and Spidey has packed on some size since the sixties, where he appeared to be a thin high school student with a cool costume instead of a guy whose every muscle fiber twitches beneath the blue and red. Even Bruce Banner is ripped and ruthless these days, making me wonder why that stunning metamorphosis into the Hulk is even necessary. I think Bruce looks quite capable of kicking some butt all on his own.

Where does that leave us wrestling guys? Wrestlers are supposed to look like superheroes. They're our competition...and *they* don't get tested.

Not that testing is the only answer, because tests were made to be beaten. And by the looks of a few of the top stars in the business whose physiques didn't decline a bit, even after the introduction of serious, regular testing (following the death of Eddie Guerrero in 2005), these tests aren't foolproof. Back in my WCW days, probably 1994, following our first real drug test, Brian Knobbs was told that he'd tested positive for something.

"All right," the gregarious Knobbs, a notorious party animal, said—probably surprised his urine hadn't melted the sample cup. "What did you get me for?"

Anabolic steroids, he was told.

"Steroids!" Knobbs yelled, ripping off his shirt, revealing a physique most jellyfish would be ashamed of. "Does it look like I'm on steroids?"

"Obviously, there's been a mistake," the lab guy said.

I heard of an older, somewhat bitter wrestler bragging that he had once put a steroid tablet in a younger wrestler's coffee, causing that wrestler to fail a test many years ago.

And I think you have to question any test that interprets the dreaded poppy seed bagel as a banned narcotic. Don't laugh—I have a good friend (not a wrestler) who failed a drug test for that very reason.

Some wrestlers have tested positive for things they didn't even know they'd taken.

I don't want to diminish the hard work that wrestlers, or other athletes, or even actors and rappers put into their bodies. I know so many guys who work out hard and intelligently, watch everything they eat, and really treat their bodies as their temples. Their dedication is incredible. But there is still a limit to what diet and exercise alone are capable of accomplishing. And if someone looks a little too good to be true, my guess is they probably are.

The documentary *Bigger, Stronger, Faster* showed how remarkably little oversight is given to the nutritional supplement industry. According to the film's director, Chris Bell, this seems to be largely a financial decision, as the state of Utah (where a disproportionately high percentage of these supplement companies are based) reaps huge tax revenues from the supplement industry. Bell himself documented how easy it is to create, market, and sell a nutritional supplement, getting it from kitchen table to retailers' shelves with very little trouble.

With so little oversight going into the making and marketing of these nutritional supplements, is it really a surprise that a few of them may contain unlisted substances, some of which might be banned? I had one WWE wrestler swear to me, with tears in his eyes, that he was taking absolutely nothing but supplements when he failed a test, resulting in a suspension at the worst possible time in his career.

He had no reason to lie—this was several months after the suspension, and I had known the guy for over fifteen years. But his career had yet to recover, and in reality it never quite did. All for buying a nutritional supplement he believed to be good for him.

A December 2007 *USA Today* article wrote of a study in which thirteen of fifty-two nutritional supplements purchased at various retailers contained traces of steroids, and six contained traces of stimulants. The article claimed that in another study, conducted by the International Olympic Committee between 2000 and 2002, "18.8% of the 240 supplements purchased in the USA contain steroids." Obviously, this is a matter of serious concern, and with all due respect to the state of Utah, I think a little oversight may be in order.

But of equal concern to me was the article's title, "Steroids Found in Supplements," and what actually does and does not constitute a "steroid." The "steroid" most often found in the *USA Today* study was actually androstenedione (or andro, as it's commonly known), a nutritional supplement that may (or may not) boost testosterone levels slightly. Very slightly.

Classifying andro as a steroid, putting it into the classification of "real" steroids, such as deca-durabolin, anadrol, primobolan, Winstrol V, and sustanon, is kind of like lumping the winner of a kindergarten essay contest into a group of Pulitzer prize–winners and calling them all "winning authors." It's like calling both a balsawood glider and a Boeing 747 "airplanes" because both of them stay in the air for at least a little while. I asked a few people who know about these things, and they literally laughed when I told them that andro was called a steroid.

But unfortunately, it's not a joke. Because it's difficult to discover the truth when those trusted to tell it are either ill-informed or too willing to settle for the convenience of a good sound bite.

I saw an article in a leading sports magazine a few years ago that offered up sobering statistics on the percentage of high school athletes using performance-enhancing substances. Sobering—until finding out that the writer's definition of "performance-enhancing substances" consisted of anabolic steroids and creatine, a supplement that can be found in *any* health food store. This is kind of like defining lawbreakers as "murderers" and "jaywalkers."

Writers so often refer to anti-inflammatory medications as painkillers that it's almost become an accepted part of the vernacular, but anti-inflammatories and painkillers are two markedly different products. One reduces pain by shrinking swelling and inflammation, and the other masks it with a euphoric high. Not exactly the same thing. I try to avoid one of them unless it's absolutely necessary; the other I have trouble walking without. Off the top of my head, I can't think of the last celebrity who has been checked into rehab for an addiction to Mobic.

It seems somewhat ironic that so many of the things that are supposed to be good for us are probably not, while it's quite probable that many things that are banned, or even illegal, have the potential to be very useful.

Over the years, in pursuit of a way to lose weight, or to feel more energized, I have probably taken all kinds of things that weren't actually good for me. Chances are, if a supplement has been marketed as a fat burner or metabolic optimizer, or something of that nature, I've probably given it (or a product closely related to it) a try over the years—all with no noticeable results. Some of the stuff loaded with ephedrine (before it was banned, following a couple of high-profile deaths) was probably downright awful for me, but if it held forth even the slightest potential of "firing up my fat furnace" or something equally dramatic, you could probably count me in.

I thought Kevin Trudeau just might have the answer in his *The Weight Loss Cure They Don't Want You to Know About*. Sure, I'd found some of Trudeau's claims to be a little questionable in the past, and following all his advice would seem to place incredible strain on both one's time and one's finances, but much of what he'd written in previous books made sense. I thought it was quite possible that he may actually have stumbled upon the weight loss cure *they* didn't want us to know about.

Dozens of pages in, Trudeau still hadn't revealed the secret. But he'd made it very clear that he had it, and it worked! Finally, after a seemingly endless array of literary foreplay, I turned the page to discover Trudeau's glorious climactic discovery: human chorionic gonadotropin.

Yes! So all I need is a little bit of that hCG stuff, an extract from the urine of pregnant women, and I'll be cured. Unfortunately, Trudeau then explains that "in America hCG is one of the only pharmaceutical compounds that the FDA has specifically said should not be used in the treatment of obesity!" Despite that fact, Trudeau suggests that "in America you have a constitutional right to do what you feel is best for your own body." So, if I can travel overseas and find a doctor to prescribe it for me or happen to find a doctor here who shares Mr. Trudeau's interpretation of our constitutional rights, human chorionic gonadotropin might still be the cure for me after all!

A few days after reading Trudeau's book, I saw that a raid of the Orlando-based Signature Pharmacy had snagged a handful of WWE wrestlers who were attempting to purchase banned performance-enhancing substances over the Internet. Among those banned substances? Human chorionic gonadotropin, apparently a cure they *really* don't want you to know about. I don't think *they* wanted baseball slugger Manny Ramirez to know about it, either; a positive test for hCG resulted in a fifty-game suspension.

I really wonder what would happen if the cure Trudeau wrote of were to become legal in the United States. The hormone hCG is just a derivative of the urine of pregnant women. How bad could it be for you? Could it be any worse than those proprietary blends of heart-racing stimulants sold in nutritional stores? Could this cure, as the book claimed, really reset the brain's hypothalamus, eliminating the insatiable cravings that have plagued me for as long as I can remember? If it could, there would likely not be as much of a need or desire for those stimulants/supplements—which would prevent a lot of people in the weight-loss industry from making large amounts of money.

Sometimes, I'm not really sure if substances are banned because they are bad for us, or if taking them constitutes "cheating." As politicians have so often told us, cheating is bad . . . unless it's on their wives, on their taxes, or in the form of bribes, hiding cash in a freezer, suppressing voters, miscounting votes, attempting to romance a would-be suitor in a Minneapolis toilet stall, and so forth and so on.

I believe that much of this has to do with the sanctity of the major-league home-run record.

Sure, it seemed odd a few years back when guys who had shown little home-run power in their careers were suddenly hitting forty or more in a single season. Then there was Barry Bonds, who, even before packing on thick slabs of muscle, was one of the greatest players in the game. But this new, massive Bonds made breaking the single-season home-run record look ridiculously easy. I mean, Barry Bonds hit seventy-three homers in 2001, and possibly could have hit a few dozen more if he hadn't been walked 177 times that year, most of them at least semi-intentionally.

Maybe the guy was a cheater. Clearly, he was also something of a jerk: rude to reporters, aloof to his teammates, even a little intimidating to the Hardcore Legend when I met him in the Giants clubhouse a few years ago. As it turned out, Bonds was reportedly rubbing some kind of cream into his body, some kind of new, undetectable performance enhancer that was no doubt the sole reason he was able to see and detect a pitch so quickly, get his wrists around so fast, and drive a ball so far, so often.

Look, I'm pretty sure Barry Bonds is guilty of using some kind of banned substance, even if it may not have been technically banned while he was using it. He may have been using something other than those creams, too. Who really knows? But by some estimates, half the league was on some type of gas. Bonds may indeed have been guilty of using performance-enhancing substances, but he's probably guiltier of being a jerk. If he'd been a heck of a guy, nice to old dogs and children, there's no way the public would have taken such joy in his downfall. I think people wanted Bonds to fail, personally and professionally. And I think just about everyone, if given the chance, would have used that cream. I think I would have, too. A needle? Get that away from me! A cream? Why not? What could be wrong with a little cream? We've got skin cream, pimple cream, suntan cream, moisturizing cream, Mandelay (go ahead, say it a couple times) prolonging cream—performance enhancers, all of them!

It just seems to me that there's this kind of mob mentality surrounding celebrities and scandals, whether they be substance related or otherwise. Just ask Tiger Woods. The whole thing reminds me of poor Boris Karloff in *Frankenstein*, fending off the torch-wielding townsfolk, all of whom seem hell-bent on vengeance. Careers ended, reputations ruined, legacies stained forever. Roger Clemens went from being one of the great pitchers of all time to being some kind of embarrassment to baseball after it was alleged that he attempted to stay at the top of his game by any means necessary.

I think the subject of human growth hormone takes on an added complexity when looked at through the perspective of a pitcher's arm. Anyone who knows basic baseball kinesiology will tell you that the act of throwing a baseball is unnatural and damaging over time. Each throw tears tiny muscle fibers, which then need to be repaired through ice, rest, stretching, or any other means available within the rules of the game. But who makes up the rules? And why should one substance—anti-inflammatories (cortisone, Mobic, etc.)—be permissible, while another and possibly better one—HGH—is not?

When I was a kid, basketball Hall of Famer Bill Walton was castigated for refusing to take shots of cortisone for his knees. Cortisone, a potent, injectable anti-inflammatory, was the drug of choice for getting athletes back in the game when common sense and human pain thresholds should have dictated otherwise. I've only had a handful of cortisone injections in my life, with two of them coming in a three-day period in 2004—an absolute no-no in the medical practice, but a no-no that's undoubtedly done all the time anyway. I didn't even have a choice in the matter; a well-known sports doctor in Los Angeles just stuck a needle in my knee without my consent.

A guy who willingly took a cortisone shot to step onto the field of play was considered a gutsy competitor, a hero, a team player. But a guy who takes a shot of human growth hormone is an embarrassment, a cheater, a fraud. Where exactly is the differentiation, and who decides where that invisible moral line is drawn?

Back in 1994, right before that initial WCW drug test I wrote of earlier, the wrestlers were given a little lecture about the dangers of steroids, before being given the opportunity to ask questions. The hand of a prominent wrestler shot up. "Whatever happened to being the best you can be?" the wrestler asked.

"Excuse me?" the lecturer said, a little thrown by the tone of the wrestler's voice.

"I said, 'Whatever happened to being the best that you could be?' I want to perform as well as I possibly can for the fans, and you're telling me I'm not allowed to do that."

There was kind of a stunned silence at the time, but the message I took from that experience is that most wrestlers (or football players, or actors, or even rappers) don't look at the decision to take performance enhancers as a means of cheating, but as a means of fulfilling their potential, which in many cases can be the difference between struggling on the indies and being a national wrestling star, or between languishing in the minor leagues and making millions in "the show." I'm not agreeing or disagreeing; I'm merely offering up a little food for thought for those members of Congress or the press who think the entire issue comes down to the word *cheater*.

In a January 2010 *USA Today* article, writer Christine Brennan uses the word *cheat* (or a derivative of such—*cheater, cheating*) no less than five times in regard to Mark McGwire's teary-eyed steroid confessional. Ms. Brennan is an award-winning journalist, and I personally enjoy her work, but that whole "cheat, cheating, cheater" thing just seems to be a far too simple and incomplete explanation when examining Big Mac's anabolic admission. The McGwire–Sosa home-run contest in the '90s put interest back into the game and butts back into the seats after baseball's strike-shortened season threatened to greatly diminish the American public's affection for its national pastime, which seemingly created an implied consent, a sort of "don't ask, don't tell" policy for every slugger looking for an advantage in the age of the long ball.

But there have always been cheats, cheating, and cheaters in baseball…and worse. Klan members, gamblers, terrible drunks, and as Zev Chafets wrote in his 2009 book, *Cooperstown Confidential: Heroes, Rogues, and the Inside Story of the Baseball Hall of Fame,* "a convicted drug dealer, a reformed cokehead who narrowly beat a lifetime suspension from baseball, a celebrated sex addict, an Elders of Zion conspiracy nut, a pitcher who wrote a book about how he cheated his way into the hall, a well-known and highly arrested drunk driver and a couple of nasty beanball artists" have been enshrined.

Speaking of home-run records and the steroid era, many will point to the recent testing in major-league baseball and the subsequent decline in home-run numbers as proof that the numbers put up by Barry Bonds, Mark McGwire, Sammy Sosa, and others are questionable. Perhaps this is true, and I'm glad that baseball finally decided to deal with what was obviously a growing problem. But more than one major leaguer has pointed out to me that the dramatic drop in home-run production has far more to do with the banning of amphetamines (often called greenies) from the game than the crackdown on steroids. Without benefit of an occasional greenie, players just can't concentrate for the duration of a long season without taking a day off every now and then. The number of at-bats just isn't there to put up those huge power numbers, with or without the gas.

Should baseball put an asterisk next to the name of every player who set some type of record while performing on amphetamines? I guess they could, but that's an awful lot of asterisks denoting the "greenie era" in major-league baseball.

Look, I want to reiterate that I'm not pro-steroid. Definitely not! But so much of the talk regarding performance-enhancing substances seems to be ill-informed, or illogical, or coming from people who have no idea what it's like to compete for a job that is so highly competitive; a job where the tiniest edge can be the difference between success and failure, wealth and poverty.

A recent episode of HBO's *Real Sports* left me wondering if the U.S. Anti-Doping Agency's stringent testing might not be a bigger problem than the cheating it aims to curtail. I watched the episode open-jawed as it showed top finishers at the Houston marathon immediately corralled after their 26.2-mile run and given a chaperone who would stay with the athlete, always within easy viewing distance, until the first postrace urine could be produced for testing. There was no time to relax, to savor the moment, rejoice at a job well done—just the constant ingesting of liquids (under personal surveillance) until that elusive urine could be coaxed out.

This, apparently, is the price one must pay to compete at the top level in today's "cheat, cheating, cheater" world. A world where the U.S. Anti-Doping Agency requires athletes to inform them of their whereabouts 24 hours a day, 365 days a year. Where athletes must consent to testing on demand, any time, any place. You pee...I see.

When HBO journalist Jon Frankel noted that only 87 of 32,000 tests during the past four years had come back positive, roughly one quarter of one percent (25 percent of those for what HBO noted was the "decidedly non-performance-enhancing drug marijuana"), the USADA noted the testing's "deterrence factor"—one of those completely unprovable theories, kind of like that pro wrestler who performs to an utter symphony of silence and then comes back bragging about how he had the "silent heat" out there.

As I watched, I couldn't shake the feeling that this was Big Brother run amok. The very idea that a desire to compete requires the mandatory relinquishing of the most basic human right to privacy is absurd. We did win the Cold War, right? So why did this HBO program make me feel like I was looking at some repressive midseventies Soviet policy?

I remember those great post–Super Bowl moments where the winning team's most valuable player would be asked the big question as he jogged off the field triumphantly: "You just won the Super Bowl. What are you going to do now?" The answer used to be so easy: "I'm going to Disneyland." What might next year bring? A chaperone? A piss bottle? A cloud of suspicion eventually raining on every parade? That "guilty until proven innocent" forcing down of liquids until that postvictory whiz? Yes! "Now that I've been stripped of my dignity and my rights, I'm going to Disneyland!"

If only we could monitor our politicians with such zeal. But I'm sure they'd pass a law against that.

Look, I know all of this must seem like an awful lot to digest. Basically, these are thoughts I have been gathering in my head for several years, and this book just seemed to be the most likely place to throw them all out in a public forum. I know many will interpret this chapter as being either pro-steroid or anti-testing; in fact, it is neither. I believe that testing has been beneficial in many ways, in wrestling and in other sports, especially in regard to prescription medication, which continues to be the biggest problem the wrestling business faces—as well as a huge problem with society in general. But I am just hesitant to fully embrace a testing system that has so many flaws and that exists in an environment where one is always guilty until proven innocent, and where the court of public opinion is deaf to anything but the blanket apology.

Unfortunately, I am not hopeful when it comes to solving the problems involved in this very complicated issue. Not as long as testing seems to catch largely the less informed and/or less well compensated. Not as long as many journalists either don't know, refuse to learn, or choose to mislead a public that celebrates both the rise and the fall of the athlete. Not as long as congressional members resort to moral grandstanding, unable, I believe, to place themselves in the shoes of a desperately poor prospect from the Dominican Republic, for whom the slightest edge might mean the difference, literally, between rags and riches. Not as long as those caught continue to supply the blanket apology, the "young and foolish" confession (with or without tears) that seems to be part of the mandatory forgiveness process. Not as long as the supplement industry goes largely unscrutinized and so many people make so much money marketing products that don't seem to work. Not as long as a desire to compete at the highest level means reducing our right to privacy and dignity to its lowest level.

No, I think this substance problem is going to be with us for a long time.

COUNTDOWN TO LOCKDOWN:
4 DAYS

April 15, 2009
Long Island, New York
11:42 p.m.

I may not be able to salvage this match, but at least I've got some tights. Yes, after a long search that included three sporting goods stores, a dance supply store, and a Sears, I finally tracked down the classic Cactus tights I'd promised (sans the Cactus lettering) at a Target…in the ladies' section. So if you do happen to see *Lockdown* and like it, you can sleep better at night knowing the Hardcore Legend doesn't need to go into his biggest match in years with any fancy, expensive, custom-made stuff. No, the Hardcore Legend will do just fine in a pair of women's triple-X activity leggings for the grand total of seven dollars.

I saw Lindsay Lohan's face peeking out at me from the checkout counter magazine rack, on a copy of *Us Weekly*, underneath the words "I Am So Alone." Poor kid. Honestly, I mean it. I remember meeting Lindsay when she really *was* just a kid, twelve or thirteen—backstage at an Aaron Carter show. The night A.C. called me out onstage and had me dance in front of seven thousand onlookers (while wearing a hugely oversized purple foam cowboy hat), in what was surely not a comfortable moment for anyone involved.

Months later, I sat next to her for three hours, signing autographs at the Marty Lyons Foundation Christmas party. Lindsay was just tremendous, posing for photos with every kid—a big smile for every child who'd seen her in *The Parent Trap*. And she was so innocent; sneaking in a call to A.C. on her cell phone, asking yours truly for romantic advice. It was very much a "big brother, little sister" vibe. As the years went by and she'd make big movies and bigger problems for herself, I'd feel sad thinking about the little girl with the freckles—knowing that part of her was still there inside a young woman's body. To this day, there's part of me that still thinks I could put a stop to her troubles with a stern talk and a hug.

It sure was a busy day, from my six hours of radio phone interviews to promote *Lockdown*, to my prematch massage with Jessica, to paying my dreaded taxes, to watching my son Hughie cheat his way to another victory in Candy Land. Yes, Hughie cheats at Candy Land. He loads the deck in his favor, picking all the double color cards and all the cool object cards—Queen Frostine, the Green Lollipop—leaving me to do what I can with the Purple Plum and the Candy Cane.

Those taxes stung a little bit. Actually, *stung* might be understating things a little. *Stung* would be like an openhanded Flair chop to the chest. This was more like a brutal, hands-free, "look at me, I'm early-nineties Cactus Jack, too stupid to put up my hands" chair shot to the head. Yeah, that one's going to hurt for a little while. I could have sworn I'd kept up with my quarterly payments. But I don't think I kept up with my book and video game royalties. When my accountant did the math, well, let's just say I was not emotionally prepared for the enormity of the numbers Uncle Sammy required of me.

I spoke with a guy today who might be able to help me with my long-anticipated charity auction to build a secondary school in rural Sierra Leone. I remember seeing all these children walking so far— many of them barefoot—just to continue their education. Many of the children need to stay with relatives along the way, and some drop out to assist their struggling families, most of whom work all day as subsistence farmers, simply to provide the means for staying alive. These farmers need their children to help in the fields, and the many hours children spend making their way to and from school every day is more than most parents can spare.

I did some rudimentary math in my head, trying to figure out how much collective time and energy could be saved if a new secondary school were built closer to some of the more-remote parts of the village. Some of these kids were walking up to fifteen kilometers a day. The results were enlightening. Four or five saved hours per child, multiplied by hundreds of children, multiplied by a few hundred days a year. That's a lot of time and energy. Time and energy better spent helping at home or out in the fields, or finding water, or maybe, just maybe, being a kid.

Right now I'm working on meeting the promise I made to build a primary school in the community. That secondary school seems like a far-off dream. Unless, of course, I can find a solution...like selling almost all of my wrestling career memorabilia and raising one hundred thousand dollars. I'm not sure if a bunch of boxes of tights, shirts, action figures, programs, and knickknacks is going to bring in 100 Gs, but I can certainly try, right? I mean, how many old pairs of boots do

I need to remind myself that I used to be a wrestler? Besides, I have a neat trick I do every morning that reminds me of my wrestling past. It's called getting out of bed. I'll let you know how the auction works out.

I think the guys at TNA felt bad about dangling that beautiful blue cage in front of me for so long before cruelly pulling it away, leaving that crummy mesh one in its place. Sure, it's similar in some respects, but it's just not the same. Like thinking you had a hot date with Christy Canyon, the natural-double-D film icon, and opening the door to see massive mat star Chris Kanyon, of the famed Jersey Triad. Just a few letters off, but oh, what a world of difference. Unless, you know, the lights were way down...and I'd been drinking heavily...and he put on a tape of my favorite D.D.P. matches. By the way, Chris is a friend and won't mind a sophomoric laugh at his expense.*

So they tried to make it up to me. "How about some barbed wire, Mick," they said.

Hmm, barbed wire, that could work. "How much could I have?" I asked.

"How much do you need?"

So, I've got that going for me. Which is nice. Honestly, I was way too busy today to do the slightest bit of thinking about the match. But tomorrow should be easy. I've got a lunch appointment with journalist Rita Cosby in New York City, and then I'll head about two hundred miles north to watch *Impact* with my buddy Tyler, a great kid I met a couple of years ago when *WrestleMania* came to Detroit. Tyler suffers from Duchenne muscular dystrophy, and the past few years have been real rough on him. I'm hoping that hanging out and watching our show will be good for him and his dad. I know it will be good for me.

I got a call from J.B. a few hours ago, wondering how I'd feel about a camera crew hanging out at my house the day after *Lockdown*. By "camera crew" I mean J.B. and Vince Russo. Sure, why not, even

---

*Sadly, Chris Kanyon passed away shortly after the completion of this book. Several of his friends felt that he would have appreciated the mention.

though it means driving three hours back to Long Island instead of crashing in style at the Hyatt, ordering room service, hopefully basking in that postmatch glow of accomplishment. I used to bask in that glow quite a bit back in the day, like almost every month. These days? Not so often. Wow, I think I'd have to go back to *One Night Stand* in 2006 for my most recent basking experience, the night I proved absolutely nothing by proving Vince McMahon wrong.

I asked Colette how she'd feel about a camera being around, capturing our every move. I think there is a part of my wife that never quite got over our reality show's pilot being rejected by A&E, the same people who green-lit *Billy the Exterminator*. So Colette started asking questions: What is the tone? What are we trying to accomplish?

"You know, Colette, it's just J.B. with a camera. Just be yourself, only a little nicer to me than usual."

Still, my wife insisted on possible scenarios, poking and prodding until I finally caved in.

"I've got it," I said. "What if I come back home after the big match just to surprise you?"

"Yeah," my wife said, obviously interested.

"And I find you in the arms of another man."

"You mean like one of the wrestlers?"

With that, my son Dewey managed to pry his eyes away from the Mets game. "Yeah, Dad," he said. "It could be Sabin and Shelley, the Machine Guns!"

"Both of them," Colette said, laughing.

"Yeah, both of them," Dewey confirmed. But he wasn't laughing. He was dead serious. This seemed like a good story line to him.

Call me old-fashioned, but I'm going to put the brakes on that one. An Alex Shelley faux hawk? Okay, what the heck. A birthday card with their likenesses on it? Sure, why not? But wanting both Guns to double-team his mom? Probably just a little more support than the guys really need. But hey, you gotta admire that type of enthusiasm.

COUNTDOWN TO LOCKDOWN:
2 DAYS

April 17, 2009
Clarks Summit, Pennsylvania
1:36 p.m.

I met Tyler Zielinski in Detroit in 2007, after hearing of the unfortunate predicament he found himself in at *WrestleMania* weekend. Let me make it clear that the following story is in no way supposed to be a shot at WWE, which for over twenty years has done an amazing job at fulfilling the wishes of children battling life-threatening conditions.

After leaving WWE, I even called Sue Aitchison, the company's director of community relations, and thanked her for all the great work WWE had allowed me to be part of during my time with the company. And you and I can blast Vince all we want for certain things (i.e., the necrophilia story line, the "Vince is dead" story line, making fun of J.R.'s colon surgery, etc., etc.), but when it comes to supporting the Make-A-Wish Foundation and groups like them, Vince and the WWE sure have made a lot of kids happy.

But, as I wrote earlier, *WrestleMania* is kind of like the Super Bowl—it's a tough ticket. And so many kids out there want to make *'Mania* their wish that requests have to be made months, even a year, in advance.

Well, Tyler wanted *WrestleMania* to be his wish, too, but unfortunately his request had been made too late, prompting a well-meaning member of the TV production team to try to make it happen. And it did. Kind of. Tyler and his dad did get *WrestleMania* tickets. But there was no hotel reservation—no room at the inn, so to speak. No meal vouchers, no Hall of Fame tickets, no "Bagels, Brunch, and Biceps" luncheon.

I heard about his plight from my wonderful little friend Danielle Ruffino, fifteen, who I'd met on Long Island several years ago at a fund-raiser. Danielle, who was also having her wish fulfilled at *'Mania*, told me about a boy she'd seen in tears at the hotel, a weekend he'd hoped would be his greatest having turned into his worst.

I don't want to say I leapt into action, but I did move pretty quickly. I'd met a few of the Detroit Tigers an hour or so earlier—they had stopped by Ford Field to say hello before making their way down the block to Comerica Park for a little batting practice. Their home opener was the next day.

I called Sean Casey, the Tigers first baseman about whom a sportswriter had once written, "There is no argument, there has never been an argument, there will never be an argument. Sean Casey is the nicest player in baseball. Ever." Wow, that's quite an accolade. Maybe I can one day be thought of as the Sean Casey of Wrestling, which might be difficult as long as Bobby Eaton and the Ultimate Warrior are still around. Okay, maybe Warrior's name doesn't belong there.

I explained the deal to Sean Casey, and within an hour I was watching batting practice with Tyler and his dad, also named Shawn, but better known in biker circles as the Medicine Man. A bunch of Tigers came by: Casey, Pudge Rodriguez, Gary Sheffield, Ray Ordonez, Joel Zumaya, even manager Jim Leyland—signing baseballs, talking shop, basically making Tyler feel like he was the most important kid in the world.

Then it was off to Ford Field, where I hoped to introduce Tyler to some of his favorite wrestlers: John Cena, Batista, the Undertaker, Jimmy Wayne Yang. All right, maybe he never specifically mentioned Yang.

There was only one problem: Tyler and the Medicine Man didn't have proper credentials. So we sat in a golf cart for ten minutes, maybe longer, waiting for the proper credentials. It was several hours before bell time, but a few thousand fans had already made their way to the building, milling about, hoping to make the big day last as long as possible. There in that parking lot, sitting in a golf cart, waving to 'Mania fans, I had a sudden recollection of a conversation I'd had several months earlier. I had asked Anne Gordon, of WWE talent relations, a veteran of some twenty years at Titan Towers, if I might be able to arrange a little meet-and-greet for my buddy Justin Tsimbidis, a wonderful little guy that I'd also met at the Marty Lyons Foundation Christmas Party. Justin suffers from progeria, the rare aging disease, so he looks a little different, but he is truly one of my favorite people.

"You know," Anne said, "you're Mick Foley. You can do anything you want around here."

"Really?"

"Yeah, pretty much."

So I've got that going for me, which is nice.

"Go ahead," I told the driver. "I'm not going to wait any longer."

"But what about the passes?" the driver said.

"Sir, I'm Mick Foley and I can do anything I want around here. Let's go."

Go ahead, admit it, that line gave you goose bumps.

So we rode down that long ramp, parking the vehicle right outside the lunch room, setting up shop and catching a photo and an autograph from every Superstar and Diva who passed through. Jimmy Wayne Yang, too.

I was talking to Kane, the most politically well-informed monster wrestler to ever record commercials for Libertarian congressman and former presidential candidate Ron Paul. Kane and I don't agree on everything, but we do have some cool discussions.

WWE Diva Melina came walking up and gladly posed with Tyler for a photo. "Mick, can I ask you an important question?" she said.

"Yes...I am married," I deadpanned.

Tyler and his dad loved it, and even Kane let a little chuckle loose. Melina's face turned bright red. It turned out to be a question about her match.

That's probably going to be it for Melina mentions in this book— unlike *The Hardcore Diaries*, where I appeared to be just slightly smitten with the lovely young Latina.

So was I? You know, smitten? Yeah, probably, but I think it would be easier to list the Divas and Knockouts that I *haven't* been smitten with than the ones I have. It would be a much shorter list. Hold on a minute, lest anyone get the wrong idea about my marriage. Not only is my wife cool enough to tolerate my fleeting schoolboy crushes on Knockouts, Divas, and film stars, but after all these years, she's still the most beautiful woman I've ever met. And as I remind her constantly via text message, she's getting hotter every day.

That time at 'Mania with Tyler and his dad left me with an incredible feeling of accomplishment. With just a little perseverance and several small acts of kindness on the part of the wrestlers and ballplayers, Tyler's worst weekend turned into one of his best.

Unfortunately, there has yet to be a happy ending to the life story of a child suffering from Duchenne's. It's essentially a death sentence, the worst possible news a child or parent can hear. Worse, even, than cancer, where there's always the chance, often a good chance, for remission and victory. As Tyler's dad told me last night, every day he watches his son die.

I was up to see Tyler about a year ago, when his dad told me that things weren't looking good. But he's still hanging in there. Just a few days ago, when I found out I'd be in his general neck of the woods, I gave him a call, asking if he'd like a little company for *Impact*.

He's some tough little guy, a big smile on his face despite his obvious problems. His poor little body is twisted and gnarled, his torso so curved it almost doesn't look real. I don't understand how life can treat a wonderful kid with such cruelty. But he's proud of his new Mohawk haircut. And he loves his wrestling.

"Hey, did you guys put all this stuff up when you heard I was coming?" I ask, noting the sheer volume of Mick Foley memorabilia adorning Tyler's walls. I mean it as a joke, the same weak joke I use when I see anything with my likeness on it in a family's home.

But the Medicine Man is strictly a no-BS guy. "Yeah, we did," he said, laughing. "I told Tyler we'd better take down some John Cena stuff and put Mick Foley up." I appreciate the honesty, but I wonder if it's necessarily the best policy in this particular case. So what if I'm on the wrong side of that confidence/delusion line. I'm happy there.

I enjoy a pizza—just two slices, which is quite an accomplishment for me—and text a few of the wrestlers I know, telling them about Tyler, asking them to send a text to him at my number. Jeff Jarrett and Edge come through. Jay Lethal stiffs me.

Then, it's *Impact* time. I warn Tyler that my promo on the show might be a little scary. He tells me that he thought I was scary when he was little, but that he knows better now. For the next hour, I laugh, listen, tell stories, and drop names of celebrities—George Steinbrenner, Alec Baldwin, Tina Fey, etc., etc.—like my very life depends on it. Then it's time for me. A little visit to Promoland. The room gets very quiet while I watch my most important promo in years.

Nothing but wrestling.

WHEN CACTUS MET MICK

I really didn't know how this thing was going to turn out. "You're going to interview yourself?" a couple guys would ask. "Well, if anyone can make this work, it would be you." Which was kinda sorta encouraging, I guess.

The basic idea had been Russo's, and it struck me immediately as one of the worst ideas he'd ever had. "Bro, you are gonna mess with Sting's head," he'd said. "I mean you're gonna treat this whole thing like it's a joke." Except I had the sneaking suspicion the joke was going to be on me.

I called Russo back a few hours later. "I think I can make this work," I said. "But I'm not going to treat it like it's a joke. I'm going to try to have a serious conversation between Mick and Cactus."

"Bro," Russo began, a little taken aback. "How you gonna do that?"

"Well, I'm going to treat this like it's the first time Cactus and Mick have ever actually met...and Cactus doesn't like Mick a whole lot."

It was kind of true, too. Cactus Jack was the guy who took back body drops on gymnasium floors in front of twenty-six fans in Poca, West Virginia—home of the dreaded Poca Dots. Mick was the guy who said, "Wow, that sounds a little dangerous. You sure you want to try that here? It's only *WrestleMania*."

I might hit this promo out of the park, or I might swing and miss in embarrassing fashion. This was really not the type of promo that could be a ground-ball single through the hole. But at least I'd gotten my wish. This was no "brother, I respect you" way to go home.

And remember—if anyone could make this work, it was me.

Let's take a look.

I am introduced to the crowd and walk down the ramp with a little extra pep in my step, doing my best to accentuate my nerdy qualities— waving, pointing to fans—so as to better juxtapose the darker, more serious Cactus I hope to expose in the next few minutes.

I step into the ring and walk a complete circle, smiling and waving to the fans in the Impact Zone. Apparently, someone forgot to tell me I'm the bad guy here. I sit down in one of the two director's chairs in the ring—another Russo idea. There's a chair for me, and a chair for my guest.

By now, as a reader, I guess you've caught on to the idea that I regularly go from past to present tense when I write about the in-ring stuff. Now, as an added task, try to remember that, for the sake of this chapter, when I refer to "I," I am referring to Mick Foley. Cactus will be "Cactus," even though I'm well aware we're the same guy. Kind of.

"Oh yes, it feels so good to be back in the Impact Zone. Thank you, thank you so much." Basic pandering, a good start. Because Cactus, at least this 2009 version I plan on presenting, would never pander.

"As you guys saw, things got a little crazy in the Impact Zone last week. Foley was *busted* wide open." A little nod to the announcing of an early eighties Vince McMahon. No one ever was simply bleeding. No, in Vince's world, which Gorilla Monsoon also inhabited, they were *busted wide open*.

"Things are going to get even crazier at *Lockdown* on April 19, when Sting and I are locked inside the Six Sides of Steel. So I thought what I'd do in the interim period was kick back, relax, and interview one of the true greats that the world has ever known. For those of you who said it couldn't be done, oh, it's going to be done! Put your hands together. All the way from Truth or Consequences, New Mexico, say hello to Cactus Ja-hackk!"

My heart is pounding. I've always maintained that different is good. But perhaps this is a little too different; like sneaking an AC/DC tune into a Baby Einstein video.

Our fans actually look up at the entrance ramp, as if they expect Cactus Jack, or some facsimile of him, to come strutting to the ring.

"You think this is funny, Mick? You think this is some kind of a joke?" It's me, Mick, sitting in the chair, but the voice is a little deeper, a lot more serious. This, apparently, is Cactus Jack.

Mick finds it kind of amusing. "Huh, huh, I thought that—"

But Cactus cuts Mick off. "Shut your mouth!" The selection of camera shots is great here. Two different close-ups, two entirely different perspectives. As I watch from Tyler's living room, I get the distinct feeling that this could actually work.

"You don't think the people know that we walk with the same legs, breathe with the same lungs, talk with the same mouth?" Cactus asks. "Yet there are distinct differences between the two of us, Mick, because you . . . have no heart . . . no guts . . . and no spine."

The camera is back on Mick. Somehow, the two characters are lit differently. Mick is fully illuminated, while Cactus is bathed in shadows. I don't know how they do it, but I like it.

"Ho ho ho. Hold on there, hot shot," Mick says, stealing a line from Warren Oates's Sergeant Hulka character in *Stripes*. The Oates line is a perennial favorite and is bound to come up any time (sometimes lots of times) Stone Cold and I speak. "You're talking about the guy who lost an ear in a match in Germany and continued to wrestle." Good point, right? Except Cactus isn't buying it.

"No, I'm not talking about that guy!" Cactus yells, as he begins to unbutton the red and black flannel, revealing the classic Cactus "Wanted" T-shirt beneath. "Make no mistake about it, Mick—that guy was me! You? Losing an ear? You'd find solace in the nearest banana split, you gluttonous son of a bitch!" Sure, the 1994 Cactus had once tipped the scales at 317, and the Mick he was deriding fifteen years later was under three bills, but let's continue to suspend disbelief here.

"Wha, wait a second now, just hold on," Mick stammers. But Cactus isn't buying it! Not for a second. Our fans, on the other hand, do seem to be buying it, or at the very least, are considering the possibility of buying it. As I've written earlier, they can be a jaded bunch, having seen just about everything there is to see. But...they haven't seen this.

"I'm calling the shots around here!" Cactus is in full command. Bathed in those effective shadows, he is about to make his best point, by raising a contentious issue. "Why don't you tell me where you were, Mick, on the night of July 22, 2007?"

Actually, I have no idea where I was on July 22, 2007. July 22, 2008, was the date of the Con I wrote about earlier in the book. And the issue I'm raising in the Impact Zone took place in 2006. But such are the perils of winging it. Sometimes the details get fudged, sometimes you mess up a word, lose your train of thought. Still, I'll take a heartfelt promo over a fact-checked, homogenized, memorized, rehearsed one just about any day.

Mick looks around nervously, like the date is a familiar one, and not a happy one. "Well, how am I supposed to remem—"

"You know where you were!" Cactus yells, angry, disgusted with this other guy who shares his body. "You were in San Diego, weren't you, Mick?" Cactus is calmer now, no longer yelling, but he's onto something big here. "Well, why don't I tell you where you were? At the Comic-Con, signing little pre-copies of your book, trying to create a little buzz of excitement for your next sellout. You had dinner at Croce's, your favorite place [true, the only restaurant in the country that I actually plan on eating at], and when you walked out the door, you heard the words 'Thief, stop, thief,' and you looked up and you saw two youths run by [they were carrying a purse], and you know what you did? You did nothing, Mick! You let them run by. You let it transpire, and you didn't lift a finger to help! Why?"

This was a real-life scenario, and I'd asked myself that same question about it many times. Why hadn't I helped? Why had I just let those two youths with the purse run on by?

Mick tries to answer the question and doesn't fare too well. "Well, because there was no way I could get to—"

"Shut your mouth," Cactus yells. Actually, Mick's point had some merit to it; there was no way I would have caught those kids. But Cactus isn't interested in excuses. "The fact is, you didn't even try because you lost the heart, the guts, and the desire a long time ago." Here comes the meat of the promo. I feel like I'm taking my best swing here, and that I've made solid contact. I just need to follow through, see how far that figurative ball goes.

"I am so tired of *you* cashing the checks *this* body wrote. Of *you* writing stories about *my* life. Of *you* living off the reputation *I* forged.

"You want to be the shareholder, Mick, that's fine . . . but keep the little sneakers at home; I'm lacing up the leopard skin." A nice round of applause for the leopard boots, a nice close-up of the Otomix sneakers. "Keep the sweatpants in the closet; I'm opting for a little classic Cactus Jack." A nice round of applause for the riddance of the sweatpants, too. "Because I will not let you have my moment of glory when I vanquish my greatest rival."

Cactus has laid out a pretty solid case. But Mick attempts to raise one more feeble objection. "But don't you think—"

"Shut your mouth!" Cactus punches Mick above the eye, right around the eyebrow. It's not a particularly good punch, even though it's a real one. In truth, if not for the sound of fist meeting bone, I don't think it would have seemed real at all. Then I threw a flurry of them, each of them real, each of them eyebrow shots, each of them designed to "hardway" the eye.

The rapid punches are a tactical mistake. They come in such quick succession that not one of them has the impact it should. Each one should have been followed by a several-second pause, a way to let the viewers digest what was being done on-screen. Instead, that great entrée was just wolfed down, like a Big Mac at a stoplight.

Up until the moment I threw that first punch, I was sure I was going to go under the eye, create a little swelling, irrefutable evidence in the whole fake-versus-real debate. No way to claim the punches weren't real if you actually see the swelling—which, in a best-case scenario, will actually get more pronounced as the promo goes along.

In the end, I let my weakness/fondness for the hardway get to me. Oddly, when it came to *The Hardcore Diaries* my description of a hardway was the only thing Vince objected to. He didn't even care about things that would have seemed far more objectionable from his personal standpoint. But he really didn't want me talking about hardways. "But Vince," I'd said, "books from our other guys talk about cutting up razor blades and using them to get blood in matches. If anything, this adds a little legitimacy."

But Vince was not to be swayed. He wasn't comfortable with the hardway exposé. So we compromised—I called it a hardway but never defined it. So, for the sake of deliberately disobeying Vince McMahon, I will define *hardway* in this book as "the act of deliberately splitting open an eyebrow with hard bare-knuckle punches." I believe it's called a hardway because the "easy way" would presumably be going the razor blade route. Hey, it's kind of tough to deny the existence of the blade in the business when so many guys talk about it so openly, and when Randy "the Ram" practically gave an arts-and-crafts how-to demonstration in *The Wrestler*.

Hardways aren't done too much anymore. They've kind of gone the way of eight-track tapes. Blading is kind of like the phonograph album: almost obsolete, but still played from time to time and talked about reverently by its old-school practitioners.

Anyway, one of those punches must have found its mark, thank goodness, for as Sting's music plays, signaling the obligatory interruption of a wrestling promo (every wrestling promo of the past decade, maybe more, has been interrupted this way—the Latins referred to it as "promus interruptus"), I am deeply relieved to feel the tiniest rivulet of blood charting a solitary course down the cheek.

Sting steps into the ring and walks a small circle around me. I make the decision to stay seated and follow Sting with my eyes, as he begins his final pitch for *Lockdown*.

"Mick, you are turning a twenty-year friendship into an out-of-control three-ring circus. I can't believe what I just saw, but you know the scary thing, Mick? *I* believe that *you* believe what you just did."

I love that line, and I love the way Sting is pacing behind me, allowing the camera to catch both our mannerisms simultaneously. Believe me, I want that hard-earned hardway blood on camera as much as possible.

The Stinger sits down next to me, taking advantage of that extra director's chair. "Have you lost your mind, Mick?" he asks, as I smile intently. I look a little deranged, which is a good thing. A close-up reveals that the blood has already dried; the little gash over my right eyebrow is like a tiny maple tree that has simply given all the sap it can.

"Is this an act, Mick? No, I really believe that you're convinced by what you just did, Mick!" Some idiot keeps yelling out "Sting, you think you're the Joker," but we have to both ignore it, remembering we're playing to a television audience of a couple million in the United States alone, not just the live crowd.

"But I don't want you to think I'm going to be intimidated, Mick," the Stinger continues. "Because steel cage, ladders, tables, chairs, barbed wire, bats...lions and tigers and bears, oh my...it doesn't really matter to me, Mick." I love, just love that lines from a 1939 children's movie are being used to promote pro-wrestling matches over seventy years after its filming. But it's time for me to cut the Stinger off, state my final case, tempt our viewing audience to get excited enough to make a thirty-dollar investment during the worst economic crisis of our generation.

"That's...the Sting...I want to see," I/Cactus says, getting up from the chair, throwing it to the canvas. Cactus starts to pace before stopping just behind Sting to make his point. I'm feeling good about this promo, watching that ball sail into the horizon, pretty sure it's going to clear that metaphorical fence. "That's the Sting I want to see, because you were never...intimidated by me. Even so many years ago, when everyone else had the good sense to run in fear, when J.R. would say things like 'Ron Santo has a family and Cactus Jack doesn't care.' [Actually, I was looking for the name of Larry Santo, the longtime preliminary wrestler with the worst tights in the business, not *Ron* Santo, the great Cubs third baseman from the seventies.] He was right, Sting, I didn't care about human life, but you were never afraid. But there was one time, all those years ago—among all the little Stingers—you know it, Sting, in Philadelphia. The first remnants of a Cactus Jack chant."

Damn! I know that *remnants* was wrong the moment I said it. A remnant isn't associated with beginnings but endings, like a carpet remnant, a leftover. As I wrote earlier, it's no wonder politicians are so scripted these days. A mistake like the one I just made would be cable news fodder for a week if the president had said it. Fortunately, this promo is going so well that it doesn't even matter. This promo is going to clear the wall—the only question is how deep this thing is going to go.

"You may not have been scared, Sting, but it threw you off your game. You may not have been intimidated, but you sure as hell were concerned. So let me ask you a little question, Stinger. What's it going to be like for you when you're trapped inside a steel cage—locked inside—and those chants aren't faint remnants but seven or eight thousand fans, all of them, *all* of them, Stinger, chanting my name! Cactus Jack, Cactus Jack, Cactus Jack."

The Main Event Mafia's music plays, interrupting Sting's

interruption, and I have a moment to think of how many verbal mistakes I've made in the last couple of sentences. I had said *remnants* again, even though I knew it was wrong, just because it was already out there, and for the life of me, I can't think of a more appropriate correct word. Maybe I should have packed a mini-thesaurus with me. Also, I'd said *seven or eight thousand*, which is likely to be an exaggeration, instead of saying *thousands*, which nobody would dispute. Plus, if this were anyplace other than the Impact Zone, home of the jaded, a "Cactus Jack" chant would have been a cinch. But it's tough to induce an interactive baby in that place, no matter how much figurative Pitocin you crank up.

Sting turns to greet his MEM cohorts, but they never do make it. Instead, I blast the Stinger from behind, knocking him down, before proceeding to rain down a few quality forearms to his head as he struggles to get up. I'm very pleased with what I'm seeing. The forearms look good. That tired old man decided not to show up at the Impact Zone, after all.

"Don't you get it, Sting?" I yell into the microphone. "There's no Main Event Mafia coming to help!" I blast him with a couple of decent boots to the head. Decent, not great. Technically, they're not *boots* to the head, either, but Otomix athletic shoes. But they will be boots in Philadelphia, leopard-skin boots.

"I can hit anybody's music I want, Sting, because I—I—I—" I drop to my knees to deliver a cool-looking forearm and conclude my sentence while I'm down there. "I run this place!" I've also managed to get a little verbal jab in at Jeff Jarrett for future reference.

"Go ahead, play me a little...Curry Man!" The recently departed Curry's music plays, complete with entrance, video, and lighting. Nice. Very, very nice! I drop a nice elbow, personally painful from the Stinger's perspective, and yell "Spicy!" I'm really in the zone now, enjoying this thing.

"Give me some Shark Boy," I say, and the familiar refrain of "Give me a shell yeah" rocks the Zone (the Impact Zone, not the mental zone I just made reference to). What the hell, why not one last sneaker to the head of the fallen Stinger? *Bam*, there it is.

"Last but not least, cue up a little Sting," I say. As the lights flash and the music plays, I step outside the ring, reach under the ring apron, and produce my weapon of choice—the barbed-wire-wrapped baseball bat. Without the benefit of that special cage to work with, I'm going to need this bad boy in Philly. Really really need it.

Man, Sting is still trying to get up. I remember being a little frustrated at the time, wondering if the Stinger had morphed into Michael Myers or Jason Voorhees behind that paint. But as I watch it, I'm thankful for his resilience, for it not only keeps him from looking like a dead fish, but it allows me to get in some fairly formidable stuff while working the microphone. It looks very effective.

"Don't you get it, Sting?" I reiterate, looking down on him, the bat in close proximity to his face. "I run this place and I can do any damn thing I *want*. And at *Lockdown*, I *want* to tear you apart."

I raise the bat in the air and watch that metaphoric ball land way, way up in the upper deck. I mean I really crushed this promo. If I hadn't made a couple of those little mistakes—*remnants, seven or eight thousand*, stumbled on *banana split* a little—it might have gone clean out of the stadium.

The other wrestlers actually cheered me when I came through the curtain. Actually cheered a promo. Some of them even stood. I'm talking about seasoned stars like Booker. A standing O for a promo. It happens all the time for matches. But promos? Not that I can recall.

Sting told me it was the best promo he'd ever heard. High praise indeed, given some of the guys he's been out there with and how long he's been around.

I might stink up Philadelphia, but for tonight at least, I'm the King of Orlando. Or at least the backstage area of a sound studio that is part of a huge amusement park complex that is located in Orlando. Yes, if that couple-hundred-square-foot area was a country, then for one night, at least, I'd be its ruler.

COUNTDOWN TO *LOCKDOWN*: 1 DAY

April 18, 2009
Clarks Summit, Pennsylvania
1:15 a.m.

Just one day. Hard to believe. Just one day until *Lockdown,* and I have no idea what to expect—from the fans, from the match, from Sting, from myself. I'm fairly sure that I can pull off a pretty good match, although for a match of this magnitude I'd feel more comfortable without those words *fairly* and *pretty.* Let's try it again. I'm sure I can pull off a good match. Yes, that's better. Much more confident. Except it's not true. I'm not *sure*. I'm *fairly* sure. About pulling off a *pretty* good match.

But all that driving has been good for me. Driving and listening. I think those tunes I picked are really making a difference, allowing me to *see* the new picture, *think* it, eventually *be* it. And you know what picture I saw more clearly than any other? Margaret Hamilton, the *Wizard of Oz*'s Wicked Witch of the West, taunting Dorothy and her pals with the flaming broom. "How about a little fire, Scarecrow?" the witch cackles, moments before meeting her own doom at the hands of Dorothy and that cursed bucket of water.

An aversion to water? Seems kind of silly. *Soap* and water? That I can understand.

Maybe all this seems kind of pointless—loading up the minivan when a new rental would have been paid for, picking out so many road-tested tunes—unless you substitute Cactus Jack for the witch and a barbed-wire bat for the broom.

That's the picture I kept *seeing*. Kept *thinking*. The picture I hope to *be* tomorrow night at *Lockdown*. I've even got a way to introduce the bat into the match that is likely to be well received. Go ahead and read my lips when you watch this match back and look for "How about a little fire, Scarecrow?"

I really think I can build a match around that one image. Provided, you know, that I can swallow and that my legs will hold me upright.

But I had a pleasant little surprise when I weighed in yesterday at the hotel fitness room: 292 with clothes. It seemed kind of impossible. I lost twenty pounds? In just three weeks? The maintenance guy peeked his head in to say hello, and I inquired as to the scale's accuracy. Within a pound or two, he said. But how was this dramatic weight loss possible? Sure, I'd been eating good and exercising moderately (probably too moderately, but I guess we'll find out tomorrow), but not enough to account for the loss of twenty big ones. I guess I could find another scale and get a second opinion. Nah, far better to convince myself that I'm lighter. If I think I'm lighter, I'll move like I'm lighter.

Maybe after the match I'll weigh in again, get that second opinion. Maybe I'll look for feedback, too. About my promo, about my match. Until then, I will consider reality my sworn enemy.

Maybe I pooped it out. Maybe there really was twenty pounds of fecal matter clinging to my intestinal wall.

Speaking of the Wicked Witch of the West, I vividly recall a conversation I had with Al Snow several years ago. It remains vivid, perhaps because it was the sole instance of Al making meaningful, memorable points during conversation.

"Who was the heel in *The Wizard of Oz?*" Al asked.

"The Wicked Witch of the West." Duh!

"No, she wasn't," Al said.

"Yes she was."

"Why was she the heel?" Al asked.

"Because she was trying to kill Dorothy." Another simple, declarative answer.

"No she wasn't."

"Yes she was."

"No," Al said, correcting me. "Dorothy was trying to kill her."

"Oh yeah," I said, stunned, realizing I was losing a battle of wits with Al Snow.

"But the witch kept trying to get the ruby slippers," I reminded Al.

"And why did she want them?" Al said.

"Um, because they were, um, her sister's?" Still losing that battle, only now it's a massacre.

"Who do you think the owner of the slippers would want them to go to when she died? Her sister? Or the person who killed her?"

"So what are you saying, Al, that Dorothy is the heel?"

"The Wizard."

"The Wizard?"

"Yes, Mick, the Wizard. For bribing an innocent pawn into carrying out an assassination of a political rival."

"Wow."

Al had been reading *Wicked: The Life and Times of the Wicked Witch of the West*, by Gregory Maguire, later turned into a smash Broadway musical. I took Colette and my two older kids to see it, and I was blown away: by the story, the music, the scenery, and especially by the Wicked Witch, as played by Eden Espinosa.

I even dragged former ECW ring announcer Stephen DeAngelis with me to see Eden do her one-man (or one-woman, in this case) show at a small club in New York last week. She was at Joe's Pub in front of 150, instead of the majestic Gershwin theater in front of three thousand. And guess what? No one felt sorry for her. No one felt like her career had nose-dived, that she'd fallen from grace since leaving the cast. I think we all felt fortunate to see such a wonderful performer, to hear that wonderful voice in such an intimate surrounding.

Say what you will about this book, but you'll have to admit—it's probably the only wrestling book out there to mention Eden Espinosa. Plus, of all the wrestling books you've read, I bet this is the most recent. Yes, I do realize that's the second time I've used that joke in the same book. And maybe not the last.

My friend Gretchen is the manager of a hotel in Clarks Summit, and she was able to get me a good rate, which is important, even though TNA will be picking up the tab. I just hate wasting money. Back in my novel-writing days, I was on a thirty-city book tour to promote *Tietam Brown*. By about the fifth or sixth city, it was pretty obvious that the book wasn't going to be a big seller, meaning I just had to accept that I had a couple dozen cities to visit for free (as book tours are promotional, unpaid appearances). But some of the perks were free travel, free beautiful hotels, and free food.

A few weeks into the tour, I received a call from my publicist at Knopf, wondering if I was okay, making sure I was eating.

"I'm fine," I said.

"Then why aren't we getting billed for any food charges?"

"Well, you know, I bring some protein bars, or get a little fast food, or go to grocery stores. That hotel food just seems too expensive."

My publicist laughed. "But we pay for everything."

"I know," I said. "But no matter who's paying for it, I will not order fifty-dollar scrambled eggs."

I didn't. I won't. I never will.

I've known Gretchen since I was nineteen, when I was a sophomore in college. I think she was the first actual feminist I really knew. I remember my mom reading some of those feminist books when I was growing up—*Our Bodies, Ourselves, The Feminine Mystique* by Betty Friedan—but my mom was a ravenous reader with two master's degrees she got just for the fun of it. She read everything. I don't know if she necessarily agreed with it all. Although I do remember her cutting a scathing promo on a guest in our home who suggested that "we might all be a lot better off if Martin Luther King Jr. hadn't poked around in everyone's business." But I don't really remember feminism being a major issue in our house.

It definitely was Gretchen's issue, along with organic food and all that talk about the atmosphere, pollution, and oil addiction that didn't seem all that important back then. I found her fascinating, though, which is probably why we're still friends twenty-five years later. Yesterday, we laughed about our mutual friend Melanie, who was a serial boob flasher, whipping out those April Buchanons at the slightest provocation. Or without any provocation at all.

I shared a class with Gretchen, "Literature in Theatre." Now that I think of it, Melanie, the unprovoked flasher, was in that class as well. One day after class, Gretchen mentioned that she was way behind on her daily journal for her class in "Feminist Social Thought" and worried that her missing journals might hurt her grade. "Hey, Mick," she said. "Want to help me?"

Would I, she wondered, be able to write a couple journals for her?

I would only need to think like a woman and write like a woman on a couple of topics that escape me now, so many years later. But I remember tearing into those journals, using the right hand that would later pen so many towering best sellers to chart a course into the modern-day feminine mind. Proud of myself, proud of my work, I handed in my finished journals.

Gretchen thought they were awful. "Mick, you've got it all wrong," she said. "How could you possibly think that way?"

I rebutted her quickly, eager to defend my newfound feminist positions. "Look, Gretchen, it's just that as a woman, I think—" I stopped and thought about the words that had just crossed my mouth, taking my time before saying anything else. Then decided I'd probably said too much already.

There you go—the Hardcore Legend as a woman. Kind of a scary thought. That's probably enough of getting in touch with my feminine side. Because tomorrow's match is going to require all the testosterone I can muster. My kids get to see my gentle side all the time. Mickey's nickname for me is Snuggly, a name he uses at least a hundred times a day. But something tells me the fans in Philly aren't going to be interested in my snuggling abilities when I'm locked inside the Six Sides of Steel tomorrow night. I think it's time that I got reacquainted with my masculine side.

Or, as masculine as I can be while wearing a pair of women's triple-X leggings.

COUNTDOWN TO LOCKDOWN: 18 HOURS

April 19, 2009
Philadelphia, Pennsylvania
2:20 a.m.

I couldn't wait to get back to my hotel room to let all of you know just how stupid I am. What was I thinking? Between the early morning drive from Clarks Summit to Philadelphia for Fanfest, to the drive to Honesdale, Pennsylvania, and back to referee a match for Northeast Championship Wrestling, I was behind the wheel for eleven hours today. Eleven! The day before my biggest match in years? Stupid. Just plain stupid.

I should have just cleared my whole weekend. That's what Sting did. I'm sure the Elmira house show would have done just fine without me. I should have canceled the show in Honesdale two months ago, the moment I heard that I might be wrestling at *Lockdown*. I still could have done Fanfest—just come in on Friday night, done my deal for a couple of hours on Saturday, and had a full day off to rest and think about the match.

Sure, I listened to some great tunes and came up with a couple of good ideas for the match, but I think I actually peaked creatively on Friday night, on the way home from Elmira. I was so busy being mad at myself this past night that I never really did get back into that zone. Plus, I was driving for hours on winding back roads, worried about running out of gas, hoping I didn't hit any of the fifty or so deer I saw grazing alongside the road during the course of my drive.

Still, it's hard to claim that any road trip that included hanging out with my buddy Tyler was a mistake to embark on. Even if I should have waited a week, after the *Impact* tapings in Orlando, and headed up for the visit.

Heading into *Lockdown*, there are still quite a few question marks hanging over my head. My mouth has gone dry several times over the last few days, without any assistance from a fog machine. My conditioning is suspect, stemming from erring way too much on the side of caution in regard to my back injury. I sincerely hope I don't turn into a breathless, weak-legged, quivering mess out there tonight, but I think it's a distinct possibility. And last night I got my first little waves of anxiety about the match.

I still think we can pull this match off, but I am more aware of the prospects of failure than I was just a night ago. I'm hoping to see the picture, but unfortunately, my clearest visualization right now is of the pint of Ben & Jerry's Chunky Monkey I'm going to reward myself with when we fly into Orlando on Monday.

My little guys are excited about J.B. coming over to film us after the show. Mickey loves Jeremy, or "Germy" as he pronounces it, because it was J.B. who filmed Mickey farting "Take Me Out to the Ball Game" under his arm for TNA's webcast of *The Spin Cycle*. Colette will be going to bed with her makeup on so she can be ready to go in the early morning. And I think Dewey is still hoping that the Guns will show up.

Look, I better get some sleep so I don't stink up the place tomorrow.

Let me just repeat these words before hitting the sack:

1. See the picture.
2. Think the picture.
3. Be the picture.
4. Don't be afraid to make mistakes.

and most important of all:

5. How about a little fire, Scarecrow?

LOCKDOWN

April 19, 2009
Liacouras Center
Philadelphia, Pennsylvania

Thank goodness I fit. Without the benefit of the blue steel cage, specifically tailored to suit my strengths, I was already at a distinct disadvantage. Even at my physical peak, I was a lousy natural athlete. At a height of six foot four (maybe a half-inch less these days, due to the twin miracles of disc compression and gravity), I had only once touched the rim of an official basketball hoop. And I'm not even sure that was a *touch* as much as it was a *graze*. My biceps, while never quite as pathetic as the Fonz's in late-seventies bench-pressing mode, were never much to brag about—and they were my most impressive body part.

If only I'd had that blue cage with the platform to walk across, to exchange punches on, to drop an elbow off of. Things might feel different. I'm going to have to follow some mighty athletic match offerings with my half a thimbleful of athletic ability. At least I have that "how about a little fire, Scarecrow," thing going for me—provided I can fit through the little hole in the mesh that one of the cameramen shoots through. Really, it was quite an innovation on TNA's part—a way to bring an unobstructed view into the wrestling fan's living room without putting a cameraman in the ring itself.

I get to the arena about an hour late, due to a rookie GPS mistake that took me through some pretty rough neighborhoods in Philadelphia, and head straight to the cage. Can I? Can I? Yes, I slip right through. Good thing I'd done that organic cleanse. Next, I approach Dirk, our venerable handheld cameraman, and ask him a question that must have seemed new, exciting, and a little bit crazy. "How do you feel about me drop-kicking you?"

Dirk looks at me in horror.

"I'm pretty sure I can do it without hurting you," I say, although even as I say it, I'm aware of the sheer dishonesty of my words.

"Okay," Dirk says, and after figuring a way he can land without breaking either himself or the camera, I've got my big spot—my Margaret Hamilton spot. I might be able to piece this thing together after all. If only I knew how to start the match. I literally have one idea, courtesy of Burt Reynolds in the original *Longest Yard*, a classic that, with all apologies to Kevin Nash, Stone Cold, Goldberg, and the Great Khali, wasn't really crying out to be remade. After whipping a close-range spiral directly into the general area of all-pro linebacker Ray Nitschke's balls, Reynolds huddles his teammates and says, "Worked once, should work again."

That's kind of how I feel about those hardway punches on *Impact*. That promo, including the punches, had created a minor buzz, and, at a complete loss for ideas on how best to begin, I wonder if Reynolds's words of wisdom will hold true if applied to pro wrestling as it pertains to hardway punches.

Out of respect for my opponent, I run the idea by the Stinger first. Sting laughs and throws up his hands. "You want to start the match by punching yourself in the face, Mick? Go ahead." Suddenly, I see some light at the end of the tunnel. We might, just might, be okay.

But what if I can't reopen that eye? What if I throw a bunch of punches and there's not a drop of blood? If *Impact* wasn't taped so far in advance I might take that chance. Two or three days after the fact, I'd be pretty sure I could bust that bad boy open. But twelve days out? Not too good a chance. So, I take the easy way out and, looking in the mirror, like a teenage girl applying eyeliner before a first date, gingerly trace over the twelve-day-old scar with a tiny remnant of a razor blade. Yes, I knew I could use that word—*remnant*—correctly in a sentence! The cut bleeds just a little, requiring a few seconds of pressure before drying up. I slap a little tape on that eyebrow, and as Randy "the Ram" said in *The Wrestler*, "Brother, I'm good to go."

Well, not quite. I've still got an hour or so to get ready, stretch my legs, soothe my nerves, try to get to that emotional zone I was in during that Mick Foley–Cactus Jack interview. Those punches to my eye will actually be of great service to me; as in each of my recent comeback matches, I've needed to absorb some kind of big move to remind me of the person I used to be. Yes, I do believe these punches will work out nicely.

I spend a little while talking with Sting, going over a couple of key moves and possibilities, but largely establishing a theme, or story line, for the match—taking our advanced age and combined collection of ring injuries into consideration. I thank him for the match ahead of time and take the opportunity to once again tell him how much our matches in '91 and '92 meant to my career. Really, who knows where I would have ended up without him? Maybe things would have worked out just fine. But I think there's a pretty good chance that without those marquee matches with WCW's top star, I would have been back on the independent scene within months, toiling in obscurity within a year or two, waiting for a phone call that would have likely never come.

I had just finished rubbing Vicks VapoRub on my chest and in my nostrils (don't worry, I washed my hands) when panic strikes. Where's my piece-of-crap yellow Sony Discman? The one I inherited from my children when they steadfastly refused to listen to something so embarrassing and antiquated. Apparently it's hard to be a cool teenager without the latest in gadgetry, which doesn't include the yellow CD player. Maybe it was an embarrassment to them, but that Discman was my lifeline to Tori Amos, who I was counting on to guide me through this thing—to conjure up some of that "Winter" magic that had been so invaluable to my prematch visualizations against Randy Orton in 2004 and Edge in 2006.

I'll listen to it in the car, I think. I am literally on my way to the Chevy Venture (the Sony Discman of motor vehicles), keys in hand, when I stop and think of a specific line in "Winter":

I hear a voice, you must learn to stand up for yourself, cause I can't always be around.

Was I crazy, or was Tori Amos talking to me through her lyrics, telling me I was going to have to go this one alone? I was certain of it. Almost as certain of it as I was certain that my "Meeting Tori Amos" chapter would be ruined if I listened to "Winter," then went out and stunk up the place. You have to understand—I love that chapter. Along with a chapter about God and Santa Claus from *The Hardcore Diaries*, it's my personal favorite among all the things I've ever written. Besides, "Winter" was there for me in cases where I faced the near certainty of injury. I'm not sure if it's fair to expect any song, even my favorite one, to provide the antidote for being old and out of shape. I put the keys away.

Ten minutes before bell time and I'm nervous as hell. I have no idea how long my legs are going to hang in there. The possibility of dry mouth is a legitimate concern. At least I'll be able to punch myself in the face soon. I have that much going for me.

Time to take that walk to the table behind the curtain. The place where the show is timed, where wrestlers take their cues, and where, for some reason, a huge bowl of candy is omnipresent. In WWE, it was called the Gorilla Position in honor of longtime wrestler/broadcaster Gorilla Monsoon, who had gone from monosyllabic Manchurian brawler to expert in human anatomy, regularly referring to the "external octuberal protuberance," also known as the back of the head. We don't really have a name for it in TNA. Maybe "Bob Ryder's Happy Place" would work.

I jog in place, do a couple hindu squats with terrible form, and slap myself a couple times while my prematch interview plays. Thankfully I'd utilized my role as executive shareholder to pretty much make rules and plant seeds that will help me tell the story I want inside the ring. The match can be won by pinfall, submission, or escaping the cage. But a cage match should never be won by walking out a door. Nope, if I'm going to escape, I'm going to do it by climbing over the top. Although I am carrying the trusty barbed-wire bat in both my interview and my entrance, I make it clear to J.B., the interviewer, and the audience that I don't actually *need* the bat to vanquish the Stinger. Got it? Good. Let's get to the action.

It's a good reaction for both of us, and a definite big-match feel as Sting and I look at each other, sizing each other up, listening to the crowd as they begin dueling chants. "Let's go, Sting! Let's go, Cactus!" I'm so glad I took the chance and went out on a limb with my character. The build has been so much fun and has been so personally satisfying. It's hard to criticize Vince McMahon's track record, but damn, that period of time detailed in *The Hardcore Diaries* was one of the most frustrating periods of my career—like every ounce of joy had been wrung out of life's hand towel. This period of time has been like a polar opposite. Life's hand towel was positively full of joy. "Life's hand towel"? Pretty weak.

But now I have to produce. A happy ending to this story is just fifteen minutes away. But in order to write that happy ending I'm going to have to make it happen first. Terry Funk once told me that every match is a great one until it actually begins. So I bide my time, enjoying the greatness of the match, worried that I will put an end to the greatness as soon as I make my first move. The first move, after all, is mine to make.

Bam! There it is. A good shot to the eyebrow followed by a few more. I'm not sure if the fans know the legitimacy of the punches, but I sure do. As I land more—four, five, six—I actually start to feel a little light-headed. Seven, eight, nine—yes, there it is, the telltale warmth of my own blood. It's an oddly comforting feeling, not just in this match, but in many over the years. Hey, if you're going to have slight psychological issues, you might as well be in a line of work that welcomes them. I throw the tenth punch, then suddenly turn and level the Stinger with a big clothesline.

I believe this opening spot has worked well, not so much for the fans but for me personally. It does indeed remind me of the man I used to be, and the blood, flowing fairly freely, is a strange motivator/ security blanket.

Wow, it's really coming down now, I think to myself, a marked contrast to that little trickle of blood I got on *Impact*. A closer examination after the fact would help solve the mystery. I had pretty much missed my tiny sliver over the eyebrow completely and had opened up an entirely new one. After the match, I would require twenty-five stitches (which I would refer to repeatedly over the next few days) to close the wounds of this particular brand of warfare. Nine or ten came from this barrage of self-directed haymakers. The fifteen or sixteen others? We'll get to them soon enough.

Those nine or ten big ones are a small price to pay for getting me back into the zone. I start to *feel* like Cactus Jack again, and the sub-sequent two boots (leopard skin, of course) I lay in on the head of the Stinger are crisp and convincing.

I try to seize the moment by attempting an early escape. But as I get to the second turnbuckle, Sting climbs to meet me and sends me back first to the canvas with a series of patented backhands. *Bam!* The fall kind of surprises me and really rings my bell. The bump looks wicked on camera but is another legitimate cause for concern, as once again I haven't tucked my chin properly, and once again my skull pays the price. Statistically speaking, not a lot of men my age are taking this type of a pounding.

Now it's Sting's turn to dole out a little punishment. He puts a couple of boots to my midsection, followed by a rake of my face into the mesh. It's pretty standard stuff, but it's well done—and even better, I'm animated, really selling the blows. I don't feel or look tired, and even though the match is still in its infancy, I feel like I'm in control of my surroundings—a far cry from that brief match just six weeks ago where I felt so helpless and naked.

I return fire for a moment, some more basic offense, stopping the Stinger long enough to make my second escape attempt of the evening. Once again I'm stopped, and once again I'm propelled backward off the second rope, this time courtesy of a back suplex. It jars me, but not as badly as the same move administered by the Dynamite Kid twenty-three years earlier, in only the second match of my career. I had heard that one of the guys had already done the move in an earlier match but I took it anyway, thinking that we'd somehow make it mean more by better displaying the physical consequences of the move.

At the time of this match, wrestling fans were rightfully still gush-ing about the Shawn Michaels–Undertaker match at *WrestleMania*. Like I said earlier, it was a great match, an all-time '*Mania* classic. But part of what made it so great was the ability of both guys to make every big move count. So many guys are in such a big rush to get in their big moves that they diminish each move's effectiveness, thereby eliminating the drama of the match. Michaels and Undertaker were all about the drama at 'Mania. I thought Sting and I were capable of creating some of our own at *Lockdown*.

Wait, wait, wait, don't get all up in a tizzy. Don't go thinking that I thought we could top what they did at 'Mania. I was almost sure that we couldn't. Because part of what made that match so great was the prevalence of each man's finishing moves. Those moves that all fans *know*, just *know*, spell the end of a match. I mean, *no one* kicks out of a Tombstone piledriver. I know I never did. *No one* kicks out of Sweet Chin Music. Then, when someone does, in this 'Mania case, repeatedly—and when it's done well (which it most certainly was), it can make for an incredible viewing experience.

I'm at a distinct disadvantage here. You see, I don't actually have a finishing move. Not one that works. Not one that has yielded victories, at least not in this decade. Look, I'm thrilled that WWE and later TNA have done such a good job of portraying me as a legend. In my eyes, they both have allowed fans to view me as a bigger deal than I actually was. But the truth is, a whole generation of fans have most likely never seen me win a match. So it's incredibly tough to produce drama on the level of Michaels-Undertaker when not a single move in my arsenal is likely to produce that Pavlovian response. Sure, the sock is fun, and it's a cheap, easy prop, but it hasn't done much this decade. And the decade's almost up.

I'm still a good storyteller, though, and unlike Michaels or Undertaker, I'm going to be channeling Margaret Hamilton.

Sting goes for the cover, but I kick out on one, and in a matter of moments I am back on the offensive, dishing out a little more solid if unspectacular punishment. I know my stuff is limited, but at least it looks good. Nat King Cole's voice only reached a couple octaves, but he entertained millions by working within his limitations. There you go—kind of hard to refute that kind of evidence.

I attempt to escape once again, and this is where things very nearly take a real-life serious turn for the worse for me. I'm once again at the second turnbuckle when Sting cuts me off—this time with a Stinger Splash to the backs of my knees. This is a new twist on a patented move, and it's a creative cutoff spot. But as I fall, my toes become wedged into a hole in the mesh, and my body falls, leaving my ankle and knee torqued at hideous angles. I feel the strain on my ACL (anterior cruciate ligament) and it feels like it's about to pop. I literally scream for help, but both Sting and referee Earl Hebner, along with all of the wrestlers backstage, think it's just ol' Cactus reaching into his deep bag of tricks. "Wow, how'd he do that?" Boy, are they giving me too much credit.

Finally, Sting realizes that an opponent screaming "Stinger, please help me!" just might be in big trouble, and he and Hebner simultaneously free me from this modified tree of woe.

From this point on, I am really proud of myself. Readers of *The Hardcore Diaries* might remember that I was extremely disappointed in myself following my match with Ric Flair at *SummerSlam 2006*, because I felt like I'd taken the easy way out by passing a couple of important steps in our match as soon as I got a time cue from the referee.

Three years later, I get my time cue from Earl Hebner. Ten minutes until *Lockdown* goes off the air. My knee is hurt, I'm getting tired, and I'm pressed for time. It could have been so easy to start cutting corners, to take the easy way out and start heading home early. No one would have thought less of me. Except me. I still have a lot of things I want to do—and I want to do them well. I'm sticking it out.

Sting and I go back and forth for the next few minutes. I'm doing a good job of selling that knee, and announcers Mike Tenay and Don West are picking up on it well. It's going to be tough for me to climb. A couple of pin attempts don't bear any fruit, and Cactus Jack is starting to worry. The poor guy is running out of options. He can barely climb, so escaping over the top is unlikely. He apparently can't pin the Stinger, not even after a double arm DDT, which ten years earlier had been my move of choice when vanquishing Stone Cold for my prestigious second run as WWE Champion—a reign that would last for less than a day.

I clearly reach into my front flannel pocket and pull out what appears to be some small object. What could it be? What nefarious act do I hope to accomplish? I place the object in my mouth. Could it be? Yes it is! It's a Fisherman's Friend menthol cough drop, a trusted partner in my battle against dry mouth. I'm tired but thankfully still in control, even as Hebner urges me to hurry things up.

So, what's a guy to do when things seem to be slipping away on him? Looks like cheating time, brother!

I wish, really wish, that I'd had the presence of mind, the energy, and the time to really work the next move, to really manipulate as much emotion and *history* as I could out of it.

To the best of my knowledge, I have never won a single match by submission...ever. Nonetheless, I'm about to try it here, maneuvering Sting into position for my own sloppy version of a Scorpion death lock. This should have worked on so many levels. Not only was I using Sting's own move against him, but the Scorpion also happened to be Bret Hart's key move—known in "Hitman" circles as "the Sharpshooter." This had been the move involved in the most infamous match of all time; the 1997 "Montreal Screwjob"—where Bret Hart had lost his world title to Shawn Michaels. Shawn applied a Sharpshooter of his own, and referee Earl Hebner instantly called for the bell—then ran for a waiting limo, having cost Hart his title on a phantom submission.

My version of the Scorpion/Sharpshooter gets an immediate wave of recognition from the Philadelphia fans. Philly, after all, has been a hotbed of hardcore wrestling fanatics for as long as I can remember, which for me would be 1990, the beginning of my Tri-State Wrestling feud with "Hot Stuff" Eddie Gilbert.

I immediately attempt to abuse my authority by demanding an end to the match from Hebner. "Ring the bell!" I yell. "Ring the bell!"

Hebner is poised, his arm in the air, ready to call this thing at my request.

Unfortunately, we don't do the move long enough for Tenay and West to pick up on the Hebner/Hart intangible, and the exercise ends far less fruitfully than it should have. Damn! We're down to five minutes to go before leaving the air, so I've really got to get moving. Unfortunately, this time constraint and my lack of conditioning are both beginning to hurt the match just a little bit. First, I shortchanged the big submission attempt. Then, I just lacked the wind to throw the full-fledged tantrum the situation called for. Things aren't looking too good for poor Cactus. Pins won't work, he's unable to climb, and now he's been unable to sway the shifty Hebner with his feeble submission attempt and implied threat to his job. Now it's time to change the rules, to go back on my word.

"Open the door, Earl," I say, thankfully loud enough for the viewers to pick up on "Open the door."

"Wait a second," Mike Tenay says. "I thought he said you *couldn't* win this match by stepping through a door."

"He didn't say you *couldn't*, he said you *shouldn't*," Don West helpfully points out.

I shove Hebner to the ground and attempt to persuade Slick Johnson, the chrome-domed referee on the floor, to do my bidding for me. "Open the damn door!" No dice from the Slickster.

Time to ratchet things up a notch. Time and hope are both running low when I make a mad dash for the fence, drop-kicking Dirk the cameraman, doing my best not to damage either Dirk or his camera in the process. If you watch it back in slow-mo, you'll see I catch mostly cage, not the actual Dirkster. The change in atmosphere at the Liacouras Center is palpable, an appreciative but drained crowd is now on its feet, anticipating a special treat from the two ring legends—three, if you count Hebner.

With that pesky cameraman out of my way, I attempt to exit the cage through the camera hole. I'm halfway out when Sting makes the save, like a one-man cavalry riding to the rescue. He drags me back through Dirk's camera hole and immediately hooks on the Scorpion—the much cleaner, more effective version. The crowd is now fully alive, possibly because the Scorpion is a legitimate finishing move—the difference maker in many a Sting match. Unlike me, the Stinger has won many matches during the past decade, many of them with this very move.

A city like Philadelphia is hard to excite with wrestling moves, even big ones, which are not likely to either injure a human being or end a match. They've seen so much wrestling over the years that they've gotten a little complacent; they remind me a little of myself back in the midseventies, when I'd seen *Rocky* over thirty times in the theaters. I mean, I loved Balboa, but I knew from experience not to get too emotionally invested until the middle of the fourteenth round.

Well, welcome to the middle of our fourteenth round. I throw a couple punches at the laceration over the eyebrow, attempting to block the pain of Sting's submission hold with some pain of my own doing. At least that's my theory. I paw for the side of the cage and attempt to climb through once again. But this time I've got another motive besides escape. I see my bat outside the ring, my security blanket, my Rosebud, but alas, it's just beyond my grasp.

I have one last chance. Dirk, the drop-kicked cameraman. "Give me the bat, Dirk, give me the bat!" It's an odd request, given my recent actions toward him, but Dirk responds favorably to my request, handing me the barbed-wire beauty just as Sting pulls me back through the would-be escape hatch.

Sting lets go of his hold, momentarily frustrated, and turns his back to me for just a moment. When he turns around, I've got a little surprise in hand—a little fire for the Scarecrow, if you will. Go ahead, put in the *Lockdown* DVD and read my lips. "How about a little fire, Scarecrow?" I say, waving the bat at the Stinger, toying with him.

I've *seen* this picture, I've *thought* this picture. Now I *am* this picture. I feel a little rush of energy as I see my vision playing itself out live in Philadelphia. Man, I could have used that little energy burst a couple of minutes earlier, when I lacked the wind to throw a tantrum.

I take a few good swings with the bat and miss each time. The onus is on Sting to move or get hit—I'm not a big fan of anything that doesn't look like it's meant to connect. Sting retaliates with a few of those big backhands, knocking me down, and attempts to scale the cage. He makes it to the top rope before I gain my bearings and mow him down with a bat to the back of his knee, followed by a good one to the hamstring.

Two minutes to go. I'm cutting it real close here. I want to do justice to the match, but I certainly don't want to go off the air before the match reaches a conclusion.

I charge the Stinger with the bat, but he thwarts the advance with a drop-toe hold—an old-school move I learned on my first or second day at Dominic DeNucci's wrestling school in western Pennsylvania. The move is not really a big deal, unless the recipient falls on something besides canvas. Like ring steps, a chair, or a barbed-wire bat. Bingo! I land hard on the bat and immediately hold my fingers. It's not a move that will yield any Honjo-like pinkie scars, but nonetheless yields a couple small cuts that will take a week or so to heal.

Sting grabs the bat and prepares to receive the easiest audience pops in the business. Sure, the bat shots to the back and gut induce some pain, but the huge reaction they create, those distinct *oohs* and *aahs*, are so far down on the risk/reward scale as to make the pain almost negligible. Gut shot, gut shot, back shot, back shot. Pop, pop, pop, pop! It doesn't get much easier than that. I mean, it's a move that hurts a little, but it's way down there on the risk/reward flow chart. Lots of reward, almost no risk.

The Stinger is a real pro. Even though we are down to a minute left, he doesn't rush the shots. He lets each one get its reaction, then he prepares for the rudimentary grinding of the bat—that ultra-easy gross-out move where jagged barbs meet forehead and a little grinding ensues. Gross, right? Except I cut the Stinger off, connecting with a kick to the nuts that the camera unfortunately misses.

I guess I'd better hurry. There are all of forty seconds left before *Lockdown* is history. Earl Hebner is practically begging us to take this baby home. But I've got one more move left in me. It's a classic "Foley running knee," in which I don't really connect with my knee at all—but *knee* sounds so much cooler than *flaccid inner thigh*. This knee is a little special, however. I drop the bat down at the last second, so that the bat, not the flaccid Foley thigh, makes contact with the Stinger.

Oohh! Even those heartless bastards in Philadelphia felt that one, and with good reason, as a laceration requiring sixteen stitches opens up immediately . . . over my right eyebrow. What the heck? You see, in all the hundreds of instances where I'd charged in with the knee, I'd never had a steel cage to stop my momentum. Look, here comes a charging Foley. See, there's my head bouncing off a steel bar. Down goes Foley! In go sixteen big ones, sixteen bad boys, sixteen stitcheroonies.

I had hoped to pull off a move so devastating that even a physically exhausted has-been with bad knees like me could have the time needed to mount one last valiant climbing effort. Which would have been perfect if I'd just had a little time to spare. But I'm down to twenty seconds. I might need to forsake the drama of a slow climb in favor of a quick exit.

I think back to 1986—to the words spoken by an eighty-four-year-old woman when she awoke to find me sleeping in my underwear on her couch. "You've got to get out, Mickey, you've got to get out now!" I was supposed to be a guest at the house for the entire summer, but a few weeks into my stay, a heat wave struck the area, and all of that clothing seemed somehow unnecessary.

Heeding those words, I find the fortitude to attempt one last escape and am shocked at how easily I am able to climb the mesh. I had anticipated big trouble and was quite pleased to be proven wrong. Sting shakes off the effects of the running bat to the face and mounts an escape attempt of his own, climbing the cage in the corner to the right of me. I have the head start, but the Stinger is gaining.

I'm reminded of the children's classic *Race to the Outhouse*, by Willy Makeit, illustrations by Betty Dont, which, along with *Tiger's Revenge*, by Claude Bawls, was probably my favorite bedtime story. Not counting the timeless Chinese fable "Spots on the Wall," by Who Flung Poo. I guess it's about time to end this match, and this chapter.

Look, the TNA World Heavyweight Championship (like the WWE Championship I held on three occasions) may not be a "real" title in the truest sense of the word. But holding it is an honor, and anyone who says they're not excited about winning it is either a liar or someone who needs to find a new line of work. I won't lie—I am absolutely thrilled about the prospect, even as I try to figure out how to land in a way that is exciting but not overly dangerous. But Sting is almost at the top of the cage. If I don't find an exciting way to climb down, I'm going to screw this thing up. So I just decide to let go. A moment later, I'm tumbling backward awkwardly, free-falling for what *seems* like minutes, even though the actual impact occurs less than a second later.

The TNA World Heavyweight Championship Belt (I'll call it a belt if I feel like it) is handed to me. I give the belt a kiss . . . and . . . cut, we're off the air. Wow, we finished the match with literally seconds to spare.

I'm tired but I'm happy, relieved, maybe even ecstatic. I know I'll be hurting tomorrow: my knee, my ankle, my eyebrow, my hands, will all pay the price. But backstage I just kind of bathe in the warm glow of a job well done. By both of us. Sting's happy, I'm happy. In a moment of most sincere sappiness, he thanks me, I thank him, there are a few awkward hugs, maybe even an ultramanly "I love you, brother."

The Stinger really wants to know what I think—he really respects my opinion. "You know, Steve [and I rarely call him Steve, even backstage], maybe we could have done a few things differently, but all things considered, I think we did pretty well."

All things considered: my age, my weight, my knees, my back, my thighs, my nerves, my dry mouth, the blue cage that wasn't meant to be, the Sony Discman I'd forgotten to pack. Maybe I'll forever remember *Lockdown* as the night I learned to stand up for myself, because after all, Tori Amos can't always be around.

There is a bigger triumph to be taken from all of this, however. I get to write a happy ending to a story that has been so much fun to tell—in the ring, with the microphone, on these pages. There is really only one proper way to celebrate a personal and professional triumph of this magnitude—drive the four hours back to my house with twenty-seven guests in my Chevy minivan. Twenty-seven? Sure. J.B., Vince, and the twenty-five stitcheroonies! Twenty-five big ones. Twenty-five bad boys.

I concluded my last book by both asking and answering my own question (which I'll paraphrase here): If I had known then what I know now, would I have still gone through with the idea, the buildup, the match? My answer? "Oh hell, no!" For better or worse, *The Hardcore Diaries* documented one of the most frustrating times of my career.

I will always be grateful for the time I spent in WWE, and, in the event I never get the WWE Hall of Fame platform to do so, I would like to thank both Jim Ross, for staking his reputation and possibly his job on his belief in me, and Vince McMahon, for allowing an unlikely tailback to take the WWE ball for a run now and then. Without those two men, it's highly unlikely that so many of the good things in my life would have been possible.

But I honestly felt like my days of making a difference in WWE were over. TNA has given me that chance. My opinion is respected, my contributions are appreciated, and my boss looks like a movie star. And she's never dropped an F-bomb on me.

So, if I knew then what I know now, would I have gone through with this whole *Lockdown* thing? Absolutely—it was one of the best experiences of my career. I wouldn't have tweaked a thing.

AFTERWORD

April 2010
One year later

For several hours a day, my home is filled with the sounds of human suffering. As early as six o'clock some mornings, one can hear the telltale *ohhhhs* and *aaghs* of Hughie and Mickey at play, a mountain of action figures about two hundred wrestlers deep in front of them, five or six different rings (steel cage, Hell in a Cell, Punjabi Prison, official Mick Foley hardcore ring, etc.) at their command, waiting to play host to unrivaled agony. Once in a while, those sounds of suffering will momentarily cease, just long enough for a "Let's take another look at that, J.R.," or a "Right in the family jewels" to supplement that aforementioned collection of *ohhhs* and *aaghs*.

My little guys have turned into big-time wrestling fanatics, just like their brother and sister before them, and the Impact Zone has become something of their own little theme park (a theme park within a theme park) where they even got to bear witness to that inevitable first-ever singles match with their dad and Kurt Angle. Thankfully, I got through it, I survived it, and while it most likely won't be remembered as one of Kurt's classic confrontations, it was far from the embarrassment I'd feared for so long. Mickey even consoled me by farting an emotional, somber version of "Jingle Bells" under his arm following the big contest.

Ordinarily, that would have been it for me for a while as an active wrestler. After all, that's my deal: I do my one big match and go back into wrestling hibernation, emerging every so often from my regular on-air nonwrestling role to talk a big game and attempt to back up about 40 percent of what I've said. But not this time. I lost the TNA championship in June (after a two-month reign as TNA World Champion) in a four-way "King of the Mountain" match, then followed it up with that first-ever singles with Kurt.

The match with Kurt came at a time when I was suffering from a particularly acute case of professional vulnerability. The "King of the Mountain" had been something of a career lowlight for me. It had been a good match, but I'd clearly been the weak link in the contest; appearing only in sporadic bursts, protected from the potentially embarrassing prospect of trying to go toe-to-toe, move for move, with guys (Angle, A. J. Styles, Samoa Joe, Jeff Jarrett) whose league I clearly wasn't in anymore. On three separate occasions, I had that distinct, disturbing feeling of getting my bell rung, but unlike other occasions throughout my career where I could look back and pinpoint the obvious sources of the bell ringing (stiff chair shot, bad landing) on video, none of the three shots that had nearly separated me from my senses seemed to be particularly impactful. I watched the three blows several times over, thinking that the camera angle must have been to blame, thinking "they must not have caught it," before considering the sobering possibility that I simply might no longer be the guy I used to be when it came to absorbing punishment in the ring.

At one point during the "King of the Mountain," Joe launched A.J. high over the top rope to the outside, where I was waiting to absorb the blow to slow A.J.'s momentum; keeping him safe while simultaneously selling the spectacular move. Any good wrestler takes pride in being a dependable "catcher"—it's the only thing that allows the highfliers in the business to perform such high-risk maneuvers on a regular basis without seriously injuring themselves. In my prime, I considered myself to be one of the best catchers around, the type of wrestler that anybody could trust with their riskiest stuff. But on this occasion, my guts and pride just kind of went on hiatus, and in what can only be considered an act of self-preservation, I put my head down and closed my eyes, hoping for the best. Poor A.J. barely grazed me before crashing to the floor. I went down hard as well; despite the fact that I'd failed to look out for the well-being of my opponent, my neck would be sore for several days from my decision to block his momentum with my head.

I apologized profusely to A.J. a few days later, telling him that I was deeply sorry and personally embarrassed to have put his health in jeopardy with such a poor display of professionalism. I may have been guilty over the years of taking risks with my own body, but refusing to look out for the best physical interests of my opponent was an unacceptable affront to everything I thought I stood for in the business. I really wondered after "King of the Mountain" whether I should ever step into the ring again.

Yes, I was feeling pretty down before I locked up with Kurt, pretty sure that I might be participating in the most embarrassing Pay-Per-View main event of all time. But I dodged a bullet that night by not stinking up the place, and I was looking forward to that much-deserved and long-awaited wrestling slumber. But wait, what's this? In a real-life scenario that seemed lifted right from a wrestling story line, Jeff Jarrett's previously clandestine relationship with Kurt Angle's ex-wife, Karen, became public, leading to Jeff's departing TNA for several months. Literally overnight, the carefully constructed Foley/Jarrett power struggle for control of TNA was over, flushed down a figurative Bemis; leaving me with absolutely no story line and Kurt with no upcoming opponent.

In an attempt to kill two birds with one stone (rectify two problems at once, in case that metaphor is a little dated), I become Kurt's opponent for the entire set of *Impact* tapings, and he becomes part of my story line. Essentially, I inherit the matches with Kurt that Jeff was supposed to have, bringing my three-day total of matches with Kurt to three—a series that leaves me exhausted, aching…but oddly thankful. Thankful to Kurt for helping me find my confidence. Despite the fact that Sting and I had pulled off a good match at *Lockdown*, I really thought any semblance of in-ring confidence was a thing of my past. But midway through that second match with Kurt, I was struck simultaneously by two distinct and welcome images: an image of my two younger children no longer booing but wildly applauding me, and an image of myself as a wrestler who no longer either sucked or lived in fear of sucking! I was actually pretty good, really "feeling" the action, selling the blows, doing what came naturally; no longer feeling quite so naked in that lonely wrestling ring.

I'm not under any illusions of grandeur. Unlike past years, I'm no longer sure I have that one really great match left in me. In fact, I tend to doubt it. Mother Nature and Father Time have hit me with some pretty devastating tag team moves, and my head, lower back, and knees (not to mention those gross-sounding pubis and ischia bones I wrote of earlier) are most likely not going to allow me that one last truly great moment in the ring. But I think I still have a few *pretty* good ones left. As a matter of fact, following those Kurt Angle matches, I've come to believe that all of my matches have the potential to be pretty good.

Looking back on the past year, some of those matches really were pretty good; a couple of them—the big match with Sting, a "Monster's Ball" match in October 2009 with Abyss—even got a respectable number of votes from TNA fans for match of the year. In 2004, I beat myself up pretty bad emotionally for settling for "good enough" in my comeback match at *WrestleMania*. It had been my first match in four years—an eternity in the wrestling world, and I was bitterly disappointed in myself for settling for anything less than my absolute best. A month later, I came back and avenged that emotional defeat; coming through big with the best match of my career. I firmly believe that every wrestler, after retiring, should feel entitled to one honest-to-goodness comeback match—if it's done for all the right reasons. After that, every comeback is at least partially about the money. I did that honest-to-goodness comeback match with Randy Orton in 2004. This is 2010. And in 2010, unfortunately, "good enough" really is going to have to be good enough—at least in the ring.

I was mildly disappointed with the post-*Lockdown* ratings, which remained strong but showed no appreciable overall increase (although the ratings were up considerably from where they had been at the same point a year earlier), and with the *Lockdown* buy rate, which did increase, but not to the type of numbers I had hoped for. TNA actually had a very good 2009, not only surviving but turning a considerable profit in an incredibly tough economy; 2010, however, might turn out to be a different story. The January arrival of Eric Bischoff and Hulk Hogan seemed to inject new energy into TNA, and the decision to go head-to-head with WWE on Monday nights created a temporary buzz around the wrestling business that had been missing for several years. But the 2010 version of the Monday Night Wars didn't work out well for TNA, and *Impact* is back on Thursdays, its ratings well down from where they were a year earlier—though international ratings have seen a sizeable increase. Despite the addition of huge stars to its roster, TNA as a brand has had trouble gaining any real traction outside of its core audience.

Looking back on *Lockdown* now, almost a year after the fact, what strikes me most is how fast the wheels of the wrestling machine move, and how much fuel—in the form of ideas and matches—is needed to fill those weekly two-hour television shows and monthly Pay-Per-View extravaganzas. All the moments that fed the machine in those weeks leading up to the big match with Sting—the vignettes, the matches, the promos (even the one where Mick interviewed Cactus)—are largely forgotten, as if they'd never existed at all. I mean, really, how much different would the wrestling landscape look if I had opted not to turn heel, if I'd just extended my hand and said "Brother, I respect you" to the Stinger, instead of leaping headlong into this great adventure I've chronicled for you? More than likely, the landscape would look just about the same. Maybe even exactly the same.

So I think it's fair to ask if any of this was important at all. I had my doubts, even while writing this book, wondering whether a fourth wrestling memoir was important enough to *write*, let alone important enough to expect people to read. Yet, for the past several months, while going through rewrites and edits, reading and rereading this book a half-dozen times over, I keep coming back to how much I like it and, in a few different ways, how important it feels to me.

With over three hundred annual hours of first-run weekly programming (*Impact, Raw, SmackDown*), and another ninety or so yearly on Pay-Per-View, the pro-wrestling business rarely has time to look back and appreciate its components. It serves so many people at such a fast pace—kind of like a massive, daily luncheon buffet, where customers are rushed through a never-ending line as they grab what they can, with each daily buffet seeming identical to the one before it and the ones to follow. Hopefully, with *Countdown to Lockdown* I've allowed TNA diners to sit back and really enjoy just one little part of that huge buffet, to savor the flavor of one homemade piece of apple pie, to taste the cinnamon, or the nutmeg, or the allspice, or whatever the hell Grandma used to put in there. And hopefully you, the readers, will remember this particular piece of pie, and perhaps recall years later just what it was you liked about it, regardless of whether the pie won official "pie of the year" honors, or was purchased by a dozen, a thousand, or a million pie-eating customers.

Some of my favorite sports books are that way; stories that chronicle a single baseball season, like *Ball Four*, by Jim Bouton; two weeks in the NFL, like *Stop-Action*, by Dick Butkus; or a single NBA game, like *48 Minutes*, by Bob Ryan. Each of those books captured the sights, the sounds, the smells, the *essence*, of their respective sports. I hope that's what I've done here with this book: captured a little of the *essence* of what it means to be a broken-down wrestler still trying to make a difference in his strange little world. As with those books, hopefully you can take this book down off the shelf a year from now, or a decade from now, or maybe even further down the road, and immediately feel the sights, the sounds, and the smells of that six-week countdown to *Lockdown*.

I never did get around to holding that big online career auction—the one I hoped would bring in a hundred thousand dollars. The rough economy made me think that holding off on having such an auction would be a wise move, and in truth I was probably guilty of highly overestimating what my career memorabilia would be worth on the open market. So I loaned some of my best stuff (original Cactus Jack, Dude Love, and Mankind gear) to the Pro-Wrestling Hall of Fame in Amsterdam, New York, and just kind of accepted that the junior secondary school I'd hoped to build in Alimany's village was not going to happen.

But one day, I received a letter from ChildFund International, telling me that the junior secondary school was under construction. The village elders, knowing the need for a secondary school was greater than the need for the elementary school I'd pledged funding to, had simply decided to use my money to construct a *smaller* junior secondary school. How cool is that? A report from Sierra Leone said, "Mick Foley is a household name in Bombali, and villagers often stop Alimany and thank him for bringing blessings into the community." Really, that whole thing couldn't have worked out better. I plan on going back to Sierra Leone later this year, to do a little more nurturing in my little corner of the world. Hopefully, a few *Countdown* readers can help me in that nurturing process. I just heard from Kari Barber, one of the journalists I watched the U.S. presidential election with, and I may even get to participate in the making of a documentary about some of those Bombali schools.

As it turned out, I *didn't* ruin "Winter" for Tori Amos. Against the advice of my agent, manager, editor, wife, and friends, and with the invaluable help of her good friend Chelsea Laird (who was indefatigable in dealing with my steady parade of odd little inquiries), I'd managed to make the chapter available to her, after worrying for weeks that Tori Amos might not particularly *want* her very own chapter in a pro-wrestling memoir. Fortunately, she liked it, she really liked it (she said it made her laugh and cry), and she didn't have any reservations about appearing in a book written by someone of my dubious professional lineage. She even referred to me as "my friend, Mick Foley" in a recent NPR interview (in front of a live crowd, no less), a quote I'm sure I can work into a conversation or two over the next several years.

Best of all, she sang "Winter" for me during a show at Radio City Music Hall. At least I was pretty sure she did. I mean, she *said* she did...kind of. Maybe you can be the judge. Here's the deal—after watching Tori's wonderful performance, my wife and I were invited backstage where the following conversation took place:

TORI: (smiling just a little mischievously) I played "Winter."
MICK: (in stunned disbelief) You played that for *me*?
TORI: She felt like she needed to come out.

I walked out into the hot August night elated; knowing I now had the perfect ending to my book. I wasn't the only Foley who was feeling a little special, either. "Okay, Mick, I completely get it now," my wife said, finally better able to understand the "spell" she claimed Tori Amos had put me under a year earlier.

A book in one respect is like a wrestling match: a great deal of imperfection can be excused if a perfect ending is employed. It can't make a bad one good, but it can make a decent one better, and a good one great. Conversely, a bad ending in writing or wrestling can make a great one good, and a decent one lousy. Trust me, I've been there, in both wrestling and writing. *This* book, however, was going to be the beneficiary of a perfect ending (not to be confused, under any circumstances, with a "happy ending"). So forget for just a moment how uneven some of the storytelling has been, how bitter I sound about that announcing experience, how over-reliant I am on the semi-colon as my punctuation mark of choice. The moment I write "She sang 'Winter' for me...The End," everybody heads for the literary exit with smiles on their faces. I mean, for me, this was like Babe Ruth promising that kid in the hospital a home run, like the Undertaker saying "Hey kid, this one's for you" before tossing me off of the cell. It was perfect!

But try as I might, I just couldn't write it. At least not with a clear conscience. Because I wasn't really *sure*. I *thought* she had sung "Winter" for me. But her words, like many of her songs, are open for interpretation. I just didn't feel like I could go to print with "she felt like she needed to come out," no matter how beautiful or poetic those words might be. I had to be sure. So, with ferocious female wrestler Awesome Kong by my side, I tracked Tori down in Düsseldorf, Germany. Wait, that sounds kind of creepy. Actually, as fate would have it, I was on a TNA European tour, and we had a night off only fifteen minutes from Düsseldorf.

Tori couldn't have been nicer, putting up with my exaggerated tales of wrestling greatness until her tour manager reminded me nicely, for like the fourth time, that Tori really had to go. I was halfway out the door, when I realized I had yet to address my daunting dilemma. Like Ralphie in A *Christmas Story* making his valiant climb back up that steep slide to see Santa, I willed my way back into the room, saying "Tori, Tori, please wait, Tori." Then, in a tone only slightly less rushed and panicked than that of Ralphie's Red Ryder rant, I said, "Can I write in my book that you sang 'Winter' for me in New York?"

If you remember correctly, Ralphie got a "you'll shoot your eye out, kid," and a boot to the head from Santa for his trouble. I received slightly different treatment for mine. Tori Amos lightly took hold of both my hands and smiled that magical San Diego smile. "You can... because I did," she said, sending me out onto the streets of Düsseldorf on an impossibly large cloud, secure in my knowledge that I had— really had—in my possession the perfect ending to my book.

Look, I know I've written quite a bit about Tori Amos already, and the last thing I want to do is (in wrestling terms) "put heat on her," to make readers think, *Hey Mick, enough with the Tori Amos stuff.* But it would be impossible to overstate how instrumental she was to the writing of this book. I had no interest, absolutely none, in writing another wrestling book, or writing about anything at all before I sat down in a Dublin hotel room and wrote "Meeting Tori Amos." But after Dublin, I kind of remembered what it was about writing I had once enjoyed so much—and within three days' time, I went from not thinking about writing at all to thinking I just might have another book in me.

I have been so incredibly lucky to have made a good living doing what I love for such a long time. I know the end of that road is in sight, but man, it's been an incredible trip, financially and emotionally rewarding on levels I never would have dreamed of. Even though the book world in general has struggled in recent years (people just don't accept reading as a viable entertainment option like they used to), the success I've had with past memoirs helped ensure that I received a pretty substantial guarantee (an advance against royalties) for my *Countdown* concept. I really saw this book as something of a gift, an opportunity I had stumbled across largely through unique circumstance and the inspiration I found in the work and words of one exceptional performer. Perhaps I could use this gift as a way to give back, to make one last real monetary difference in the world, before reverting back to my legendary thriftiness. I decided to go all out, to venture farther out on a limb of the giving tree (not the one Shel Silverstein wrote of) than I ever had before—agreeing to donate a cool 50 percent of my guarantee.

Upon returning home from Sierra Leone in November 2008, I had expressed interest in funding a project for the SEFAFU girls, the survivors of rape and sexual assault I wrote of earlier. A few months ago, I received a proposal from ChildFund: a chance to provide microloans and scholarships for up to two hundred of these women and their children, many of whom were the products of those civil-war rapes.

This proposal was exactly the type of thing I was looking to do. Unfortunately, it came with a fifty-thousand-dollar price tag, almost exactly what half my advance (minus agent's and management fees) worked out to. Very little money would be left over for RAINN (the group Tori had cofounded in 1994), which somehow didn't seem right.

I did a lot of thinking—wondering just what kind of book I'd have written if not for that initial San Diego meeting with Tori Amos, if not for that "Time in a Bottle" moment that had caused me to put pen to paper six months later in that Dublin hotel room. In truth, I wouldn't have even had a thought, let alone a book. And the more I thought about it, the more I became convinced that I could climb out just a little farther on that limb of the giving tree.

Interpreting this feeling to be a sign from God, I walked into the RAINN offices in Washington, D.C., announcing my intention of donating those other 50 Gs to the invaluable work—education, prevention, crisis intervention—they provide in the fight against sexual abuse.

Since that day, I've often wondered about that sign from God I thought I'd received. Most likely, it wasn't actually a sign from God— probably more of a sign that I should have brought my hands up when I saw all those chair shots coming over the years. But even acknowledging that I most likely don't have any real sign-interpreting abilities, I've still never regretted that decision to donate the rest of the money. In fact I'm thankful I made it...every single day. Maybe a hundred thousand dollars (fifty for RAINN, fifty for ChildFund) isn't exactly a Warren Buffett or Michael Bloomberg type of donation, but, even so, it's going to help a lot of people, at home and overseas.

I recently completed a forty-hour training course to become a RAINN online hotline volunteer, learning to help victims on a one-to-one basis. I'm far from a natural, and it's only for a few hours a week, but I honestly feel like it's as important as anything I've ever done—up there with winning my first WWE championship, becoming a *New York Times* best-selling author, and being invited to Christy

Canyon's Super Bowl party. If I've learned one thing in life, one *truly* important thing—it's not to allow anyone else to define what success is. We get to do that for ourselves.

A little earlier in this afterword, I questioned whether anything in this book was important at all. From a purely business standpoint, the six-week period leading up to *Lockdown* may seem somewhat insignificant. But from a personal standpoint—from the decision to take chances with my character to the decision to write again, to take that fateful climb onto the outer limb of the giving tree, this has been one of the most important times of my life. Maybe I don't have that one last great in-ring moment left in me, but writing this book, and experiencing the journey it's taken me on, has made me believe that I just might have a few great moments left *outside* of the ring, where *good enough* will hopefully never be good enough.

So maybe this wasn't the best wrestling book in the world, or even the best one I've personally written. I'm happy with it nonetheless. Luckily, I get to define for myself what success is—in life, in wrestling, in writing. I worked hard on this book, I'm happy with it, and I will forever consider it both important and successful, whether it sells one copy or a million. And I'm glad I was able to chronicle such a particularly enjoyable and fulfilling time in my career, especially when compared to my last book, which chronicled a pretty frustrating one. I'm guessing this is my last wrestling memoir (certainly it's the last one I'll write with pen and notebook pads), but one never can tell where inspiration might strike.

So, as you come to the end of this last page, feel free to express your emotions out loud. Unless, of course, your emotions are not positive, in which case I'd prefer you keep them to yourself. Say something like, "You know, that Mick Foley guy wrote a pretty good book." Go on, don't be shy. You can say it. You can...because I did.

ACKNOWLEDGMENTS

There were so many people who helped make this book such a positive experience for me. Thank you to my editor, Ben Greenberg, for accepting this book into the Grand Central Publishing family based on one unlikely chapter and a vision. Thanks to my agent, Matt Bialer, for believing that a wrestling book could still be relevant the fourth time around, and to my manager, Barry Bloom, for always looking out for my best interests.

To my wife, Colette, for twenty wonderful years together.

Thank you to my typist, Karen Bohner, for not only enthusiastically deciphering my handwriting, but for serving as fact-checker, punctuation and grammar corrector, and a valuable sounding board for ideas.

Jill Thompson, my primary first reader, as always, had great judgment and insight.

Thanks to the gang at TNA—my boss, Dixie Carter, for her unwavering support; Lee South for all the great wrestling photos; and the promotional team who I just know will leap into action to support this book.

Thanks also to the good people at Grand Central: Jamie Raab, Deb Futter, Tanisha Christie, Leah Tracosas, Flag Tonuzi, Dana Trombley, and Pippa White.

A special thanks to Chelsea Laird for going above and beyond the call of duty on so many occasions just to help me out.

And to Tori Amos, whose music, spirit, and kindness were such a big inspiration in the writing of this book.

Lastly, a debt of gratitude to all the great people at RAINN and ChildFund International for their heartfelt belief in me.

INDEX

Note: The abbreviation MF in subheadings refers to Mick Foley.